THE MASTER SHOWMEN OF KING RANCH

ELLEN AND EDWARD RANDALL SERIES

The MASTER SHOWMEN of KING RANCH

THE STORY OF BETO AND LIBRADO MALDONADO

BETTY BAILEY COLLEY AND JANE CLEMENTS MONDAY,
WITH BETO MALDONADO

FOREWORD BY
STEPHEN J. "TIO" KLEBERG

UNIVERSITY OF TEXAS PRESS
AUSTIN

Printed in the United States of America
First edition, 2009

∞ The paper used in this book meets the minimum requirements
of ANSI/NISO Z39.48-1992 (R1997) (Permanence of Paper).

LIBRARY OF CONGRESS CATALOGING-IN-PUBLICATION DATA
Colley, Betty Bailey.
The master showmen of King Ranch : the story of Beto and Librado Maldonado /
Betty Bailey Colley and Jane Clements Monday, with Beto Maldonado ;
foreword by Stephen J. "Tio" Kleberg. — 1st ed.
p. cm. — (Ellen and Edward Randall Series)
Includes bibliographical references and index.
ISBN 978-0-292-71943-9
1. Mexican American cowboys—Texas—Biography. 2. Maldonado, Librado. 3. Maldonado, Beto. 4. Mexican American families—Texas. 5. Ranch life—Texas—Biography. 6. King Ranch (Tex.). I. Monday, Jane Clements, 1941– II. Maldonado, Beto. III. Title.
F395.M5C64 2009
976.4'472009236872—dc22
2008053524

CONTENTS

FOREWORD

When Beto first came to see me and said he was interested in writing a book about his experiences on King Ranch, I was very enthusiastic. Through the years, Beto has kept meticulous records about all he has seen throughout his travels and experiences and has kept wonderful notes. You see, there have been volumes written about King Ranch, the rich history of its founding, the cattle industry, its founders and shareholders, but far less about the people, the Kineños (King's men), as they are known. None of the story would be complete without the Kineños and their dedication, hard work, devotion, innovation, and their noble cause. The people *are* King Ranch.

The Master Showmen of King Ranch gives the reader a look at the people who made King Ranch what it is today. For over six generations, Kineños have worked side by side in the hot South Texas sun to generate products of quality synonymous with King Ranch, the birthplace of the American cattle industry. The first skill in animal husbandry is observation, and Librado and Beto Maldonado were masters. Looking at the breeding cattle they were preparing either for sale or show each day and evaluating their merits or flaws became common.

There have been many Kineños over the 150-year history of King Ranch who have added immensely to the success of King Ranch from the time of their arrival in 1853 alongside Captain Richard King. Two men stand out whose efforts, success, and expertise have no equal in their work, loyalty, and dedication, and those two are Librado and Beto Maldonado, master showmen. No one family has made a greater contribution to the success of King Ranch cattle than the Maldonados.

Beto continues today to enrich the lives of those with whom he comes in contact in our visitor program. Beto takes groups and families who come to visit King Ranch on nature and agricultural tours to expose them to the land and its assets. Beto wants the visitors to leave the Ranch with one message: that six generations of men and women working the land and its assets can improve them and leave them to the next generation better than they found them. This is a noble cause.

Stephen J. "Tio" Kleberg
Member, Board of Directors
King Ranch, Inc.

PREFACE

Life sometimes offers unexpected surprises that become rewarding experiences to be cherished. Such a surprise came to us when Alberto "Beto" Maldonado called one day and asked if we would help him write his life's story. Beto has been on the fabled King Ranch for seventy-eight years. He and his father are the legendary showmen of King Ranch who took the Ranch's famous Santa Gertrudis cattle all over the world. Beto is one of the most knowledgeable people about King Ranch history alive today. He is warm, cheerful, enthusiastic, and caring toward those around him, as we learned when we interviewed him for our book *Voices from the Wild Horse Desert*. We agreed to help Beto with his story and have enjoyed many hours with him, his family, and his compadres from the Ranch while gathering information for the book.

The Maldonado family has played significant roles in the development of the Ranch and, like many of the Kineños (King's men), has had a special relationship with the Ranch owners. The ranching culture was established on a foundation of mutual respect and responsibility; employers and employees became extended family, and Beto and his family have been a part of this culture for three quarters of a century. During this time they have experienced many changes that occurred on the Ranch. Beto has afforded us, and now you the reader, the opportunity to venture behind the gates into the unique mystique of King Ranch. He has allowed us to see how life was really lived and to experience the joys and tragedies of everyday life there.

We thank Beto for sharing his memories of life on the Ranch, which began for him when there was no electricity, water had to be heated in a tub over a fire, and transportation was mostly by horseback, walking, and an occasional truck ride. We are grateful that Beto provided us the opportunity to work with his loving family, and we thank each of them who spoke with a sparkle in the eye and a warm smile while telling with pride stories of their parents, siblings, and grandparents. Sammy and Jo Anne Maldonado graciously opened their home to us for conducting interviews and photo sessions and for enjoying a delicious dinner prepared by the Maldonado family. Special thanks go to Dora Maldonado for answering repeated phone calls with a patient, cheerful voice as Beto's "secretary" and for sharing stories of their life together for almost sixty years.

The other family we thank is Beto's Ranch family, his friends that he has worked alongside for more than sixty years. They include members of the Kleberg family who graciously shared their memories and their appreciation of the contributions the Maldonado family has made to King Ranch.

To Tio and Janell Kleberg we are most grateful for one of the most enjoyable afternoons of our lives as we sat in their living room with Beto and listened as the three of them recalled stories of the adventures of Librado and Beto with the Santa Gertrudis cattle, King Ranch auctions, and the training of the bulls by Librado. We laughed and at times became almost teary at the memories they shared. The love and respect between these people were clearly evident. The insights Tio and Janell gave into the challenges and joys of living on the Ranch and in the Kingsville community were invaluable and have added a unique dimension to this book.

Special thanks go to Helen Kleberg Groves for sharing remembrances of growing up on the Ranch with the Maldonado family and to Mary Lewis Kleberg for her memories of King Ranch auctions and the showmanship of Librado and Beto. We appreciate Sally Kleberg's sharing her rich memories of Christmas celebrations at the Ranch, especially her description of the arrival of Santa Claus (Librado) each year, the only Santa most of the Ranch children ever knew.

To Jamene and John Toelkes we express our thanks for being our anchors. You were always there with a smile and willingness to help. You shared your vast knowledge of King Ranch and helped us to steer an accurate course. You did this with warmth and humor and kept our spirits up when they were low by reminding us that this story needed to be told. We thank Cathy Henry for caring so much about Beto and wanting his many contributions to the Ranch, including his expert tours, to be shared with people from around the world.

Dr. Monte Moncrief, thank you for hosting us in your home and sharing your many varied and sometimes harrowing experiences with the famous King Ranch stock. It was a pleasure to hear you and Beto recall the times you experienced together and to see the deep friendship and respect that remain today. We also appreciate the late R. P. Marshall for sharing memories of his work with Beto as they showed the best of the Santa Gertrudis breed in some most unusual places, and for his gift of *Geneva Remembers*. Norman Parish and José Silguero, our thanks go to you for sharing your valuable information. A special thank-you goes to Linda Hillin, John Carter, and Janet Pollock for taking over and doing an excellent job of editing and producing *The Franciscan* during the writing of the manuscript, and to Fr. Jerry Sneary for his understanding. Lisa Neely, King Ranch archivist, read the manuscript and made significant contributions to the accuracy of the King Ranch information.

Finally, we are indebted to our families for their patience and support. To our dear husbands, Charles Monday and Burnham Jones, who have believed from the first in the value of this material and supported us all the way, we express our heartfelt appreciation. To the Monday family—Kimberly, Lauren, Jack, Ellie, Julie, Buddie, Sarah, Ben, Sam, Jennifer, Adam, Annie, and Caroline—we express our thanks for your continual love and support. Our gratitude goes to the Colley family, especially to Jill, for her sound professional advice and steady belief in us and the value of this project. To Steffen, Julia, Philip, Alexander, Carey, Mike, Jessica, and Cameron, we say a special thanks.

Once more we turn to our excellent editor, Theresa May, and her magnificent staff to say that it is a pleasure to work with you and the University of Texas Press. Our admiration for your professionalism, guidance, and expertise continues with this, our third UT Press book. Lynne Chapman and freelancer Rosemary Wetherold made the book better in so many ways, and we thank you.

Our goal in preparing this work was to step aside as writers and let Beto's voice be heard; although there are three voices in the text, Beto is the main storyteller. We added introductory and historical material with the intention of placing the lives of Beto and Librado in greater perspective and of adding interesting details about the Ranch and the area. In addition, the quotes of family, friends, and King Ranch cattle buyers add a variety of perspectives to the fabric of the story.

We hope you will enjoy this unusual opportunity to step back in time and personally experience the unique culture of King Ranch through the eyes of this exceptional family who helped make it one of the most famous ranches in the world.

INTRODUCTION

Since the development of the West was forged by the ranching industry, the American cowboy has been immortalized around the world in print, in movies, and on television. Some media even portrayed the intricate skill, expertise, and hard, endless work of the Mexican vaqueros, the "real cowboys" on whom the myth was based.

Although the vaqueros are rightly celebrated for the success of King Ranch, arguably the most famous ranch in the world, there is another story. While thousands of vaqueros working cattle from horseback did create the astounding success story that is King Ranch, thousands more worked on the ground in strategic support of the entire operation. A Hollywood axiom is that there would be no stars without supporting actors. Likewise, the success of the Ranch has depended on the men working to clear brush, build and mend fences, tend windmills, make and repair equipment, keep meticulous records for the up-breeding programs, cook for the *corrida* from chuck wagons, and perform countless other tasks necessary for the Ranch's smooth operation. They worked with the same pride, loyalty, and dedication as the vaqueros. Hollywood missed them, and their stories are mostly untold. This book is about one of these families, the Maldonados. It is a story about the family as they grew up on the Ranch and about their everyday life with its challenges, tragedies, and joys. Their story is a rare opportunity to experience a moment in time, gone forever.

Librado and Alberto "Beto" Maldonado, a father-son team, tamed the two-thousand-pound Santa Gertrudis bulls and showed them to the world. Sometimes they wore tuxedos as they paraded "their" sleek, beautifully behaved animals in prestigious hotel ballrooms in Texas, and sometimes they wore khakis while showing the prized animals on the African continent. They have shown the bulls in TV studios high above street level in Chicago and in livestock shows across the nation. At least one of them led the bulls into the ring of every King Ranch auction sale from 1950 to 1986, where famous and near-famous buyers and guests gathered from around the world to purchase King Ranch animals. The Maldonados traveled with the animals by horse-drawn wagons, boxcars, express trains, trucks, and airplanes. Respected by cattlemen throughout the world, they were the chosen representatives wherever King Ranch showed cattle. This is their remarkable story.

Located in South Texas in the Wild Horse Desert and stretching from the Nueces River to the Rio Grande, King Ranch is considered by many to be the birthplace of the American cattle industry. Its headquarters is just west of Kingsville, in a land full of mesquite, cactus, rattlesnakes, and blistering heat. It was here that Captain Richard King established his cow camp in 1853 on the banks of the Santa Gertrudis Creek. King was a steamboat captain who knew virtually nothing about ranching when he began his new venture. He did know that his lucrative steamboating business on the Rio Grande would dwindle with the end of the Mexican-American War (1846–1848), and he was looking for his next venture.

Captain King was aware of the history of this strip from conversations while doing business along the border. The land lying to the north was dismissed as miles and miles of wasteland populated by wild mustangs, bony cattle, and fierce Karankawa Indians, with a sprinkling of Texas outlaws and Mexicans tenaciously holding on to their ranchos. From the descriptions he heard, King no doubt wondered why anyone would want this desolate territory, much less be willing to fight for it, as the Mexicans and Texans had done ever since Santa Anna lost the Battle of San Jacinto in 1836 and the new Republic of Texas declared the Rio Grande its southern border. Still, tales of this wide expanse interested him. Though he had never seen this land, King must have pondered whether a ranching business akin to the *latifundos,* immense Mexican haciendas in northern Mexico, was possible.

In 1852, Captain King had cause to travel north from his home in Brownsville, Texas, on a business trip to Corpus Christi. It was his first time to cross the Wild Horse Desert, and he finally saw the storied territory for himself. He went in April, perhaps the ideal time for making the four- or five-day trip. The sweet smell of yellow huisache blooms punctuates the air this time of year. Wildflowers like coreopsis, fire wheels (also known as Indian blankets), phlox, lantana, and lazy daisies reach as far as the eye can see. Texas prickly pear bloom profusely in yellows and shades of orange and red before critters like the Texas tortoise and birds such as green jays and long-billed thrashers, devour them. Early morning cool and moderate midday temperatures mask the searing dry, sometimes humid heat of the long summer soon to come, sometimes lasting until late October.

Even so, the relentless April sun can be blindingly bright, almost hot. Riding through rising dust in stirrup-high grass, King came upon the Santa Gertrudis Creek, and he must have been impressed with its cool, sparkling water and mesquite trees, for on this day his life took a starkly different direction. His dream of a thriving ranching business was born on this spot, which remained dear to his heart for the rest of his life. The following year he purchased land for his rancho, which would ultimately encompass more than one million acres, 825,000 of which remain today.

The U.S. Civil War (1861–1865) afforded a brisk business of transporting cotton from the Southern states to foreign ships in the Gulf of Mexico and moving supplies for Confederate troops, enabling King to finance his dream. He was successful beyond his most ambitious expectations.

King Ranch developed the Santa Gertrudis breed of cattle, the first American breed and the first anywhere in the world in more than a century. The new breed was soon spread across King Ranch holdings on four continents. The Ranch also developed the King Ranch Santa Cruz composite breed and bred its own Quarter Horses, recognized as some of the best in the world. Its Thoroughbred program produced the only Texas-bred Triple Crown winner and one of only eleven in history when Assault won the Kentucky Derby, the Preakness, and the Belmont Stakes in 1946. Numerous ranching innovations—such as the invention of the root plow and dipping vats, which resulted in the eradication of Texas tick fever—were on the cutting edge of the industry.

This success did not just happen. To conquer this desolate land, Captain King needed men who knew about ranching, so he turned to northern Mexico, where he persuaded about one hundred people to leave the area known as Cruillas and come north with him to help establish his rancho. King and his descendents formed a bond with these original worker families that laid the foundation for the Ranch's success for six generations. Together they built a legend noted for both the accomplishments of the Ranch and the remarkable culture they created as a ranching family.

Not all ranches are the same. King Ranch established a blending of Hispanic and Anglo heritages that forged a unique ranching culture. An extended family relationship developed between the owners and the workers, characterized by a bond of loyalty and of responsibility for each other. This relationship was built on pride in the work and on respect and admiration for each other.

The workers became known as Kineños but kept their own culture. Spanish became the language of the Ranch. The Kineños ate their own foods, such as tamales, enchiladas, *buñelos*, and tortillas, and their cuisine soon became regular Ranch fare. They continued to practice their Catholic religion. Their relationship with the Ranch was one that lasted from birth to death. Kineño families were provided free housing, free utilities, a monthly food ration, wages, medical care, and education for their children. Protected behind the gates of King Ranch, they did not have to worry about seasonal layoffs common on other ranches or about economic depressions or any of the outside forces that concerned other vaqueros and residents of the Wild Horse Desert and the West. In return, the Kineños worked long hours from dawn to dusk the entire year except for Christmas holidays. Their children grew up expecting to join the workforce as soon as they were able, following in their parents' footsteps. They provided the Ranch with a stable workforce. Many of these families intermarried, resulting in what was truly an extended family. They looked out after each other and the owners, and the owners looked out for them.

This was the culture of King Ranch until sweeping changes overcame it in the 1980s. No longer could the Ranch continue the birth-to-death relationship with its Kineño families. Many Kineños were offered early retirement as the workforce was greatly reduced. King Ranch is no longer the same; a page of history has turned.

We are fortunate to have had the opportunity to step behind the gates and hear the story of what life was like before the changes came to the Ranch. We gleaned our story from Beto Maldonado, a meticulous record keeper who, through his written notes and remarkable memory, told us about his seventy-eight years as a Kineño on King Ranch.

The story of dedicated vaqueros doing grueling work from horseback, rounding up and branding cattle during long days and weeks on the vast pastures of King Ranch, is already familiar. Now Beto tells another side of the story.

THE MASTER SHOWMEN
OF KING RANCH

PROLOGUE

Beto's Tour

On a cool fall day in 2006 Beto Maldonado took the authors on a private tour of King Ranch. Thousands of visitors from across the United States and eighteen foreign countries have taken this tour from the Visitor Management Department with Beto as guide since he led the first one eighteen years ago, but for those who have not, we offer here the opportunity to share vicariously this unique experience, one of several tours offered through the Visitor Management Department of King Ranch.

We arrived early for the tour at the Visitor Center, near the entrance of the Santa Gertrudis Division, just west of Kingsville, Texas. There, on top of the hill where Captain King founded his ranch in 1853, we could see miles and miles of mesquite-dotted pastureland, with some of the finest cattle and horses in the world peacefully grazing. The tall stately Main House commanded the surroundings, overlooking vast lands spreading in every direction.

Beto took up his microphone and, with a sparkle in his eye, love in his voice, and memory for every detail, began his driving tour.

Welcome to King Ranch. My name is Beto. We'll be going on the Loop Road. Feel free to ask questions, and I'll do my best to answer them for you.

It's a beautiful day. We're located on the Santa Gertrudis Division, which encompasses more than 200,000 acres. It's one of four cattle divisions here in South Texas. The Santa Gertrudis and Laureles are located in the Kingsville area. Kingsville is sitting right in the heart of King Ranch. Mrs. King donated 853 acres of land to establish the city of Kingsville and nearly 42,000 acres around the Kingsville site, and nearly 35,000 acres around what is now Raymondville to bring in the railroad. So traveling from west to east, you drive through Kingsville five miles, then you go back to King Ranch all the way to Laguna Madre on the coast. The other two divisions are south of here, near the Rio Grande Valley. Together in the four divisions there are more than 825,000 acres of land, 32,000 head of cattle, 360 head of horses, 57,000 acres of farmland under cultivation in cotton and milo. Another 56,000 in Florida, with 36,000 in citrus. King Ranch is the largest citrus producer in the United States. Another 20,000 acres produce sugarcane, turfgrass, and sweet corn.

Captain Richard King founded King Ranch in 1853. Captain King was a steamboat pilot in the Mississippi-Florida area. He came to Texas in 1847. He and his partner, Mifflin Kenedy, founded a successful steamboat business in the Port of Brownsville, Texas, 120 miles south of here near the border. It was in 1853 when Captain King attended a Gulf Coast fair in Corpus Christi. To reach Corpus Christi, he had to cross what was called the Wild Horse Desert. He rode for more than 120 miles before he encountered any good water; it was right here at the Santa Gertrudis Creek that we are about to approach. They stopped here and rested, then continued on to Corpus. It was in Corpus where he and [Gideon K.] "Legs" Lewis got together and decided to start a cattle venture in this area. So this is the Santa Gertrudis Creek, where he stopped and rested on the way to Corpus Christi 150 years ago.

The name "Santa Gertrudis" came from a Spanish land grant, the name of the Headquarters, creek, and later, the breed of cattle. The Santa Gertrudis breed, the first American breed of cattle developed in the Americas, was done here. It is a cross between a Brahman and a Shorthorn—three-eighths Brahman and five-eighths Shorthorn. It was recognized as a true breed in 1940 by the U.S. Agriculture Department. My dad was the first man to show the breed to the pub-

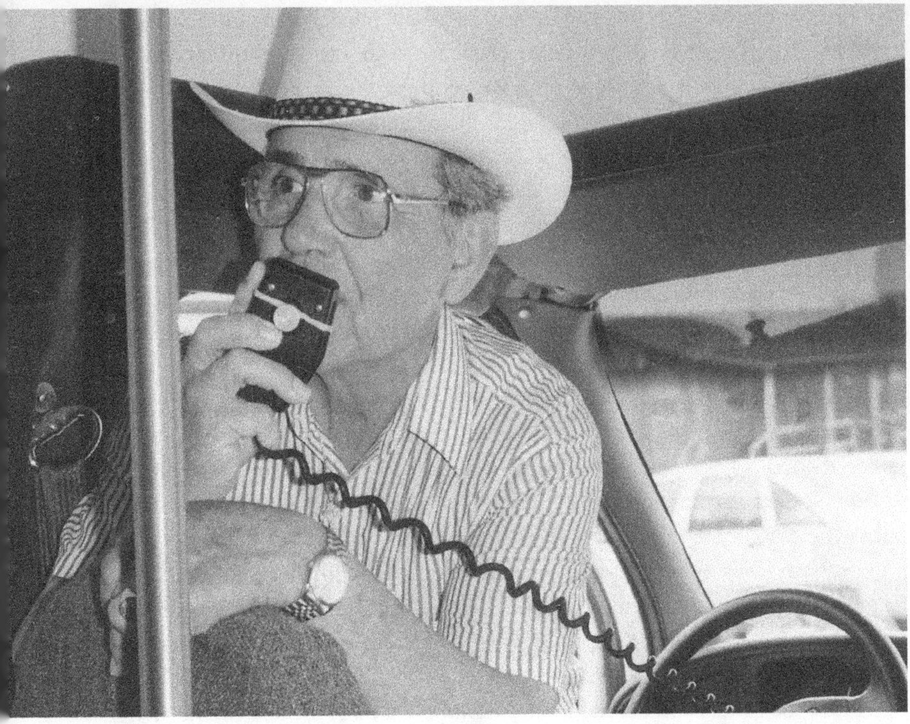

Beto Maldonado leading the King Ranch tour. Photo by Betty Bailey Colley.

lic in 1928 in Houston, and I was the first to win a blue ribbon in 1940, when the breed was recognized as a true breed. And my brother Lee got second place.

My dad showed Jersey cattle at the International Livestock Exposition in Chicago for the first time in 1918; in 1954 he was showing the new breed, Santa Gertrudis. People wanted a Santa Gertrudis bull on TV, so he loaded this 2,000-pound bull—Buen Amigo—and took him to downtown Chicago, put him in the elevator up to the twenty-first floor to be on TV at six o'clock one morning. He was in trouble after that happened—a whole bunch of people came looking for him at the livestock show.

In 1985 a group of Santa Gertrudis breeders got together to make their first airborne cattle auction on the way to Hawaii. We had a bull that we named Macho. Macho was weighing 2,900 pounds at the time. Those people asked Mr. Tio Kleberg and Mr. R. P. Marshall the possibility of me taking Macho to the airport in Dallas. So they told me, "Beto, get Macho all shined up and take him to Dallas at a certain date." I had traveled with my dad throughout the country and foreign countries showing cattle for many years. I learned lots from my dad. I took Macho off grain three days before we left and off water twenty-four hours before I paraded him inside the airport. We got there the day before, we spent the night there, and next morning I got Macho all shined up, went to the second floor to the ticket counter. There were 251 people making the trip, plus all the other people that were there already. Got to the ticket counter and everybody wanted to have their picture taken with Macho. So poor Macho stood there for the longest time on one leg, then on the other. I had two men with me, Bobby Silva and Ruben Rodriguez. We were prepared; we had brooms and shovels, but Macho behaved like a gentleman. He was on TV nationwide and in newspapers throughout the country.

We'll be driving through some of the small breeding pastures of varying size from 400 to 1,000 acres. The biggest pasture on King Ranch is 32,000 acres. It's on the Norias Division. This is where we run some of the cattle and Quarter Horses. The net wire fence that you see is made for King Ranch specifications. There are more than 2,000 miles that surround the Ranch and divide it into pastures, long enough to stretch from here to Boston. The metal posts in between the cedars are put there in case of a fire. That post will hold the fence up until it can be repaired. You put up a fence like that, it will last you thirty or forty years.

Notice the squares on the net wire. Of course, that was the design, the idea of Mr. Bob Kleberg Jr. Mr. Bob would do everything in the world to keep his livestock from getting hurt. As you can see, the square is big enough for a horse to stick his leg in there and pull it out without any problem. It's small enough for a cow not to get the head in there. You will also notice that we use no staples. We actually drill a hole, and the slick wire is wrapped around the post and will stay there forever.

We recycle the old tractor tires, convert them into horse feeders. Best ones money can buy. A horse will find a way to get hurt—they can't do it with this rubber tire. We invented an apparatus that turns it inside out hydraulically. We put a bottom on the one we use for grain; the one we use for hay, we don't. They last forever.

We are getting to the Quarter mare barn. It's where we run some of the mares, fillies, and colts. We normally run an older horse with a group of young ones as a guide—he knows where the goodies are, so he takes them around. Also manages to settle them down when they're running and acting up.

Ahead of us on your right you can see part of the main residence. General Robert E. Lee helped Captain King pick that site for his house—he was Colonel Lee at the time. It is the highest point on this division of the Ranch. We will drive in front of the house on the way back.

This country is so pretty and green. We've had an abundance of rain, and it really put us in excellent shape.

We lost a retired stallion, Peppy San Badger. He was thirty-one years old. His papa, Mr. San Peppy, was the first to win $100,000 in cutting. Peppy San Badger won even more. Now Peppy San Badger's offspring have earned more than $23 million.

Standing on your right, ahead of us, is Taquito Sugar, one of our younger studs. The one next to him is Ritas Sweet Badger.

King Ranch purchased a colt from George Clegg in Alice, Texas. The Kineños later named him Old Sorrel—he was the foundation sire of the King Ranch Quarter Horse family. In 1940 the American Quarter Horse Association decided to start registration. They decided that the No. 1 horse would be the Grand Champion stallion at the Fort Worth Stock Show in 1941. It was a King Ranch horse by the name of Wimpy. In 1984 they registered the two-millionth horse. It was a King Ranch filly, descendant of Wimpy and Old Sorrel.

The metal band on the fence is put there so the horses will be able to see the fence from a distance. A lot of times they go to running, run into the fence, and get injured. That was Mr. Bob's idea. Like I said, he would do everything in the world to keep his livestock from getting hurt.

King Ranch's brand is the Running W. Nobody really knows why Captain King picked the Running W for his brand; he acquired more than thirty-five different brands when he was buying land. There is a name on the list by the name of Mann; some think Mr. Mann might have used an M for his brand and Captain King used it upside down. Or they say that he might have seen a lot of snakes, but I think it's a very neat brand. The very first brand that he used was an R with an arrow and then later HK for "Henrietta King."

These are sites of the first feedlots on the place, on your left. There is nothing left there today, as you can see.

Ahead of us—some of the heavy equipment we used in the past to clear the brush with. The chains were used or pulled with our two D-8 Caterpillars to knock the brush down. They later invented the yellow apparatus to go in front of the D-8 that would do the same work. The very last piece, the blade, would go behind the D-8 and root them out. And next to the last is a rake. We very seldom do any raking; we let it rot to fertilize the land. The first apparatus and the blade have been enlarged almost twice as wide. Placed into a twin D-8 Caterpillar, two D-8s welded together—it's a fifty-two-ton piece of equipment that can clear up to four acres of land per hour. In the 1890s they hired some help to start clearing some of this land; one person could only clear less than an acre per week by hand; today one person can clear a lot of acres, maybe 200, per week with that machine. We have cleared as much big brush as we need to, about 600,000 acres after the Second World War. We have to stay on top of the newly cleared ones; otherwise in fifteen years' time we have nothing but brush back to the pasture. We try to keep 65 percent cleared and 35 percent with brush.

There're times that we see wild turkeys around this area. They come around, of course, to get their share of the feed. We have a lot of wild game on the place—a lot of turkey, javelina, quail, wild pig, dove, and deer. The main cause of death of deer was screwworm. After they got rid of the screwworm, the deer have really multiplied.

As you can see on your right, half of that pasture is already being cleared, the other one still has to be worked on. We now leave some of the mesquites for shade for cattle.

You're looking at mostly King Ranch Bluestem, the most popular type of grass on the Ranch today. There are others, but anyway, the popular grass of the Ranch is King Ranch Bluestem. It's a hearty grass that has just about pushed the other ones out.

On your left about a mile from here is a windmill. That windmill supplies the four corners with water. The water well with a submersible pump ahead of us supplies the other four. Some of the mares, Quarter mares, on your right.

The trees along the road are what we call salt cedar. They're also called Athel pine [tamarisk family], and they're from Australia. Make an awful good windbreak and shade. They stay green pretty much year-round.

That old silo has been standing there for the longest time—I'd say it's been sitting there for the last hundred years. They used to farm this area when they had that feedlot back at the Rancho Plomo.

Santa Gertrudis heifers on your left, the first American breed of cattle developed in the Americas. It was done on King Ranch. We breed heifers as yearlings. We like for them to weigh 750 pounds when we put a bull with them as yearlings. They are two years old when they drop the first calf. We have a spring and a fall breeding season.

This is where we normally run some of these Santa Gertrudis herds. We also run some of the Quarter mares, fillies, and colts—on your right. The number tag in the cows' ears has the same number that matches with their firebrand and their tattoo number. When you keep records of cattle—and some of the time the brand numbers have been covered one way or another, especially in winter, when they shed more hair—they are not that easy to read. The ear tag is a big help. Of course, it's something new. I worked with cattle before ear tags, and it was a problem reading those fire numbers. We would actually stamp the numbers on the horns to avoid branding the numbers on the hides of those animals. This was Mr. Bob's idea. Then later the ear tags were out, and they have done wonders for us. There is a number printed on them.

Every pasture has a name. When I was keeping records, every offspring from those pastures was identified with a butt letter brand showing the pasture that they came from, but that's no longer being done. That was one way to control inbreeding of cattle at the time. Santa Gertrudis single sire, or pedigreed cattle, were identified by sire and dam, so they took one [brand] on each side. The Santa Gertrudis cows take a Running W on the hip, number right below, and the year that they were dropped right below the number. On the Santa Cruz, the Ranch's composite breed, the year of birth is on top of the hip with the Running W beneath.

The average weight on those baby Santa Gertrudis calves is 79 pounds; weaning weight on the heifers is 525 pounds and 550 pounds on the bull calf.

A water well with a submersible pump ahead of us on your right supplies these four corners with water. There is some type of a water well in most four corners of pastures to supply the four corners. We also make ponds to hold rainwater. We like for wild game and cattle to have water as near as possible.

The windmill on your left about a mile from here supplies the other four corners. Water was one of the biggest problems back in the early days. They had all kinds of problems with bandits and Indians, but water was the main problem. In the 1890s these people were going through a drought—hundreds of cattle were dying. Mr. Kleberg was looking for all kinds of drilling equipment that he could find to find good water. It was not till 1899 that they discovered the first artesian water well. Today we have over 400 windmills of water throughout the Ranch. In 1980 we had a hurricane that destroyed most of the windmills. Left a lot of cattle without water. Since then, a lot of the windmills have been converted to submersible pumps. We have to drill 700 to 800 feet to find good water in this part of the Ranch.

These cows are kind of lonesome because their babies were pulled away from them not too long ago. Consider the condition they're in—carrying a calf for the last seven or nine months—because of all the green pastures. We normally supplement them when they are dropping calves, but that's the only time—but, of course, when we're undergoing a drought, we actually have to do it. But as you can see, it is as green as can be, but there's times that it's not that green but that dry grass will keep them alive. The maintenance department does the mowing, most of the road, around the main buildings, the main residence.

Another water well with a submersible pump on your right supplies these four corners. There's a pond I was talking about that we dig to hold that rainwater when it rains. This land is very well fertilized—the only thing lacking is phosphorus. So one of the easiest and cheapest ways of doing it is to put it on a feeder. Rainfall is twenty-five to twenty-seven inches per year. When we get enough rain, this country is in good shape; some of the mature mama cows will be weighing over 1,500 pounds.

Cattle on your left are the Santa Cruz, the new composite breed. We started the crossbreeding about fifteen years ago. They're half Santa Gertrudis, a quarter Gelbvieh, and a quarter Red Angus. The breed is popular; there is a demand for it.

Fence on your left that you can see—that fence has been there for forty years. See how the posts are wearing out? So is the wire. The fence crews are working on it now. As you can see, not any more trees on your left; they've been cleared. I remember the time when there were three crews of people building fences. They would be living under a tent—of course, that was back in the '30s and '40s. And now it's very modern. It will be cedar posts and steel.

There's a water pond I've been talking about.

This bunch of cows—their babies were weaned just recently. I think there are maybe two- and three-year-old cows in that bunch.

When we did single sire, there was no more than forty cows to one bull. Multiple sire is no more than twenty cows to one bull, a lot of cattle in one huge pasture.

Here are a bunch of Santa Gertrudis heifers.

There go the cowboys. Ahead of us is a cowboy camp house. You find a lot of these houses throughout the Ranch; at one time the cowboys would come work cattle and be away from their families for three or four weeks. They now come and go the same day. Ahead is a set of working pens; you also find a lot of these pens throughout the Ranch so cowboys won't have to drive cattle far to get them worked.

A popular gate on the place is—we call them bump gates. You stop right against that gate and push it open with your vehicle. It will swing back to the same position. We have over 600 miles of paved roads throughout the Ranch, and a lot of these gates. Makes it very easy and convenient to get from one spot to another. Mr. Bob revised the design to make it better. The very first ones were made out of lumber, a lot lighter, and they're now made of pipe and last a long time. They are made here on the Ranch. Our welding people do this kind of work. Rain or shine, day or night, you don't have to get out to open a gate.

There's an old dipping vat. I worked here—a lot of cattle. This is the loading chute. You back up with your trailer and get 'em loaded. You have a gooseneck, you load 'em on this side. There're times that I have dreams of working cattle in this set of pens—the Calera Pens.

The dipping vats killed fever ticks. Mr. Bob's father actually invented the dipping vat in the late 1800s or early 1900s, or something like that. But it was a problem that they would have to dip every so often. They started at one point and made a circle and went through the Ranch and by the time they finished with the last pasture, the first was due to be dipped again. So it was almost an endless job, but they managed to control the fever tick. They have been out of use for a long time. Now they inject the cattle with—I don't know what they use today—but they used to use Ivomec, an injection that keeps the flies off and worms 'em, and the whole shebang at the same time.

Everything is worked with a hydraulic chute, as you can see. You can do miracles with those hydraulic chutes. That's to brand cattle, tip horns. You push the cow in there—you can use the two gates at the front that will catch the head and you can do any kind of work with that animal's head, and then you can vaccinate any part of the body, or brand on the side or butt or whatever; you can go around the back and brand them on their butt. Called a squeeze chute. It is used now, but not the dipping vat. This chute is almost like the one you saw back there, the yellow one. You can open the top and bottom, and you can run any size animal through there. It's manufactured, built.

These calves are bellowing for their mamas. They bellow for about three days. Their mamas also look for them.

A water well with a submersible pump on your right supplies all of this area. It runs by electricity. It replaces the windmill. In case of a hurricane, it doesn't blow it away as easy as it would a windmill. [That's] some of the weaned bull calves ahead of us.

Dog kennels. At one time the cowboy wouldn't leave without his cow dogs, mainly Australian Blue Heelers. When there was a lot of brush, there were places that the cowboys couldn't go in there with a horse, and the dog would push 'em out for them.

Sometimes I stayed a week at a camp house on the Laureles and Norias Divisions when I was spraying cattle. A camp house accommodated about twenty or twenty-five people to sleep. They would normally have two cooks to do the cooking. The cooks would get up early—everybody would get up early in the morning—and the cooks would start preparing breakfast. The cowboys would go saddle up, then have breakfast, take off, and go gather cattle. They could be working maybe a mile away from the camp house. The cooks would prepare the chuck wagon and go serve lunch where they were working. Then they would head back to the camp house and prepare dinner at the end of the day. But they would always have two cooks to do the cooking for them. Mainly beef, along with beans and rice and camp bread. The rabbit syrup, Brer Rabbit, was very popular for dessert with the camp bread and coffee.

These are all Santa Cruz bull calves. See, they're lighter in color compared to the Santa Gertrudis. They are maybe nine or ten months old.

Now, this is one of the many dams that you find on the place today. Some crude ones were built in Captain King's time to hold some of that precious water, but most of them were built in the early twentieth century. You can already see that it's full from that rain a day or two ago. We had twenty-five inches of rain two months ago.

This is the arena where they work, exercise, and train Quarter Horses. It's a full-size arena. King Ranch cowboys and employees and members of the family will all get together once a year and put on a rodeo, along with a barbecue. We have all kinds of events; everybody participates. This is also where we have the Ranch Hand Breakfast every year, where more than 5,000 people come through the line for breakfast. Biscuits, scrambled eggs, sausage, coffee. And they have a roping demonstration in the arena, and other people do cooking—*pan de campo*, camp bread—and music that is good. You get to visit with friends and make new friends.

This part of the Ranch was dairy cattle country and racehorses. All the facilities except the arena—the arena wasn't there at that time—were used to train the Thoroughbreds for racing. They would train them here and then send them to New York and California. When Mr. Bob Kleberg passed away in '74, all racing stock was moved to their facility in Kentucky.

All the buildings that you see have been converted into a Quarter Horse/cattle operation. That used to be the jockey room and next door was the feed room, and the big Running W there was the blacksmith shop—that's where they would trim their hooves and put shoes on 'em and what have you. This building was the kitchen, with a dining room, and they would serve breakfast, lunch, and dinner for the racehorse people that would come to work. [That's] the veterinary department right next to those buildings, and the trainer's room and the guest rooms. And then behind was the training stable and the racetrack; on your left was a mile-long racetrack where they would train them, with the grandstands that still stand there today. But the racing stables have been out of use for the last thirty years. Everything was neatly painted with the brown and white—those were the racing colors.

But Mr. Bob had a very sharp eye for livestock. He was a genius. His chauffeur told me one day that he told him that he would like to see the day come when he can go see his horses run in New York and come home for dinner the same day. So the very first jet that was available to him, he got him a jet, and he would have breakfast here at the Ranch, go see his horses run in New York, and come home for dinner. He had a lot of big dreams, and the good Lord helped him to get 'em done.

On the left a couple of blocks, that's where I was born seventy-eight years ago. There were fifteen wood-frame homes for people that worked at the dairy and Quarter Horse barn. On the left is the kids' project barn—it's for youngsters to prepare their livestock for shows. Mesquite trees on your left, and some more of the stables that we used for the racehorses.

I live on the other side of this set of pens. When they replaced a lot of the wood-frame buildings, they built what we call the Colony. Then Mr. Bob told my dad he was going to build him a house near work, near the dairy and the Quarter Horse operation. So when I got married in '49, they built me a house right next to my dad, so we were neighbors for the longest time. That old mesquite tree is over a hundred years old. I used to climb it when I was a kid.

The dairy barn. We used to have some of the finest Jerseys in the country. We would show them throughout the nation, milk them, and supply the employees with milk. We would milk ninety-six head twice a day, run milk through a cooler, bottle it, and deliver it to the employees' doorsteps early in the morning and late in the evening. We shut it down in the '50s.

This is where some of the famous horses are buried. Their stones are sitting there: [Thoroughbreds] Assault, Middleground, and [Quarter Horses] Old Sorrel, Mr. San Peppy, Hired Hand, Anita Chica, Peppy San Badger—there's a stone for every horse.

They would keep some of the mares here and some in Kentucky. And they would bring all the offspring at a certain age and train them and would take them from here by express car to racetracks in New York and California.

This is the tack room, where the cowboys saddled up in the mornings—you can see the trailer there. They'd load 'em up in the trailers and take off. This was neatly painted brown and white at one time. Everything was painted brown and white—tubs, buckets, tack boxes—and everything was neatly kept. Floors were rubber from one end to the other, and there was a drain in every stall.

Straight from here—that's where I was born seventy-eight years ago. There were like twelve or fifteen houses for employees that worked with the dairy cattle and Quarter Horses.

There is one of those tires [used as horse feeders] that I was talking about. Some of the cow ponies on your left.

That's where a cowboy lives. Houses on the right are what we call the Colony. There are over a hundred homes where some of the help that work on this division live.

We also have a school and a chapel, but it is no longer used as a chapel. Other groups use it for meetings and what have you. They go from pre-K to eighth grade here, and then we bus them into town, where we have our own high school at the university [Texas A&M–Kingsville], or to King High School in Kingsville, or to Riviera.

There is a Colony in every division of the Ranch.

Should be some Longhorn steers ahead of us on our right. Some of these steers played a big part in working cattle in the open at one time. They would halter-break them, teach them to lead. They would normally have ten or twelve of these steers beside a working herd when they were working cattle out in the open. When they would go to weaning those calves, after they were branded and vaccinated, they would put them with the steers along with the cows they no longer wanted to keep—barren cows and what have you. At the end of the day, whenever they finished working the herd of cattle, they would turn all the keeper cows back in the pasture. The steers would lead calves to the pen, and they wouldn't have any problem getting calves away from them. There were times that they would brand as many as 800 calves in a day's work.

Captain King's men drove over 100,000 Longhorn steers and cows up the country up north to railheads such as Abilene, Kansas, in his time. What Captain King would do, he would send the men with the Longhorns up the trail, then meet them at the point of contact with the northern buyers.

Some of the Longhorns on your right in the middle of the pasture. We keep them for historical reasons. We only have maybe 50 head, but you'd be surprised how many people visit the Ranch and ask for Longhorns. Today on King Ranch we have 1,000 head of Santa Gertrudis, 23,000 Santa Cruz, 360 horses, and 60 Quarter brood mares.

Ahead of us on the right is the baseball park named after Assault. That's where the youngsters and oldies play baseball. At one time we had a popular team of players. I have a list of those; they were in the paper and the whole shebang, with Tio [Stephen J. Kleberg] with them, and I have a list of all the players that played there at one time, the ones that are still alive and the ones that are deceased.

Here's where we had a garden at school on your right—part of the Santa Gertrudis school buildings. This was the home economics department, and we would also have seventh- and eighth-grade classes there. When I was in that grade, there weren't many girls, so I actually participated in home economics—did some cooking and sewing. I had an apron that I made—don't remember where it ended up.

These buildings on your right are the maintenance department, the welding shop over there. I said something about some of these barns—every barn had a name. They were built to store hay in; there were times that we would harvest the hay and bale it and stack it in those barns. Part of these barns had places, stalls where you could stall horses and what have you, and part of the buildings had little floors so you could also store grain or whatever. That's where I kept my Shetland pony when I would ride horseback to school and back.

Right here on the right was a carpenter shop. Juan Zapata was the carpenter, and they would build those little phosphorus houses that they put phosphorus in for the cattle, brand new.

There's where we would come and eat our *taquitos.* My mama would prepare us a *taquito* for lunch of potato and eggs and what have you. And when she didn't have time to prepare a *taquito*, my mom would give us a dime each. The commissary was right across the street from the schoolhouse, and we would buy a can of potted meat for three cents and a box of saltine crackers for a nickel and have two pennies left over.

Mrs. King's carriage house is ahead of us. This was built in 1909. She would keep her carriages on the north side and her horses on the south side for the breeze. It is not in use; it's been out of use for a long time. It's supposed to be a fireproof stable. It was painted white at one time and they decided to sandblast it down to the original bricks, and I think it's one of the prettiest buildings.

The building on the right—hay barn. A picture of the front of that barn is seen in Ford commercials. There were five or six hay barns. This is the only one that remains today.

The white building is the commissary. It is one of the oldest buildings on the Ranch. That is where we used to buy some of the groceries. It was built back in 1856 to 1858; second floor was guest rooms and a kitchen at one time. Part of this building was used as an office. I don't know if they still have that little window with the round figure on the top—that's where they would pay the people. They shut it down a good ten or twelve years ago and converted it into offices.

Behind the commissary is the main residence. The original house burned down in 1912; this one was finished in 1915. Mrs. King got to live here for ten years. Nobody lives here today. Members of the family stay here when they come to the Ranch. They use it for special guests, parties, and weddings. They keep a staff of about nineteen people to run the house. After the original house burned down, Mrs. King wanted a house built almost fireproof. She also wanted floors built so people wearing boots would feel comfortable walking into her house. So you will find brick, tile, New York blue slate, and wood floors throughout the building. There are seventeen bedrooms, and there's a bathroom for every bedroom, twenty-six fireplaces, and it also has central air and heat.

We are coming to the feed yards. Some of the steers end up at the feed yards, and heifers that did not make it for breeding purposes will wind up at the feed yard to slaughter and end up on somebody's table. They take them to Sam Kane Beef Processors near Corpus Christi to slaughter. They are fattened here, then sold. They want them weighing 1,150 pounds. How long they stay here depends on how much they weigh when they get here. What we like to see happen is put out ten pounds of feed per head two times daily, hoping to get from two and a half to three pounds' gain a day. And then when they reach 1,150 pounds, they take a ride to the slaughterhouse.

This is part of the Santa Gertrudis Creek.

People that buy cattle from the feed yards send their own trucks or hire trucks to take them away. The feed yard got started in the mid-'70s.

This is the pasture where you run thousands of cows with hundreds of bulls. Ratio of one bull to twenty cows. Called multiple sire.

These are some of the commercial cattle. A unit manager is in charge of the feedlot, and he has some people under him. The feedlot has a capacity of 16,000 head—700 or more are sent to slaughter every week weighing 1,150 pounds. We buy as many as 15,000 crossbred feeder calves every year.

We clean pens quite often, as you can see, and we fertilize these pastures in the area. Those cables, as you can see, are adjustable to the size of the animal so they won't get out. Feed is put out twice a day, and then before the day is over, they make sure that there is feed in the troughs. Everything is identified because they weigh them from time to time. Most are not Santa Gertrudis or Santa Cruz. Only in dry years do we use those. Most of the time we buy heifers and steers. When they bring them in, the younger ones are put in the paddocks that are in the feed yards. They put them on grass and on self-feeders and then they bring them into the pen.

We have our own dryers, and if the price is right, we sell and buy cheaper at a later time. But a lot of the milo—the grain that we grow—we use here at the feed yards. We also buy corn. We use corn that we have to buy because we don't get enough rain in this part of the country for corn. There's times that we can buy corn, and there's times that we can't. We feed them milo. The mill processes a ton of feed per minute and a quarter of a million pounds a day. Also processes that grain sorghum to an oven that actually pops it so the cattle can digest it better. It's just like popcorn.

It's pretty full today—maybe 15,000 or 16,000 head of cattle. Most of the pens are full. Just those two that are cleaned are vacant.

Here's a set of loading chutes that I want you to see. You can load any size trailer, double-deckers, regular cattle trailers, or goosenecks or whatever. Cattle trailers are loaded a certain way. They have six sections, three on top and three on the bottom. They're called front, middle, and back. They load the top front, then bottom front; top middle, then bottom middle; top back, then bottom back. Those rails are where those men are working with those gates to get 'em loaded.

The building on the right is the office. The building ahead is where they do the processing when calves get here—the vaccinating and ear tagging and what have you.

Those cowboys on horseback work cattle, and they check pens every morning—every pen is checked every morning to make sure that everything is okay.

Cattle are brought in by truck. Everything is hauled by truck. They did away with the rail a long time ago. Of course, at one time they would haul everything by rail. The largest livestock loading point in the nation was on King Ranch.

This is the truck that puts out the feed. Every pen has a number, and they push a button and unload that many pounds in every pen. It's a small feedlot compared to other parts of the nation, but of course it's owned by one family. They're pretty expert at putting out the feed—everything is put right on the trough. They go back and forth and put out whatever amount is required for every pen.

I get thank-you notes or Christmas cards from people that I take on a tour of the Ranch, and they give me a call. And I have people that have told me that their friends have been here on a tour, and they want to know how to go about doing a tour and ask for me to do it for them. I had a couple the other day from the [Rio Grande] Valley who had purchased a King Ranch Ford pickup, and people would see them in that vehicle and would ask questions and they couldn't answer the questions—had never been here. So he and his wife or girlfriend or whatever made a point of taking a half-day tour with me to learn about the Ranch so they would be able to answer some of the questions.

Hunting season is beginning. Hunters are already excited. Lots of deer out there—good and fat too. They should be carrying an inch thick of fat on their loins.

We're headed for Laureles. This is supposed to be part of I-69 that is going to go all the way from Canada to Mexico—it will come right through here.

We're now on King Ranch all the way to the coast. Those are cotton module builders. We have some more over there. They put those module builders along the road to put that cotton in. The picking machines drop the cotton in those module builders and press it down, and each one can hold as many as fifteen to eighteen bales. A bale weighs about 500 pounds. A good harvest of cotton, you have a line of modules several miles long, you see lines of modules right along the road. And when there's a super crop, you see them all over the fields. They have to be hauled into the gin to have the cotton processed. This is primarily cotton and milo country.

This is the farm office and storage building there, the maintenance over here. Cotton pickers on your right. Forty of these cotton pickers can harvest your cotton, 30,000 acres, in three or four weeks. All the milo is done by contract labor that comes from Nebraska. Some of the farmland is used by tenant farmers, and they also help out. The Ranch does have some of the pickers, and they might hire some others to pick all the cotton. We have our own dryers and cotton gin; we can process forty bales per hour. A good harvest of cotton would be like 60,000 to 65,000 bales.

This is where they haul those modules. They back up and roll 'em into the truck and haul to the gin. There are 60,000 acres here under cultivation at Laureles. The rest is used as cattle country. These are some of the tractors, John Deere tractors. King Ranch owns the local dealership. Laureles is a quarter of a million acres. This is good farming blackland here on both sides for fifteen miles. Some of the rows north to south are a mile or more long. There's one crop a year.

You can see for miles. You can see some of the electrical lines way over there. Used to be a set of working pens ahead of us—there's an earth water tank and a water trough. There were once working pens here called *palo marcado*. There's a dipping vat over there. They burn what cotton is left along the road, but the rest is left and they do some disking. Headquarters to Laureles is about twenty miles.

There's a truck with fuel on this paved road, and there's another paved road over there. Those tractors run out of fuel, that truck goes there and fills them up and keeps them going.

This area of Laureles is called the South Texas Farm. When they had cattle here, they had names for those pastures. They were smaller pastures, but every pasture had a name, and they still have that name today. Every camp house, every windmill. When they were gathering cattle on horseback, they would enter a pasture and the man ahead of the group would assign you, you, and you to the left, you, you, and you to the right, you and you to the rear, and when they would wind up where they were taking that herd of cattle, and if they knew a cowboy was missing, they knew where to look for him. They could be having problems with a group of cows or one got injured or got bucked up or whatever; they would just know where to go look for 'em. Today if we were to have a problem, we would pick up the phone or radio and call in that we're at a certain pasture.

On the right is the Celanese Chemical Plant, north of Kingsville. Many people from Kingsville, Bishop, and Driscoll work there, and of course people go from Kingsville to Corpus to work at the naval base or with helicopters.

We're on our way back to the Visitor Center now. Thank you for stopping by for a visit. I wish you good luck on your way back home. You're invited to come back again, anytime.

It's the summer of 2008, and today I, Beto Maldonado, will once again pick up my hand mike and speak to the five gentlemen with me today on my private tour. They join more than 35,000 visitors who have come here already this year. These men happen to be from Mexico, veterinary students interested to see firsthand one of the most famous ranches in the world, my home for all of my life.

They will ask a lot of questions about how the Ranch handles its cattle and horses, about the grasses and why there is no barbed wire on King Ranch. I will do my best to give them answers. They will not know about my great-grandfather raising my father, Librado, to cowboy at Lasater Ranch or of my father dedicating his life to "his individuals," and they may not understand about the pride of the Maldonado family for working with King Ranch for most of a century.

But maybe they will leave here knowing that King Ranch has played an important role in feeding the nation for more than 150 years. And I hope that they will get an idea of the contributions that Los Kineños have made to its success, whether working cattle from the saddle of one of the famous King Ranch Quarter Horses or performing on foot those jobs necessary every day to make the Ranch work.

1

THE TRIP OF A LIFETIME

He [Librado] has paraded cattle through show rings
in twelve states from Texas to New York
and in four foreign countries.

Bob Bracher, in the *Santa Gertrudis Journal*

Alberto "Beto" Maldonado, age ten, rolled over and opened his eyes. It was not quite light, and he especially liked this part of the day. He could hear the sounds of prairie creatures beginning their day. Those little nighthawks and screech owls and the diamondback rattlers were almost ready to call it a night, and a white-tailed hawk and his mate were just beginning to think about breakfast. Streaks of yellow would soon begin lighting up the huge eastern sky, slowly bringing to life the sprawl of the famous King Ranch in the Wild Horse Desert of Texas, where Beto had lived his whole life. At first light Beto suddenly sat straight up, jumped out of bed, and shook his eight-year-old brother, Librado Maldonado Jr., known as Lee. "Come on, Lee. Get up. Hurry!"

The boys had found it almost impossible to fall asleep the night before. After carefully laying out the clothes they would wear for the big day, they said good night, turned out the kerosene lantern, and stared into the darkness, each with his own thoughts. Would they remember what to do, and how to do it so their dad would be proud? Had they done a good enough job? Would their "babies" cooperate? It was a brisk November in 1940, and tomorrow was the long-awaited day when they would finally show their calves in the county fair. They wanted to do it just right. Beto and Lee did not know that "their" calves represented what would soon be one of the most famous cattle breeds in the world.

King Ranch is known for a long list of innovations that have established it as the widely accepted birthplace of American ranching, but no other of the Ranch's contributions is more enduring than the development of the Santa Gertrudis breed, soon recognized in countries around the world for its beef quality and ability to withstand dry and often blistering hot climates like that of the Wild Horse Desert. Under the direction of Robert J. Kleberg Jr., King Ranch expanded its enterprises to Cuba, Brazil, Argentina, Venezuela, Spain, and Morocco, as well as to Australia, where the Santa Gertrudis remains the most prevalent breed.

Beto's father, Librado Maldonado, developed a unique method of presenting these huge, sleek red cattle across the United States and around the world. When Beto was a young boy, he began learning these remarkable techniques from his dad, and the two of them became the master showmen of King Ranch.

OUR FIRST SHOW

I remember it like it was today. Lee and I were up early. We ran to the dairy barn close to our house and began our morning chores, which included raking stalls and teaching the weaning Jersey baby calves to drink from a bucket. We did that by cupping our hands in the warm milk and rubbing it on the calf's lips until the calf would lick it and taste it and finally drink from the bucket. Next we went to check on "our" calves. They were the new King Ranch breed, the Santa Gertrudis. After talking softly to our "babies" like our dad did, patting and rubbing them down so their red coats would shine, we ran back home to clean up for breakfast.

We washed our hands and faces with cold water—we had bathed the night before in the big No. 3 tubs with water heated on the woodstove, just like every night, but this morning the cold water would do just fine. We combed our hair, but it didn't do much good, because we would wear our felt hats to show the calves. We pulled on our best long khaki pants and shirts—Mr. Bob [Robert J. Kleberg Jr.] always liked for the men on the Ranch to wear khaki, so that's what we wore too. Those khakis had been washed clean in those same No. 3 tubs and starched and pressed by our mama. My shirt was buttoned to the throat—I always wanted to look just right—and Lee's was open one button. We pulled on our boots, the kind that came up over our ankles. Familiar smells from the big black woodstove in the kitchen signaled that our mama had breakfast ready, just like every day. We quickly ate some fresh, warm tortillas wrapped around fried veal and refried beans and ran back to the barn to "help" load our calves. Finally we headed for the Kleberg County Fair in Kingsville in a Ford truck that the Ranch owned. My dad was driving.

We had tended to these calves almost from the day they were born. After they were weaned and we had taught them to drink milk from a bucket, we fed them some of the grain that was fed to the Jersey cows, and they also ate hay. We bathed and brushed them every day and exercised them in a small paddock where they could run. On the day of the fair we did not do anything different; the calves were always ready to be shown anytime and anywhere, like all King Ranch show cattle. We tried to train them to stand still for the judges like our dad showed us. We had been taught to handle the calves by the best—our dad was Librado Maldonado, and he was the showman of the Ranch's prizewinning Jersey cattle.

We stood very straight and still and looked the judge in the eye, just like our dad had taught us to do. When we won and our names were called, there was no jumping up and down, no high fives, no celebrating. We stayed very still and behaved like we had already been taught. The blue ribbon I won for first place and Lee's red one for second made us real happy because they were the first ones for the Santa Gertrudis, which would win a whole bunch of prizes later on.

And do you know what happened with that calf? I was so proud of that blue ribbon that I actually nailed it to the front of the stall where that calf was tied down, but I didn't tie 'em tight enough. When I came back a little later, that calf had eaten that blue ribbon! I never did think about asking the judge about giving me another one, or I would still have it. I still have a lot of buttons that we would get and had to show to go in and out of those livestock shows. I was the type person that I didn't like to wear those buttons. I would carry mine in my pocket most of the time and show it when necessary.

You know, at ten years of age when my calf won that blue ribbon, I knew that day that I wanted to pattern my entire life after my dad and show Santa Gertrudis cattle for King Ranch, very much so. I had no idea then where all we would go to show them.

THE MALDONADOS TRAVEL

My dad told me that Santa Gertrudis were first shown to the public in 1928, twelve years before they were called a true breed. He paraded them in Houston

Beto Maldonado (*left*), age nine, and his brother, Lee, age seven, tame "their" calves in preparation for showing them at the first Santa Gertrudis breed competition, 1939. Courtesy of Beto Maldonado.

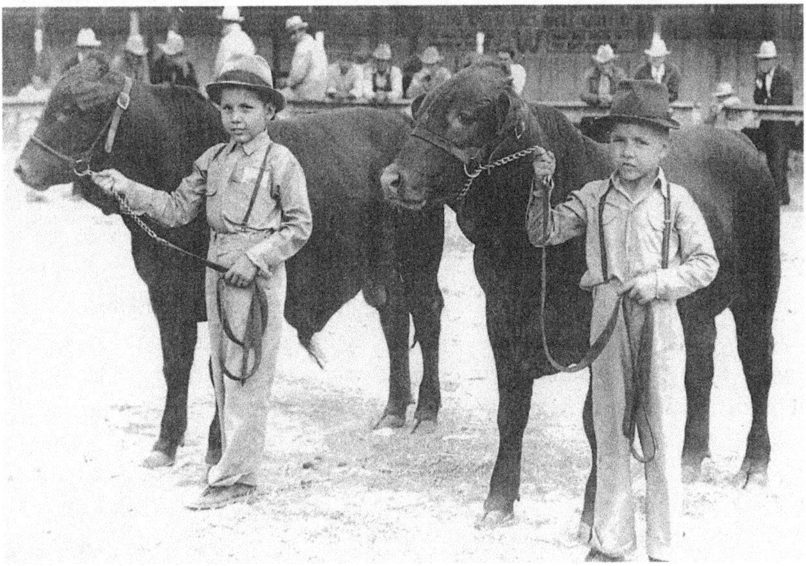

Beto (*left*) and Lee Maldonado show the first two Santa Gertrudis bulls to compete in a show ring. Beto won a blue ribbon with Bull Falfurrias, and Lee won second place with Bull Premontes at the Kleberg County Fair, 1940. Richard M. Kleberg Sr. was the judge. Courtesy of King Ranch.

at a livestock show that was held under a tent. After the Santa Gertrudis was named a true breed in 1940 by the U.S. Department of Agriculture, my dad and I would go on to show the breed in Houston, Fort Worth, Atlanta, Dallas, San Francisco, Knoxville, Coleman [Alabama], Tampa, Havana, and Casablanca. King Ranch never competed with other Santa Gertrudis breeders at those shows because it was the developer of the breed. I remember one time we left Fort Worth for Tampa and it was freezing cold, and when we got to Tampa, the pigs were dying because it was so hot.

My dad actually got to haul cattle by boxcar, express train, truck, and air during his life. Of course, he started with the boxcar. He would actually prepare those cars into a second-floor deal. He would tie all his animals and bed 'em down on the first floor, and the second floor was used for extra feed and a place where we could sleep at night. Of course, the animals were always treated and brushed like they were at a livestock show.

THE CUBAN FIASCO

King Ranch participated in a joint ranching venture in Cuba with George A. Braga of New Jersey, whose family had been prominent in the Cuban sugar business for years, to establish a Santa Gertrudis operation in Cuba. The relationship with Cuba actually began during the time of Robert J. Kleberg Sr., through his acquaintance with Colonel Harry Maud, who had a cattle operation there. Later Maud contacted Robert J. Kleberg Jr. to discuss a cattle purchase, and on December 29, 1936, King Ranch shipped thirty-five Santa Gertrudis yearlings to Cuba, the first lot of Santa Gertrudis cattle to be sold abroad. It soon became obvious that these cattle were thriving in that tropical climate, and the breeding program was resulting in improved beef quality (Lea 770).

In 1952, King Ranch entered an agreement with Compañia Ganadera Becerra, the corporation formed between King Ranch and the Manati Sugar Company, to develop a program patterned after the Ranch's Texas operation, and by 1956, a herd of 1,500 Santa Gertrudis were on the 40,000-acre spread, 1,600 of it in sugarcane (Lea 693, 770–773). Cuba was considered a farming and ranching paradise with fertile soil and near-perfect temperatures, and an investment there was generally considered as safe as one in the United States. Prospects for the cattle program, now with 4,500 head, seemed excellent for adding to the quality and quantity of beef for the citizens of Cuba. There was, however, a startling development that drastically affected the King Ranch Cuba operation.

Fidel Castro and his followers managed to seize the government of Fulgencio Batista in 1959, and Castro was named prime minister [title later changed to "president"] of communist Cuba. On January 1, 1959, Castro announced a

King Ranch truck used to transport Santa Gertrudis show cattle in the early 1950s. These same trucks were also used for transporting Thoroughbreds, such as those waiting to be loaded in this photograph. Courtesy of King Ranch.

land reform program that featured confiscating private property, including the King Ranch operation. Though the Ranch there had been operational for seven years, because of extensive clearing and improvement of pastures for breeding up the herd, building roads, and other start-up expense, the first net profit was shown in the last six months of its existence. That $600 profit was the only recovery from the Castro takeover. The total loss to the Becerra and King Ranch venture from the Communist "land reform" was $5,719,000. Of this amount, the loss to King Ranch was $3 million (Cypher 79).

My brother Plácido took [commercial grade] Santa Gertrudis cattle to Cuba, and I still have a souvenir that he brought me from there. It's a little dagger with a leather cover, and it says "From Havana, Cuba." When Plácido went, the cattle were shipped to Houston and loaded on barges that were towed or pushed by tugboats, and that's how they took them to Cuba. Dad took Santa Gertrudis purebred heifers and bulls to Cuba by plane—I believe it was in 1955. Of course, he wore cowboy boots, and people would say that those boots could kill roaches in the corner of the room. They were talking about the sharp points on Dad's cowboy boots, one-half to three-fourths inches at the toes. I never did go to Cuba.

King Ranch Cuba Memories . . .

Uncle Bob [Kleberg] was just crazy about Cuba. He bought this country up there in the north end of Cuba that was very backwoodsy. It was close to Camagüey. It opened up that end of Cuba for those poor old rancheros there; they had to take the sugarcane to the mill on mules or carts or whatever, and King Ranch built roads to where they could get those animals south to the railroads. King Ranch also built three brick homes for the operation there.

They had a boy from Falfurrias, Lowell Tash. They put Lowell Tash over the property over there in Cuba. They always had a foreman and a *segundo* [assistant], and Tash was the head honcho over there. All right, here comes that Fidel Castro on the move. He was a bandito and he wanted Lowell Tash's neck, head, whatever . . . so Lowell Tash . . . got on an airplane and escaped to Florida, just by the hair of his chinny chin chin.

MONTE MONCRIEF, DVM

When I went to the future King Ranch in Cuba, it was a tropical jungle. It belonged to sugarcane owners. I did not know Batista, but my father did, and Batista wanted to diversify the Cuban agricultural economy. There was one time of year when they harvested the sugarcane, and then no one had any work the rest of the year. There was a shortage of beef, and they were having to import beef into Cuba. When Castro came into power, King Ranch Cuba was confiscated and the cattle sent to Russia.

HELEN KLEBERG GROVES

I went to our ranch in Cuba; it was beautiful. The buildings were white and open, with lots of palm trees, and windows that could be opened to the breeze. The climate was warm and humid. They had beautiful gardens in Cuba, and we ate pasta, fruit, and vegetables. They made a special cracker that was wonderful, and I would bring sacks back with me.

MARY LEWIS KLEBERG

> In 1956 the Cuban Santa Gertrudis Association invited the membership to Camagüey to a show. The Cubans threw a lavish night party for the visitors. They literally had red carpet out to the car. After the party a big bunch of us got in the middle of the street to walk back to our hotel. We were singing and living it up. A Cuban caught up with us and suggested we break it up. He pointed to soldiers on top of buildings with machine guns, following us. We scattered like ants. (Marshall 11)

THE ANIMALS ALWAYS CAME FIRST

When we traveled on the boxcars, Dad always worried about the animals first, no matter how tired or hungry or whatever—you had to go and groom those animals, bed them down, feed and water them first, and then you could go eat. It was the same when we'd ride on the express cars. You'd feel like they were children; if it was time to water the animals, you watered the animals; if it was time to feed them, you fed them. Sometimes we would leave a fair at maybe two o'clock in the morning to get to the next one in time for the bulls to have a day or two to get accustomed to the water. If we didn't get to the next fair till three or four o'clock in the afternoon, Dad wouldn't let us stop for lunch, because the bulls were thirsty and we took care of them first. And in the morning, we had to have the animals ready by 7 a.m., and then we could have breakfast.

Dad and I always rode with the cattle, and sometimes it was real hot or very cold in those boxcars. We took canned food like sardines, beans, salmon, and crackers, and when the train stopped, we would get hot coffee. It would take forever to get from one city to the other on those boxcars.

AND WHEN WE TRAVELED

When we were on the show circuit, they [King Ranch] furnished our clothes. Three or four pairs of pants would last a long time. The only other people who had clothing furnished were the racing stable people. Mr. Bob would like for us to wear a khaki outfit, and the Ranch bought it. The commissary carried nothing but khakis. You could buy a pair of pants for $2 and a shirt for $1. The women washed and starched them.

Any expenses we had traveling, the Ranch would actually give us cash money—there were no credit cards at that time. For example, if we were to stay on the road for a month or so, or go to San Antonio and show cattle, we would go to the livestock show office and they would give us some money. Those people at the San Antonio show were well connected with King Ranch, and those people knew us. For example, if they'd give us $500, they'd call the Ranch, and the Ranch would mail a check the next day for $500. In Morocco, Michael Hughes was in charge of King Ranch operations, and he would give us dirham [Moroccan monetary unit]; that was like five dirham for one dollar.

When we were traveling and gone for a long time, we would take our clothes to the laundry. One time we were in Houston for the Fat Stock Show, and Roy Rogers was there. One of the men that helped my dad for the longest time, Refugio Rodriquez, was with us. I took everybody's clothing to the laundry. He said, "Tell them to put on mine 'RR' for 'Refugio Rodriquez.'" So when I got back I told him, "Cuco, they told me that they couldn't do that for you because Roy Rogers was in town and that was his initials." I'm the kind of a person that I always come up with something that will bring up the spirits and make people laugh.

TV AND TUXEDOS

In 1954 they [King Ranch] wanted to show a bull at the International Livestock Exposition in Chicago, and they wanted him to be on TV so the Santa Gertrudis breed could be seen all over the country. My dad showed [Jersey] cattle there for the first time in 1928, twenty years before the Santa Gertrudis breed, and he was familiar with the show. Anyway, my dad and Mr. R. P. Marshall—he was executive director of SGBI [Santa Gertrudis Breeders International]—found a trailer and loaded Buen Amigo, a big, over-2,000-pound bull and took him to the train depot. At the fair, they had a place for us to stay in a big ol' building, and they had horses and all breeds of cattle there. The other breeds were tied outside at night, and in the morning they were covered with snow. Our cattle were freezing inside. Of course, we would have to exercise them, but we didn't have to worry about getting them ready to show because we always had them in perfect shape; they were groomed, cleaned, and brushed every day. So we helped other breeders get their cattle ready to show.

We took Buen Amigo to downtown Chicago and rode with him in the elevator to the twenty-first floor of that building where the TV station was at six o'clock in the morning because there were no remote cameras at that time—TV was pretty new. Buen Amigo behaved like a gentleman. Dad, who had never been to school a day and was completely self-taught, was interviewed [in English] on TV that day, and after that, a bunch of people came to see my dad at the fair because they thought it was remarkable how he could handle such a huge animal, leading him by just a short halter rope. The first time I actually showed with my dad was at the Texas State Fair in 1950, and that was a lot easier because at least there we didn't have to take a bull up in an elevator.

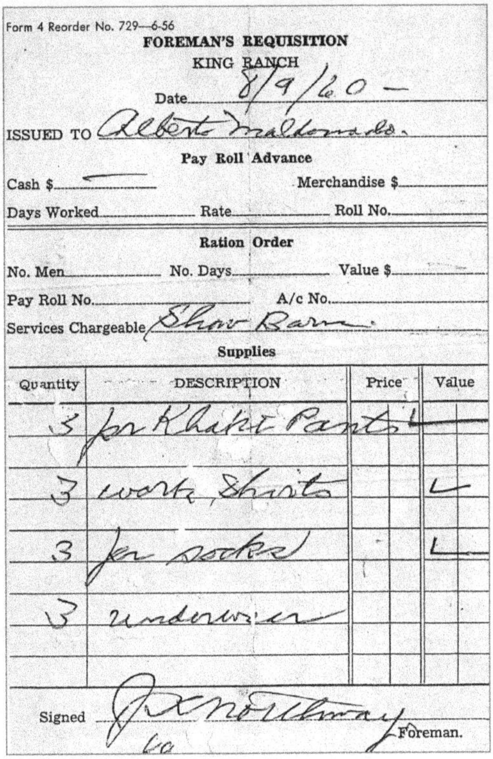

Form 4 Reorder No. 729—6-56

FOREMAN'S REQUISITION

KING RANCH

Date 8/9/60 —

ISSUED TO Alberto Maldonado

Pay Roll Advance

Cash $ —— Merchandise $

Days Worked Rate Roll No.

Ration Order

No. Men No. Days Value $

Pay Roll No. A/c No.

Services Chargeable Show Barn

Supplies

Quantity	DESCRIPTION	Price	Value
3	pr Khaki Pants		
3	work shirts		
3	pr socks		
3	underwear		

Signed J K Northway Foreman.

King Ranch foreman's requisition form. Courtesy of Beto Maldonado.

While we were at the Chicago fair, I met this young couple, Pete and Sue Secundios, who were newly married and had visited San Antonio for their honeymoon. They bought a steer calf in San Antonio and took it back to show, and that steer was named the grand champion steer at the Chicago exposition. [TV star] Arthur Godfrey was at the fair showing his Tennessee Walking Horses, and he started bidding on that steer. They sold it by the pound, and it weighed over a thousand pounds. Arthur Godfrey was the highest bidder, and Pete and Sue ended up with over $30,000 for that steer. Sometime soon after the sale, Sue was on television on a program called *To Tell the Truth*, where the judges or audience would have to pick the right person who had done whatever they told about; this time it was who sold a steer for $30,000 at the Chicago Fair. I was watching that program and I told my wife, Dora, that I knew that woman, and she said, "How in the world do you know that person?" And I told her I was there when it [the sale] happened. Pete and Sue came back to San Antonio in 1994 to celebrate their fortieth wedding anniversary, and they came to King Ranch to see me. After that, I didn't hear from them for the longest time. After my heart surgery in April 2006, they were thinking about me and gave me a call. Something was telling them that something was wrong with me, and they called me up.

BIG D

Then, in honor of the U.S. Bicentennial in 1976, the SGBI put on a sale at the Adolphus Hotel in Dallas. My dad and I took a registered Santa Gertrudis poll bull with a firebrand #1776 to that show and stayed at the Adolphus Hotel. The cattle were moved on ramps from the garage to the Regency Room, where they were penned until time to go in to the ballroom. Dad wore a tuxedo complete with that black bow tie, but he still wore his white felt cowboy hat to show that bull. Bobby Shelton [Bob and Helen Kleberg's nephew] had found that bull somewhere on the Ranch with the #1776 to take to Dallas. Everybody thought we numbered him that just for the occasion, but calves are numbered for life when they are born on King Ranch, and that was his number. So my dad took that bull to the third floor of the Adolphus Hotel in Dallas, Texas, and the former Texas governor John Connally sat next to Gerald Bowie, the auctioneer, to watch Dad parade #1776. That bull sold for $33,000 for one-half interest, and that was the top price that day. I was lucky to be able to go along and help my dad.

> I was at the Adolphus when Librado showed the bull in the ballroom, and we were never nervous as long as Librado was holding the bull. He was confident. Librado and the cattle were a pair. I never saw a bull misbehave with him. He was a classic when he was in San Francisco. King Ranch was asked to come out to a big exhibit and show some of their bulls. A bunch of us went, and Librado brought the bulls out by train and took a bull into the hotel lobby, and I believe it was the St. Francis. I was also in Chicago when they showed our bulls. He was a gentleman and kind; he spoke to me in Spanish and English.
>
> MARY LEWIS KLEBERG

My dad and I also took a bull to the Western Heritage Sale at the Shamrock Hilton hotel in Houston, also sponsored by the SGBI. It was a fancy sale—men dressed up in tux and ladies in evening dress, and they served a steak dinner before the sale. We actually had a ring inside the ballroom where the animals that were for sale were paraded. [Former] Governor John Connally was at the auction table, and again Gerald Bowie was the auctioneer. Everybody had to wear a tuxedo in order to parade the animals inside the ring, so my dad wore his tuxedo from the Willie Garza Man's Shop in Kingsville and showed a King Ranch Santa

Librado Maldonado exhibits King Ranch bull #1776 during the 1976 Bicentennial sale held at the Grand Ballroom of the Adolphus Hotel in Dallas, Texas. Half interest in #1776 sold for $33,000. Santa Gertrudis breeder Joe Marchman (*left*), former governor John Connally, auctioneer Gerald Bowie, and Bill Burford, representing the Texas Art Gallery, look on. Courtesy of the *Dallas Morning News*.

Gertrudis bull, and that bull brought $76,000 for the breeding rights. At that sale they showed Quarter Horses, Santa Gertrudis cattle, and artwork—sculpture and paintings. I saw a painting that was auctioned off for $325,000. I really enjoyed looking at those paintings.

> Ranchers and art lovers paid more than $3 million for paintings, quarter horses and Santa Gertrudis cattle at an auction held in a hotel's grand ballroom. . . . Another former Texas governor, Bill Clements, paid $56,000 for an oil painting entitled "Religion and the Pueblos."
>
> ASSOCIATED PRESS, 1976

OOPS!

It was one time when we were showing at the State Fair in Dallas that one of the bulls "fixed up" a lady's brand-new dress. She got too close to the pen, and she was real upset when that bull splattered on her. We showed her where the restroom was, and she stood in line for the longest time and came back and said she could not get in, so we let her use our room that we were able to use to get dressed. She got all cleaned up, but by that time her family had disappeared. About 355,000 attended the fair that year and she couldn't find her family, so I took her to the office and those people paged her family. She did not thank me.

I GOT TO SEE MONTREAL

I went to several events when Dad didn't go. One I remember is going to Montreal, Canada, with Dr. Albert Rhoad, the Ranch geneticist. They were having an International Congress of Genetics in Montreal at that time, so he was going to take some of the Santa Gertrudis breed to show. He actually got the cattle lined up and got Dr. J. K. Northway, chief veterinarian, to prepare the necessary papers for him, and they hired a van from Fort Worth to do the hauling all the way to Montreal. It was just the driver and me; Dr. Rhoad and his wife flew up. It took us a couple or three days to get there because we were driving until eight or nine in the evening, and then we would stop at a motel and spend the night there and then take off the next day. The animals stayed on the truck on the way up because that van was big enough for them to move around, and there was no way we could unload them.

He [the driver] was driving a fairly new van and didn't have some of those permits to go through those states. I remember spending about a half day when we entered New York because he had to wire for a permit to drive through New York.

At the checkpoint in Canada, we had to have health papers for the animals. We had to have those even to go out of the county, and we would always manage to carry what necessary papers it would take to go to any state or through customs. So we went through customs, and the border patrolman saw the sign [on the truck] that said "Fort Worth, Texas." He said, "You know, I was stationed in Texas at one time, but a long ways from where you people come from. I was stationed in Falfurrias." Falfurrias was almost on the King Ranch Encino Division. So when I told him where I was from, oh, we had a good time. He said, "Oh, my goodness." He could name the sheriff in Falfurrias and a whole bunch of others. Once we got to chatting there and they knew where we were coming from and showed them the health papers and what have you, we had no problem getting through customs.

So I actually took a bull by the name of Lunar, a gentle bull well known from his breeding, and Mama Grande, a big ol' cow, and two other cows to show. They were not groomed or the horns shined or anything like that; they were just there to show the breed to the geneticists.

We actually stayed at McGill University in Montreal, I think it was a week. There was a lot of space on one side of the campus where they actually built a

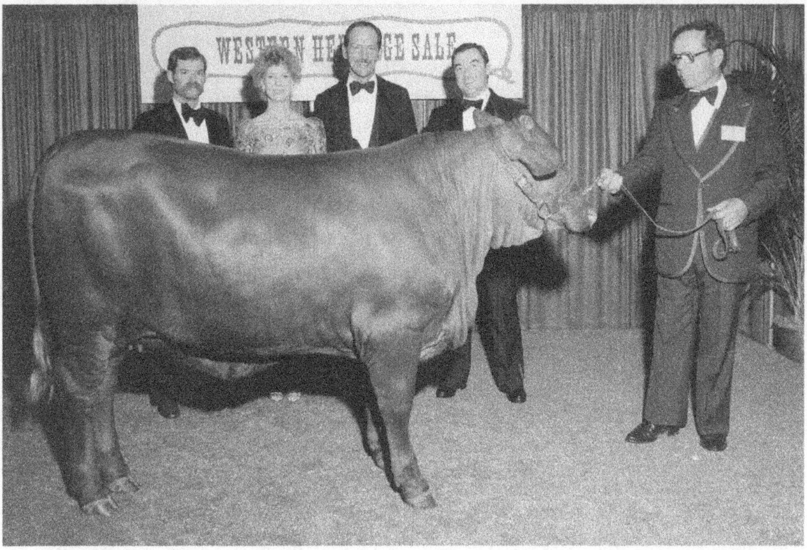

Beto Maldonado was in total control of the Santa Gertrudis bull for this picture of Tio Kleberg (*left*), the new owners of the bull, and Richard Kleberg III (*right*) at the Shamrock Hilton in Houston. Courtesy of King Ranch.

Beto Maldonado calms a Santa Gertrudis bull before parading him in the auction ring in the grand ballroom of the Shamrock Hilton in Houston in 1982. Photo by R. Reagan Atkinson.

pen so we could keep the animals and bed them down with hay, and there was water there. I stayed in a big ol' dormitory. I don't know how many thousands of rooms that building had, but one was assigned to me and they gave me a key to get in and out. It was two or three days before the rest of the people came—I think it was off school or something. I would get in line there along with the students for lunch and dinner. The kids found out that there were cattle there, so they would come look at the animals, and they found out I was from Texas. One of them asked me—I think he had seen a lot of western movies that were made back in the '20s and '30s, he asked me if we had television in Texas—this was in the '50s!

At that meeting was where we got to visit with people from Russia. Dr. Rhoad asked them about the Santa Gertrudis. They knew the breed and told Dr. Rhoad that they were doing real well in Russia. There were people there from all over, and they would show animals and a big ol' cabbage and things like that. These were geneticists—it was not a competition. Those geneticists were showing what they had done through genetics.

And I got to visit Montreal. I would go to the movies and places like that and I would go eat. Some of the people would speak French to me—I think they thought I was a Frenchman or something. I took a tour on a bus one day, and this guide was telling all about Montreal. I got to visit the Notre Dame church; it's beautiful. It's got the largest bell in the Americas, and I think it's rung a couple or three times a year. I think two or three men spent their whole lives building that church. Anyway, when we were making the tour, the guide was pointing out places and names and what have you, and we went by a cemetery. He said they just recently fenced in the cemetery and asked if anybody knew why. Of course nobody responded. He said it was because people were just dying to get in there.

Another time, in 1984, Bobby Silva and I took, I'd say, about five Santa Gertrudis bulls and heifers to a sale in Coleman, Alabama. We usually rode with the cattle, but that time, the cattle were hauled by commercial truck and we flew. And one time I got to go to the World's Fair in Knoxville, Tennessee, but I didn't take cattle. I just went for fun.

MOROCCO

In 1967, Bob Kleberg set foot on Moroccan soil for the first time at the invitation of King Hassan II, son of Mohammed V. The king had met Kleberg earlier that year in New York at a social event where they discussed ways the king might improve his country's beef output and quality suitable for the growing American tourist business. Morocco, a North African state, lacked people knowledgeable of animal science, and the land was in poor condition, seriously overgrazed from a primitive, nomadic way of caring for herds of cattle. Back on the Ranch, Kleberg wrote a paper for the king, detailing how his government might go about initiating a viable ranching enterprise. The king replied with an offer to partner with King Ranch in such an endeavor, and seeing Morocco as an economically feasible entry, eventually, into the European market, Kleberg entered for the first time into a fifty-fifty partnership with a bureaucracy holding the other half. The Moroccan government agreed to furnish 25,000 acres of land, with 25,000 acres to be added each year until the total was 125,000 acres. Kleberg agreed that King Ranch would furnish the cattle and expertise (Cypher 210).

The King Ranch operation in economically strapped Morocco ended in the mid-1970s because the mounting cost of arms to fight guerrillas opposed to King Hassan's government rendered Morocco financially unable to do anything else. A compromise plan, even if feasible, was never to develop, because the architect of the operation, Bob Kleberg, died on the evening of October 13, 1974 (Cypher 227).

> When Bob died, Kip Espy, John Armstrong, Julia and Andrew Jitkoff, and I were sent to Spain and Morocco to evaluate properties. In Morocco, we came into a valley that was fenced and fertilized. The grass was up to our waist, and the cattle were beautiful. The government was very unstable, and the king had fourteen attempts on his life, one while we were there.
>
> SALLY KLEBERG

THE TRIP OF A LIFETIME

I actually went with my dad in 1969 to show Santa Gertrudis at the International Fair in Casablanca, Morocco. This is how it happened.

My dad was preparing bulls for the 1969 cattle auction sale when Mr. Bob came over to look at the bulls. Mr. Bob had a sharp eye, a super eye for livestock. He could find defects and whatever was wrong with any animal, and he could spot it right away. The bulls were almost half gentle when he [Mr. Bob] came over to look at them, and dad had them all lined up along the fence like he always did when he was working with them. Anyway, Mr. Bob looked at them and he asked my dad, "Are these bulls for sale?" My dad said, "If the price is right, they are for sale"; Mr. Bob liked to joke with my dad like that. Mr. Bob actually looked them over from one end to the other and left, and in the next day or two he came by and said, "Librado, continue to work with these bulls. I'm gonna send them to Morocco, and I want you to go with them." My dad asked me if I would go with him, and I said yes. I told my foreman at that time, Norman Parish, what we needed to do, and he said, "Oh, by all means, yes. We will manage a way to work so you can go with your dad."

Tio Kleberg later shared why the Maldonados were chosen to take the bulls wherever they were shown:

> We had the best guy in the world. You couldn't have better. We always knew that if there was a problem—he may not be able to deal with the transportation company in Houston—but there was no question in our minds that the bulls were going to be taken care of. He may not have gone to bed for four days, you know, but the animals were going to be cared for. And that's the reason you'd send Librado. You could have hired somebody from the transportation company and say, "Take these bulls and deliver them." Wasn't gonna happen, not when you had that much invested in the breeding stock.
>
> Think about the repercussions. We were developing a whole new seed stock in a foreign country, so you wanted those bulls to get there and you wanted them to get there healthy . . . No question in our mind—he's the best guy to send.

This trust in the Kineños (King's men) goes back to Captain King, perhaps best illustrated by a fictitious story based on a revered Kineño family told by J. Frank Dobie in *Cow People*. The story illustrates why Captain King's ultimate trust was always with his own Kineños to bring his herds safely up the trail during the cattle drives.

Dobie's story was that in the spring of 1880 King had a herd "shaped up" to go up the trail to Dodge City, Kansas. Abios was late. Three days passed, and still no Abios. Young Richard King II was very impatient and wanted to know why his father was waiting on that old drunk. Finally, Abios showed up and took charge of a herd worth thousands of dollars.

Captain King and his son went on ahead to Kansas to await the herds. As the other trail bosses arrived in Kansas, the captain would ask them how the trail had been. The first trail boss reported that he had trouble at Cimarron, and some of his cattle had drowned. The second trail boss replied, when asked, that it had rained and stormed through the Indian Territory, and he had lost some cattle in a stampede. The third trail boss said that the Indians had run off his horses. Several days later Abios arrived. Captain King asked him how his drive had been. He said, "Oh, *muy bien*, Señor. No trouble at all. We came along *despacio, despacio,* slow, slow. I picked up 130 King Ranch cattle lost out of other herds. We are 130 cattle long. Look how the cattle have gained in weight. Look how contented they are." Captain King turned to Richard and said, "Now do you know why I wait for Abios?" (Dobie 219–222).

So we didn't have a sale in 1969 because the bulls Dad and I were training were going to Morocco. Mr. Bob had already purchased land there for King Ranch, and he wanted to show the Santa Gertrudis to those people and start a herd there. We continued to halter-break those bulls, and it was in April that arrangements were made; the bulls were tested and the proper papers for the consignment were ready. At that time, Dr. J. K. Northway was the chief veterinarian, and he knew just what it would take to take an animal to any part of the world. There were twenty-one head of Santa Gertrudis bulls coming to two years of age, and we continued to work with them till we loaded 'em out.

We loaded 'em on a trailer and took 'em to Houston on trucks. At that time, William Egan Jr. was the veterinarian inspecting cattle coming in and out of the United States there, and he passed us through. His father was William Egan Sr., the racehorse trainer here at the Ranch.

A big ol' Constellation four-motor plane came into Houston, and we loaded those twenty-one bulls plus all the feed, troughs, and all the equipment we had. It was a special aircraft that would haul livestock and it was already outfitted. The pens were made of aluminum. They put no more than four bulls in one compartment, one pen; that's how they were loaded. My dad and I rode right near the pilot and copilot in regular seats. Dad actually had to sign a letter to get us up into the pit of the aircraft. The Constellation is a giant aircraft.

We left Houston and went all the way to Newfoundland. It was mid-April, and when we landed, there was snow on the ground and we weren't wearing jackets. It was at the Garner's Airport. Before jets, it was very heavily used because they [airplanes] would stop there to refuel. It took seven hours from Newfoundland to Rabat, the capitol of Morocco. King Ranch already had a lot of land there, and it was bringing Santa Gertrudis cattle into that country for the first time in that part of the world.

Michael Hughes was in charge of the operation in Morocco and Spain. He didn't get a notice of us coming at that time, but he could hear the aircraft and he could guess it was us. We landed there, and there were trucks to haul the cattle to Raul Estrade's place; he was the foreman of the King Ranch operation there. But they weren't using cattle trucks—they were more like dump trucks—and I was afraid those bulls would jump over those sideboards. They put probably six bulls to one of those little trucks. I guess the bulls were tired and did not attempt to go over those sideboards because they didn't get hurt. We traveled not very far out of Rabat and unloaded 'em in a big ol' pasture. We unloaded everything at Raul's place—the feed and troughs and what have you.

The next morning, we went over to the farm, and my dad started hollering—he said his bulls were bilingual, they understood Spanish and English. So he started to call the bulls for them to come eat, and he would tell 'em, "Come onnnn, babies; come onnnn, babies; come onnnn, babies." And they could hear him because they weren't that far away from where Dad and the troughs were. People were just amazed that those bulls would answer his call and come to that feed trough and eat. We used King Ranch feed, same thing with all the show cattle. We would buy hay, but grain—we used our own because they were used to it, and if you use somebody else's, the cattle go without eating and they get in bad shape.

We stayed there in Rabat a few days, and then we loaded six or eight bulls and took 'em to Casablanca. It's funny; I remember when my brother Plácido went to war, that's where he landed—in Casablanca—then went into Italy. And I would say some twenty-five years later my dad and I were at almost the very same location he was in the Second World War.

We stayed in Casablanca for a week to ten days. The fair was on a pretty-good-size piece of ground. I would compare that fair pretty close in size to the State Fair in Dallas. It was all fenced in and very neatly kept, and exhibits were from all foreign countries. It was an International Fair, and the very first day of the fair, the king of Morocco [Hassan II] and his staff were the only ones who were inside that fair the whole day. His father, King Mohammed V, had been on a visit with Bob Kleberg at the Ranch. Mr. Bob got him into a khaki outfit, khaki pants, and khaki shirt and got him a rope, cowboy boots, cowboy hat, and the whole shebang. Pictures were made of him here at the Ranch, and when we showed in Casablanca at the fair, we took those pictures with us. His son [Hassan] was in power then, and we showed him his papa's pictures and we presented him with a Stetson hat. We got to visit the palace. At the beginning of the *Patton* movie, they showed the front of the king's palace in Morocco, and that's where we were.

They took us on a tour. We saw almost every city in Morocco, and we got to see the place they were building where they would keep those caskets there for burials. Raul Estrade knew people, and he knew how to get what he needed. We went to one building and he told us there was $3 million of gold in that ceiling. Michael Hughes would take us all around in his Mercedes-Benz. Some of those roads were very narrow. He also took Mr. Bob in his Mercedes-Benz, and he [Mr. Bob] actually liked the Mercedes-Benz so much that he told Michael Hughes to

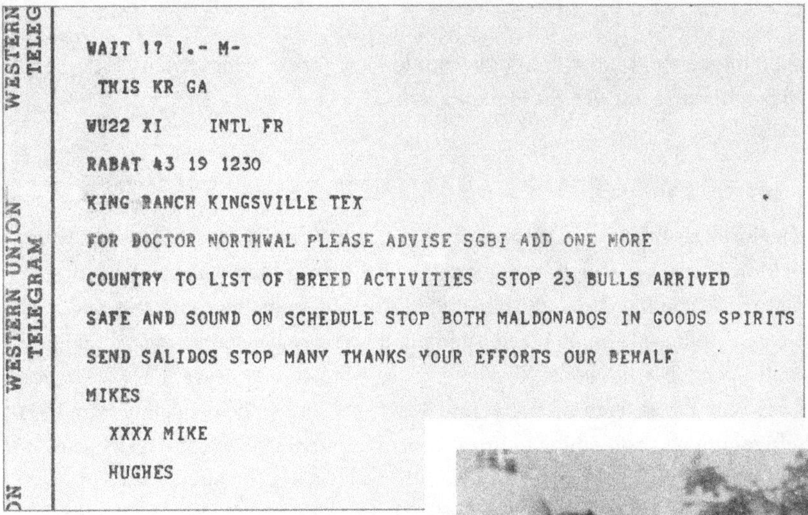
WESTERN UNION TELEGRAM

WAIT 1? 1.- M-

THIS KR GA

WU22 XI INTL FR

RABAT 43 19 1230

KING RANCH KINGSVILLE TEX

FOR DOCTOR NORTHWAL PLEASE ADVISE SGBI ADD ONE MORE COUNTRY TO LIST OF BREED ACTIVITIES STOP 23 BULLS ARRIVED SAFE AND SOUND ON SCHEDULE STOP BOTH MALDONADOS IN GOODS SPIRITS SEND SALIDOS STOP MANY THANKS YOUR EFFORTS OUR BEHALF

MIKES

XXXX MIKE

HUGHES

above: Telegram from Mike Hughes telling of the safe arrival of Santa Gertrudis cattle in Morocco. Courtesy of King Ranch.

right: Plácido Maldonado landed in North Africa in World War II near where his father and his brother Beto would introduce the Santa Gertrudis breed to Morocco twenty-five years later. Plácido was a member of the 88th Infantry Division and a life member of VFW Post 2375. He retired from King Ranch in 1987 with fifty years of service. Courtesy of Beto Maldonado.

get him one and send it to him. It went to New York or Pennsylvania or somewhere, because it never got to the Ranch.

WE STAYED AWAY FROM VEGETABLES

Dr. Northway told us to stay away from vegetables and the water while we were in Morocco so we wouldn't get sick. At Rabat no breakfast was served in that part of the country. We would eat at Raul's house. In the morning we would have a cup of coffee and some bread. At night, it was a seven-course meal, mainly mutton and fish, bottles of wine, cheese, vegetables, and dessert, but we stayed away from the vegetables. Everything was freshly done; the only thing from the refrigerator was something to drink, cola or something like that. The fish was baked. They would bring you a whole fish, and you would work on one side and turn it over and work on the other side. They would pass cookies for dessert and a cup of coffee and, at the very last, a bottle of cognac to clean the cup of coffee and drain it out. You would stay at the table two hours just eating and talking. The wine was good. They made it, or somebody made it, because you could tell by the bottles that they had been used many times.

There was a bakery next door to the hotel where they had all kinds of bread and soda pop. We could buy those breads and it wasn't wrapped, but if you wanted them to, they would slice it and give you a piece of paper to take it home, or you could go get a tray and put whatever on it, just like here. I drank Fanta Orange with the bread.

When we got to Casablanca, the temperature was nice, not hot. In fact, on top of the mountains there was still snow. We stayed at the hotel in Casablanca and got a taxi to come and go to the fair. We ate mostly mutton at the hotel because the beef was very poor; those people knew fairly well what we were going to eat for lunch or dinner. We had our own purified water at the hotel and they kept our name on it, so when we ate, we used that water.

At the livestock show we ate what was available. They had an American stand there that sold hamburgers and hot dogs. People would buy the bread; it was about fourteen inches long, like French bread, but a lot thinner, maybe a couple of inches. The only thing, they wouldn't put it in any bag—there was a little paper to hold it in your hand to carry it home. And what they would do, they would cut that bread in two, and they had a piece of round wood and they would stick that wood into that piece of bread to make a hole, and that's where they put that wiener in there and that was your hot dog. The bread would make two hot dogs and you could take them, or if you wanted only one, you could leave one there. They also had awful good potatoes, French fries, and all kinds of beautiful, white potatoes, real pretty, and good. I remember they had Coca-Cola and Fanta soda pop.

right: Beto (*left*) and Librado Maldonado in front of the Santa Gertrudis stall at the International Fair in Casablanca, 1969. Courtesy of Beto Maldonado.

below: Valentine from Beto's daughter, Dora, when she was nine years old. Courtesy of Beto Maldonado.

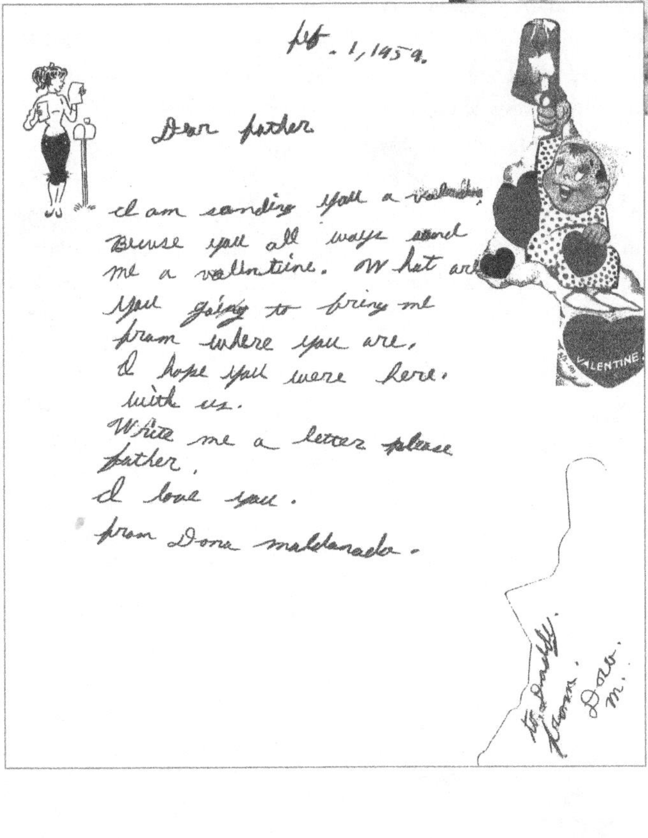

Feb. 1, 1959.

Dear father

I am sanding you a valentine, Becuse you all ways send me a vallentine. What are you going to bring me fram where you are. I hope you were here. with us.
Write me a letter please father.
I love you.
from Dora maldonado.

VALENTINE

to Daddy. from: Dora M.

FOR EVERY SEVEN DIRHAM, A WIFE

I saw a man with three wives there. For every seven dirham, you could have one wife. If you had fourteen dirham, you could have two wives; twenty-one dirham, three wives. I was told you could have as many as six wives. They used long black dresses and wrappings, and when I got there, I thought, "There are a lot of nuns here!" All you can see are the eyes. They are very serious people, and you cannot fool around with them; you don't joke with them. We had our picture taken there, and one of the pictures I have was when we were given a pass to get into the fair.

The people out in the country never come to the city. They have what they call marketplaces where people from the city bring in their busloads of goodies and exchange them for what they have in the country, like chickens, eggs, and whatever. They don't eat pork in that part of the country; there are no pigs there.

So we spent a couple of weeks in North Africa, and then on the way back from Casablanca we made a point to stop at Madrid, Spain, for a couple or three days. That's when King Ranch was acquiring land in that part of the world. It was raining, so we didn't get to see much of Madrid. A bullfight was going on one of the nights, but we were not able to go to the fight due to the rain.

We headed home, and I remember very well saying to myself, "Well, here we are on May 3rd in the middle of the Atlantic Ocean having something to eat." We landed in New York and spent a couple of days there visiting my younger brother, Lee, and some other employees of the Ranch. Lee was one of the grooms for the racehorses, and they had places to stay at the racetrack. One of the other grooms already had his family there and had a home, and that's where my dad and I stayed, with Herman and Lina Cortez. My nephew, Joe Henry Perez, from Alabama was in that part of the country and he came to New York to visit with us. Then we headed back home, landing in Houston and finally Corpus Christi. It was the trip of a lifetime.

2

THE BULL WHISPERER

He was the first and the finest—the original showman of the Santa Gertrudis cattle breed.

Mark Jones, in the *Kingsville Record*

King Ranch, often called the birthplace of the American ranching industry, is located in South Texas between the Nueces River and the Rio Grande. Its contributions to the industry are legion. Its success is a result of a unique culture forged by the interdependence of King Ranch owners and the Kineños, who worked side by side for six generations with equal pride in the work to be done. No other endeavor illustrates this remarkable culture better than the thirty years of the famous auctions, all of which featured Librado Maldonado, his son Beto Maldonado, or both.

AN EXTRAORDINARY AUCTION AT 35,000 FEET

I actually took over-2,000-pound Macho to the Dallas/Fort Worth Airport to buy him a ticket to Hawaii. When I walked through those DFW doors, it was like the president of the United States was walking in there. Macho, a huge Santa Gertrudis, was the only bull to "buy" a ticket at DFW [or any airport].

There were more than two hundred people already there, and I marched Macho right up to the United [Airlines] counter. One of the newsmen was there from New York and he put the story on the morning and evening TV news, and Macho had his picture in every newspaper in the country. Of course, I didn't actually buy a ticket for Macho. When I attempted to buy a ticket, they wanted to charge by the pound, so I told the ticket seller I couldn't afford it!

Here's what happened. In 1985, some Santa Gertrudis breeders got together and decided to make their first airborne cattle auction on the way to Hawaii. What they would do, they would go to your place and take pictures of your consignment animals and make a consignment tape. Those breeders finally got a whole bunch of consignments, and that's how it got started. They were doing an airborne auction because it was something new, something nobody had done, something to talk about, and that type of auction would be good publicity for the Santa Gertrudis breed.

The animals that would have semen or embryos in the sale were pretty well known by the breeders. King Ranch offered semen for sale—I believe it was Macho's semen this first time, and I think tiny bottles of that semen sold for $80. Everybody knew Macho so well because Macho and his papa, King 55, were the only two Santa Gertrudis bulls to be named Four-Star Superior Sire by the Santa Gertrudis Breeders International. They based that superior performance on growth, performance of offspring, beef quality of offspring, and absence of defects. Macho was a beautiful, perfect cherry red that you liked to see in a Santa Gertrudis, and he weighed about 2,900 pounds.

So what they did, they asked Tio Kleberg and Mr. R. P. Marshall about the possibility of me taking Macho to DFW the day of that departure to Hawaii.

Ruben Rodriguez and Bobby Silva went with me, and we spent the night in Georgetown at Larue Douglas's ranch on the way up. When we got to Dallas–Fort Worth, we fixed up Macho's bed in the basement of the DFW Airport. We had a king-size bed frame made for him out of aluminum pipe, and it would come apart so we could travel with it. That bed was a good twenty-four inches high, and it took ten or twelve bales of hay to fill it up because we packed it down so Macho would have a soft bed on that concrete floor. Everybody with United [Airlines] knew what was going on, and they would go downstairs to visit Macho.

We spent the night at the hotel at DFW, and the next day we got Macho all shined up and loaded him up in the trailer and brought him in front of the DFW doors, and there was the media, very heavy. Those media people found it hard to believe. Macho was a perfect gentleman. I had taken him off feed three days before and off water for twenty-four hours. When I pulled him off his bed that morning, he dropped every drop of urine he had before I paraded him into the airport, and so I was in good shape after that happened.

The plane was a big 747. Gerald Bowie was famous for conducting sales like the ones he did in the Adolphus Hotel in Dallas and the Shamrock Hilton in

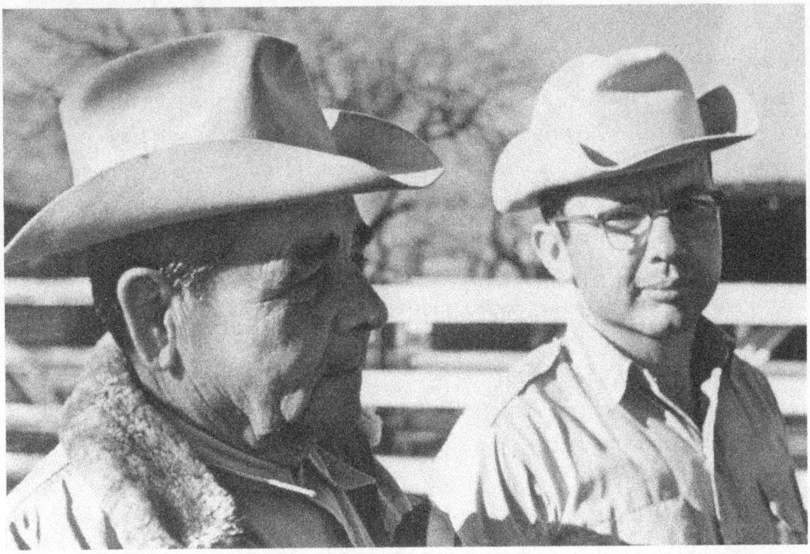

Librado (*left*) and Beto Maldonado, 1956. Photo by Helen Kleberg Groves.

Beto Maldonado and Macho, a Santa Gertrudis bull weighing more than two thousand pounds, enter the Dallas/Fort Worth Airport to "buy" Macho a ticket for the first airborne auction to Hawaii, 1985. Photo by R. P. Marshall.

Houston in 1976, and he was the auctioneer that day on the plane. He would start the bidding just like any other auction, except he was showing a picture instead of the animal. He would say, "This is so-and-so's cow, she's five years of age, and she produced so many calves, and whatever, and we're gonna sell embryos from this cow." He sold semen from the bulls like that too. I know because I have a tape of that auction.

It was January, and because of the weather, I think, the aircraft was late getting there and we had poor Macho there for a long time. He stood on one leg, then on the other. Bobby and Ruben were prepared with brooms and shovels, but Macho behaved like a gentleman.

After everybody boarded up, we took Macho outside and loaded him in the trailer, and we headed back to the Ranch. When I think about it, I can't believe we actually did that.

I still have that January 10, 1985, Associated Press release about that airborne auction on the way to Hawaii. Here are some quotes:

> More than three hundred ranchers, breeders, and guests taking the flight to Hilo in Kona, Hawaii, munched on pastries and coffee while waiting on the plane for two hours because of bad weather elsewhere. . . .
>
> The center-ring auction, sponsored by Santa Gertrudis Breeders International, would sell interests in semen from seven prize bulls and embryos from two donor cows. . . . "[T]he focus of the sale is the high technology of embryo transfer," [Steve] Harrison (chairman of the trip's organizing committee) said.
>
> "Through science, a prize cow can produce dozens of eggs for transplant to 'recipient mothers,'" said Dr. Robert Morris of the Ozark Valley Farm in Mountain Home, Arkansas. "A prize bull's semen passes on another set of high-priced genes."
>
> One passenger estimated an embryo would not sell for under $10,000 at the auction. Harrison said, "If Macho had been for sale, he could command more than $1 million."

The airborne auction was a public relations success, as judged by Steve Harrison. On January 23, 1985, he wrote in a letter to Tio Kleberg:

> The significant contribution of the King Ranch added class to "CHERRY RED." Beto and Macho were the perfect centerpiece for "The World's First Airborne Cattle Sale." The resulting PR on NBC Nightly News and numerous

other media was better than we had hoped for. Please give my thanks to Beto and his crew for an exceptional job well done.

THE FIRST KING RANCH AUCTION

Cool breezes feeling almost like autumn blew across the Headquarters at King Ranch in Kingsville that November in 1950 (Lea 652). It was a welcome break from the hot South Texas summer that lasted way too long. The wide blue skies were clear and bright, just as they are most of the time. It was a perfect day for the first auction of Santa Gertrudis bulls and King Ranch Quarter Horses, which ranchers had already begun purchasing by private treaty. As the new Santa Gertrudis breed became known and a few were sold, the demand grew. A waiting list of more than three thousand made it necessary for buyers to wait their turn because supply simply could not keep up with demand. Ranch management decided to offer an auction so that buyers could evaluate the yearling bulls and purchase them immediately if they chose.

Robert J. Kleberg Jr.; his brother, Richard M. Kleberg Sr.; his nephew and assistant, Richard M. Kleberg Jr.; Dr. Albert Rhoad, geneticist; Dr. J. K. Northway, chief veterinarian; Lauro Cavazos, Headquarters foreman; and Librado and Beto Maldonado planned that first auction. Of these people, only Beto survives today. Tio Kleberg shared some of his experiences working with the auctions over the years:

> The reason the auctions got started was once the cattle were recognized—my suspicion is that once they had a number that they could sell—I think he [Bob Kleberg] said, "You know, if we have these requests to sell them by private treaty, people coming once a month or whenever to buy bulls, instead of selling them one at a time, why don't we just have an auction and offer a number of them?"
>
> We would rank the cattle and horses. We'd walk through with R. P. [Marshall] and Librado and Beto with the bulls, and we'd try to reach a consensus on which ones were the top third, the middle, and the bottom third, so we'd know where we wanted to place them in the sale. You'd start off the sale with a sort of an average animal and run through five or six, and you'd know which ones you'd want to start with and which you wanted to end.
>
> All bulls are the same and they're all different. It's like putting twenty cars out there; they're all automobiles, but something attracts your eye to one or two of them—it's the same with bulls. There may be eight people looking at a bull, but it only takes two people to make an auction, and as long as we had two or three people looking at each animal, we knew we

> had something going. People would typically be attracted to the star. You'd have two or three that absolutely stood out for whatever reason, and the tough part for them [the buyers] was they could buy only one, and that's when they would come and ask, "Well, if you were me, which one would you buy?" We had them ranked and had a lot of notes, cheat sheets, on each one, and I'd say, "In my opinion, if I had to buy an animal, I'd buy that bull right there."

It was November 10, 1950. In the past, King Ranch had taken its famous Jersey cattle to show across this country and even into Mexico. On this day people would begin coming to King Ranch, and they would soon be coming from all over the world: Germany, Brazil, Mexico, Australia, Africa, Canada, South America, and Central America.

At future auctions, men with famous names like du Pont, Bass, Wortham, Rockefeller, Richardson, and Connally would visit the auction tent. Some of them would begin arriving in their own airplanes and landing them close by, no more than a mile from the auction on the Ranch's landing strip located between the Main House and Highway 141, across from Lauro's Hill. But the auction on that day in 1950 was mostly for locals, serious area ranchers looking to perhaps purchase an outstanding bull. King Ranch had mailed brochures featuring pictures and pedigrees of the livestock to leading ranchers, and these catalogs had done their job.

It took a giant circus tent to accommodate the two thousand people who attended that first sale. Some were serious buyers of course, anxious to upgrade their own herds. Some were neighbors. And then a lot of curious people were there, just looking for an excuse to visit King Ranch. It was one of the largest spreads in Texas and one of the most famous ranches in the world. There was plenty of room for the tent; by that time the Ranch spread across 825,000 acres, somewhat less than the 1.2 million acres that made up the Ranch at one time, after Mrs. King had almost doubled its size following her husband's death. But King Ranch was still plenty big. Some 203,468 acres made up the Santa Gertrudis Division, just west of Kingsville, which is the Ranch Headquarters and was the location of this first auction.

Row after row of wooden folding chairs covered the hard-dirt prairie floor, and there were some bleachers. Still, people stood shoulder to shoulder around the walls of the tent. Those standing could probably see the action in the ring a little better than those in chairs, though the three feet of dirt that had been added to the floor of the ring brought the cattle to at least eye level for those lucky enough to find a seat. Beto Maldonado and his father, Librado Maldonado, began that day with what would become the hallmark of showmanship of

Santa Gertrudis cattle in this country and around the world. With their uncanny ability to handle livestock, they would become master showmen. Beto remembers what that day was like.

I REMEMBER THAT FIRST AUCTION

I think those people were surprised to see on top of that dirt a layer of sawdust dyed green to make the auction ring look real nice, like a carpet. It would look real nice until five or six animals came through; then it would be penetrated with the dirt, all mixed up.

I remember Armstrong Ranch was there and, of course, John Martin from Alice. He was not a big rancher, but he was in the Santa Gertrudis business. Tobin Armstrong, John Armstrong, Robert and Tom East, members of the King family—they were all there. And, of course, Sarita East from Kenedy Ranch was there. These people were serious ranchers and were always looking to upgrade their herds, and this was the place to do it.

It was an exciting time because the tent people were kinda late, and everybody was anxious to see whether or not those people would be here so we could get that tent up in time. This happened every year until the permanent arena was built in the mid-'70s that included an auction ring. It was covered, and it had bleachers and could hold hundreds of chairs [on the floor] for the bidders. But as long as we were using the tent, our people always managed to put that tent up just in time for the sale. José Saldano would come and put up the tent. He would have about fifteen men, one of the fence crews, and they would get here soon after the trailer arrived with the tent, put it up, and put up the chairs.

The tent [auction] ring was built a standard size so you could parade any size animal without any trouble or being stepped on. Cowboys from the four divisions of the Ranch—Encino, Laureles, Norias, and Santa Gertrudis—would come help with the horse and bull sale. They would help us put out feed for 'em, move 'em around, bring 'em into the auction ring, and take 'em when the animal left the ring. We had something like fifty-one colts and fillies for sale also, and those cowboys actually kept them under the trees, with a man holding each of those horses. Martín Mendietta Jr. was in charge of the *corrida* here at Headquarters, and Lolo Treviño and other people would come and help us with the sales. Everybody helped. I would say that there were at least a hundred employees working at that first auction.

It was real exciting. Mr. Bob Kleberg Jr., his brother Mr. Dick Kleberg Sr., Mr. Dick Kleberg Jr., along with other members of the Ranch family, were seated, ready for the auction to begin. Everybody was looking and waiting for the auctioneer to climb the steps to the table high above the auction ring. He would have men to help him with the bids. Right in front of the ring there would be four men, sharp men, one for each section of the tent, and once you started bidding, you could just nod your head; they'd take your bid. The men would be closer to the buyer than the auctioneer. If there was a bid for $1,000 and you bid $1,500, the men would go, "Yip," and the auctioneer knew he had a bid. And of course at the end of the sale he would call the name of the buyer.

The auctioneer that day was Colonel Walter Britten. As he climbed those steps, the tent quieted. He was tall. And he looked real young. He wore a suit, starched white shirt, tie, and, of course, a hat. That is what he always wore when he would auction all those years after that, even when doing the junior livestock shows—a coat and tie and dress pants. Colonel Britten took the mike, looked out at the crowd, and said what he always said, "Now let's turn to him No. 1." No one knew that day that a very long friendship was started. He would be the auctioneer at every King Ranch sale until he retired thirty-three years later. The Ranch donated the first Santa Gertrudis heifer auctioned, to establish the Walter Britten Foundation at Texas A&M University, where Britten had already helped finance the education of more than thirty students who needed financial assistance.

From the 32nd Annual Sale of Santa Gertrudis at the
King Ranch, Kingsville, TX, Oct. 13, 1983.

We do a fitting thing here today, dedicating the thirty-second King Ranch Santa Gertrudis sale to our friend, Walter Britten. [Jim Clement, President of the famous King Ranch speaking. He continues with:]

I guess he's known as Colonel to most of you. So much of the institution of Santa Gertrudis herds around the world has been established under his guidance. The males and females he has sold, in this ring and others, have gone on to establish herds that have made some of the highest contributions to the breed in the livestock industry; a good reason Walter is called the "Dean of American Purebred Auctioneers." He has received the Master Salesman Award from the American Hereford Association; the Outstanding Auctioneer's award from the National Auctioneers' Association; sold every junior sale at the State Fair of Texas for the past forty-four years; has sold junior sales at the San Antonio Livestock Exposition since its beginning thirty-four years ago; and a record at the Houston Livestock Show and Rodeo of selling grand champions and junior sales for 43 years.

> Even more important to us locally, Walter has donated his time and talent over thirty-two years by selling every junior heifer in the Kleberg-Kenedy County Livestock Show.
>
> Richard Kleberg Sr., then Chairman of the board, turned to Dr. Northway (longtime veterinarian at the Ranch) and asked, "Who's the young squirt?"
>
> "A kid from [Texas] A&M."
>
> "You just git that kid for our sales from now on!"
>
> Since that eventful day in 1950, Walter has become a close friend and admired by three generations of our family.

John Armstrong [Executive Vice President of King Ranch] introduced guests from seven foreign countries and some other prominent cattlemen, then said:

> When this first Santa Gertrudis is declared sold, the Walter S. Britten Foundation will have been established. All proceeds for that lot will go to this new foundation set up to help further young people's education. That's especially appropriate since Britten's greatest pleasure is helping young people.

Stephen "Tio" Kleberg:

> There were two people who have been extremely instrumental in my life in the way I have conducted a sale and the way I prepared for a sale. One of them is standing at my right . . . and that's Colonel Walter Britten. The other gentleman was the late Librado Maldonado, but we do have his son here. Beto is now responsible for the preparation of the cattle and bulls for sale.
>
> It is with this that I would like for Beto to present Colonel Britten with a signed token of appreciation (a twenty-two-inch gavel). [Applause]
>
> You know the gavel that he started out with was this big, but now it's only four inches long. He beat the hell out of it! (Britten 171, 173)

At this first auction, my dad ran the bulls through the ring without a halter like any other auction. . . . He'd run 'em in from a gate on the left, run 'em around the ring, then let 'em out the opposite gate. The auction was a success. The best one brought $10,000 in 1950 dollars; yet, as Dad and Mr. Bob thought about the buyers who had traveled from all over to bid on and maybe purchase what was to Dad and Mr. Bob the best of the best, they began thinking that there must be a better way to show the bulls that would be better for the animals and the Ranch. Mr. Bob and my dad came up with the idea of halter-breaking those bulls and parading them into the ring slowly on a halter, like my dad had done with the Jerseys.

Dad already had a routine to prepare "his" Jerseys for show, but the Jerseys were a different, tamer breed that were shown in much quieter surroundings than the auction ring, with its hundreds of spectators. He probably wondered if his Jersey techniques would work with those huge bulls in a ring surrounded by a lot of people all talking at one time, and the yelps of vaqueros bringing bulls to the chutes, and the continuous movement and noise of the crowd. Could he train them in order to show them like gentlemen in the ring? He decided that he would try his best. Mr. Bob believed he could do it, so he began to make a plan.

Dad knew that "his" animals had already been judged and well documented on super performance in fertility, growth, performance of offspring, beef quality of offspring, and absence of genetic defects—the qualities the bidders would be looking for. He knew his "babies" measured up. All he had to do was get them ready for the ring, and he thought a lot about how to do it. He estimated that it would take him maybe nine months. It would take a lot of patience, but Dad was known for his patience with animals.

He knew he would have to begin as soon as the top bulls were selected for the auction. Mr. Bob, Mr. Dick [Richard M. Kleberg Jr.] and Lauro Cavazos, foreman of the Santa Gertrudis Division—the first Mexican American foreman—would do that job.

Sally Kleberg spoke of her father's [Richard M. Kleberg Jr.'s] reliance on Librado's expertise:

> My dad relied on Librado to tell him the personality of the bulls during the culling, as well as the conformation. Librado—he was it for the bulls. He was like the bull whisperer. He never manhandled them. He just spoke to them and clicked his tongue and walked slowly around the ring.

When my dad was finished training them, he wanted those 2,000-pound bulls to enter the auction ring all shined up, with polished horns and hooves, and stand like gentlemen and then circle the ring with him while Colonel Brit-

Librado Maldonado (*left*), auctioneer Colonel Walter Britten, and R. P. Marshall worked together for many years. Britten sold all of the King Ranch auctions from their beginning in 1950 until his retirement in 1983. Courtesy of King Ranch.

ten started the bidding. When the bidding was closed and the bull sold, my dad wanted to lead the individual calmly from the ring. That was his dream. It would take several years, but his dream would come true.

First, Dad made a schedule similar to that used for his Jerseys—but tailored to the Santa Gertrudis. They [the vaqueros] would normally bring thirty-five or forty bulls, and we would actually start with those bulls, loose. Those bulls were wild.

> "Sometimes a bull will get a little skittish and try to act up with me so I will leave him alone and try to go back and work with him the next day," the master showman [Librado] said. "You never want the bulls to get any more upset than necessary, so we will just let them alone and try again." (Bracher 65)

At first, we had a chute and we could bring in maybe five or six bulls at a time, and there would be five or six of us on both sides. And we had a wood ramp, and we would walk on and use a currycomb with a long handle to scratch them from head to rear. They couldn't kick us because the chute was solid, filled with lumber all the way to the ground, and if they kicked, they would kick the chute. We would work on them with those long-handled currycombs for the longest time; then we would turn them into the arena where we were actually going to sell them. We had enough help to get the bulls to the ring, but Dad would make a point to walk back and forth with us every time to make sure that things went well.

We would cut a tape of the sale so we could get the bulls accustomed to the sounds of the auctioneer, hand clapping and hollering and what have you, of the guys taking the bids—we would get the sounds of the auction sale. We would actually walk a bull around inside that [auction] pen for a long time, and another right behind him. We were five or six or seven of us, and we would parade one bull each inside the pen for maybe thirty minutes. We walked them around every day for thirty or forty days until we were able to know that they had calmed down, gentled down, and later we would get them out of the pen and actually walk them on the road.

No matter how hard we tried, some of the bulls just would not train and would have to be removed from the sale. That's why we started with thirty-five or forty, so we could wind up with twenty-five, if we were lucky. They were hand-picked and of course the cream top of the herd. Dad was always a little disappointed, though, when he couldn't tame one of those bulls.

But before the bulls reached the chute for the first time, my dad had already started taming them weeks before by tying them to the barn stall fence, even checking on them all through the night to be sure they did not get tangled, then untying them and leading them to water the next morning. After a month we hoped we would be able to put a halter on. My dad made those halters out of regular rope, made them adjustable to fit any size head for a perfect fit for each animal. He showed me how it was done, and I made them too. We would use sheepskin to actually cover the top of the halter for the nose. The nose is very sensitive, and after so long, the rope would rub the tender part of the nose, and if you covered it with sheepskin, it wouldn't happen. Same thing at the top of the halter where the ears were. We stayed with the halters we made for the longest time.

Later they came out with those manufactured nylon halters, I would say in the '60s, that actually had a chain on the bottom, that we liked a lot better than the ones we made. But the new ones Dad would actually have rebuilt at the [King Ranch] Saddle Shop. Jim Sedwick did that work, just like his papa, Gene Sedwick, before him. Jim would put a piece of leather on that top part about three inches wide, a heavy piece of leather that would keep that rope from penetrating the skin.

We left a long piece of rope, maybe five or six feet, on the halter that would drag, and you could step on it to make them stop, or the other bulls would step on the rope, or they would step on their own rope and self-break themselves. What we did, we made a long rod out of heavy-gauge wire, and we were able to get hold of that piece of rope and bring 'em close to the fence and wrap the rope

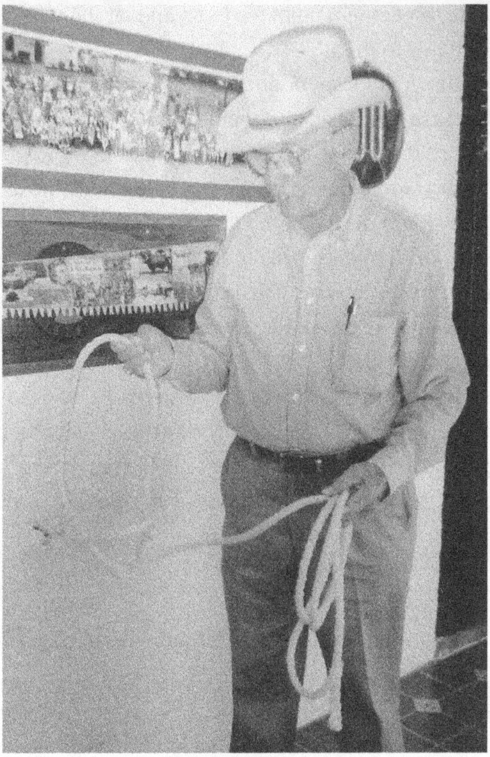

Beto Maldonado still remembers how to make an adjustable halter, designed by his father, Librado, to fit a bull's head of any size. Photo by Catalina Maldonado Yaklin.

around that post and get 'em tied up, spacing them so we could get in between bulls and not be kicked. The bulls got tamer from month to month, and they got to the point that they weren't that skittish. Gradually they would find out that we would do tender loving care and that we weren't gonna hurt 'em, so they would actually let us get close to them to the point that we could actually use a brush and a currycomb on our hand instead of on a long stick. That's how it was done.

Whenever we put a halter on those bulls before the sale, we put a three-inch number made of brass on the halter that would stay there forever. At first, though, when untamed bulls were run through the ring, we put a brass chain around the bull's neck with the numbers attached to that chain. And we weighed them from time to time to see how they were gaining and of course we kept records, and we would work 'em almost six days out of the week. At the end of the day we would drive 'em to a pasture maybe half a mile away from where we were working and they would slowly go back to the pasture and they were fed, and they would have all the grazing in the world in that big ol' pasture. Then in the morning we would bring 'em in by foot or truck all the way to the training pens, and little by little we were able to get them adjusted to us and let them know we were not going to do any harm to them.

Dad talked softly to "his individuals" all these months, just like he did the Jerseys, in Spanish and English because he considered them bilingual. The main thing is not to be afraid of them, he said. How he would control them in the show ring—way before the sale he or I would put a copper ring in the bull's nose with an apparatus called a trocar, originally designed to relieve bloating in cattle, but adapted to punch a hole the size of a large ice pick in the cow's nose for the ring to pass through and snap to close the ring. The nose ring would have a leather leading rope about five feet long, and by holding on to that rope, along with the halter rope, Dad could control the bull.

For the next two years, we worked to train and groom the keeper bulls, and we thought we were finally ready to try selling them in halter at the auction. I watched and helped my dad every day to get the animals ready for the sale. He taught me a lot. I learned all I could about using the exact same methods as my dad.

Cathy Henry, of the Visitor Center, told of observing Librado's expertise in the ring:

> Librado was extremely calm, in control, in charge—the bull knew it, bidders knew it, the ring men knew it—they didn't get in Mr. Maldonado's way. If he had an animal that was going to act up a bit and he [a ring man] was standing too close to it, if he asked him quietly to move back, he did it. He was kind of like a ringmaster, in charge of what's going on and making sure that everything happens just like it's supposed to.

THE TEST

Auction number three in 1952 was when we planned to parade the bulls. We were up extra early on that day to put the finishing touches on grooming those animals. We spent at least an hour cleaning horns with a small rasp, then smoothing them with sandpaper and emery cloth and finally using a cloth with a little oil to shine them up. We were already taking care of horns for the longest time because of the screwworm problem that we had. Any sharp point on a cow or bull could do harm to the others, and any wound would wind up with a screwworm case, so for the longest time we cut a couple of inches off the horns and smoothed them down. Then, of course, after my dad was gone and it was available, I came with an electric sander. Every time I was shining those horns with

Librado Maldonado calmly leads a 2,000-pound Santa Gertrudis bull to the King Ranch auction ring, circa 1953. Courtesy of King Ranch.

that electric sander I thought my dad should be there, because he would use a whole bunch of time shining those horns by hand.

Next came the manicures. Thank goodness for the big hydraulically operated machine that laid the animal on its side so we could clip, clean, and polish the hooves with oil. Later on, a man would come, I think from the Dallas–Fort Worth area, and he would clean and trim the hooves for us. One day an elderly couple stopped there and visited with us when people could just drive through the Ranch, and the gentleman that was doing the trimming of the hooves would do it in a hurry and he had chopped and clipped with a sharp knife and the whole shebang, and this lady said, "Ooouuuuuu, my goodness, doesn't that hurt? And that man said, "I don't feel a thing." He was a character.

We would do that about a month ahead of time because a lot of the time the bulls would cripple, and we wanted it done so if any were done [cut] too close, or what have you, they would have time to recover.

Normally the *corrida* crew of about fifteen cowboys would join us a day or two ahead to get accustomed to the routine with the bulls. They would help us lead the bulls to the auction ring from the place where we were working them near the arena, a small pen where the bulls were tied up so people could see 'em and decide which ones they would bid on.

We would have the horse sale in the morning around ten thirty, and in the afternoon about one-thirty we would have the bull sale. And then of course between the end of the horse sale and beginning of the bull sale we managed to bring everything [the bulls] just as close as we could, 'cause as soon as that bull was out of the ring, there was to be another one there for us to start selling. We knew the order, and there was a vaquero there to bring them by number. If you were a buyer, you could look on your program and see that #5 was coming in. You would have a description on that program, the pedigree and the defect that he might have, whether he's the kind of bull you're looking for, a cherry red or light in color or whatever. You could have already seen #5 because we tied them up the day before and again early that morning so people could come look at them. Even five months ahead you could look at that animal. That bull would always have the same number—he carried his number like a license plate. You could go there a month ahead and see #4 and go home and tell your foreman, "I want you to go to the King Ranch sale and bid on #4," and it would be the same animal.

It was along about the nineteenth auction in 1971 that the Ranch began listing the pedigrees of the Santa Gertrudis bulls in the program. A lot of people would concentrate on the pedigreed bulls by known sire and dam [forty cows to one bull, one pen]. There were other times when there would be bulls from multiple sires [hundreds of purebred bulls and cows in one huge pasture with a ratio of one bull to twenty cows] that you would not know the sire and dam of those animals, but a lot of times the multiple-sire bulls would bring as much money as the known sire and dam. Colonel Britten would start usually in the thousands of dollars, and then of course he could bring it lower or it could go up.

People wanted to buy those bulls. Let me tell you what happened. Mr. R. E. Smith, a wealthy man from Houston, had Santa Gertrudis cattle and Quarter Horses and was one of the first who had those outside of King Ranch. I think he was associated with the Astrodome. Anyway, he had Santa Gertrudis, and they would win in shows. We had a bull named Manzano, and Mr. Smith liked that bull so much that he told his foreman to go to the King Ranch sale and, if Manzano was gonna be in that sale, to buy him—no matter what the cost. The foreman said, "Beto, Mr. Smith told me to come over here and buy Manzano if he was in the sale." But Manzano was not in the sale, so he couldn't buy him.

We had a [dirt] landing strip in a pasture near the headquarters that was built for King Ranch's plane, and some people started flying into the Ranch for the auctions. I remember for sure Sid Richardson's aircraft was one that would land here. Anyway, it was a big event and I enjoyed every minute of it. I hope I can see it happen again.

Librado Maldonado leads a 2,000-pound bull around the King Ranch auction ring so that buyers can see the animal from all sides. This feat was Librado's trademark. Courtesy of King Ranch.

THE SALE FINALLY BEGINS

At that third auction sale day, I remember there was a short, white, foot-high picket fence with pots of some kind of flowers behind it along the front of the auction ring fence to make it look real nice and also to keep the ring men from getting too close to the ring and the bulls. The ring fence was about eight feet tall, made of four-inch pipe to be sure those bulls stayed in the show ring, but Dad did not want people too close to the ring.

The gate banged open, and Refugio Rodriquez handed that first bull's halter to my dad. I can still see him. There he stood, very straight as always, wearing those starched khakis my mama had washed on that scrub board and carefully ironed, tucked into those boots all shined up. Of course, he wore a khaki shirt with two pockets, his hat as always, and that kerchief around his neck with the Running W brand in the Ranch's brown and white colors.

Refugio brought the bull through the gate on the audience's left. Dad took that bridle rein in hand and led the animal to center ring and faced the audience. Then he began circling the bull around the arena. The audience was real quiet; those people seemed to be holding their breath. I know I was. I think they couldn't believe that a man would enter the ring with a 2,000-pound bull led only by a short halter, but this was to be the trademark of King Ranch sales for nearly thirty years.

There was this lower guard fence, maybe four feet high, at the back of the ring that formed a barrier, made of the same pipes as the ring. I was always back there when my dad was in the ring. I would have a whip, and whenever the bull just stood still, Dad wanted me to get behind that bull and make him walk around. You don't just go in there and stand still, because people want to see how that bull walks, want to see his face, his rear, the side—the whole shebang—so what you need to do is maneuver that bull around and around until he is sold. You would actually have to know how to turn him around in that ring to stay away from the side of the fence, be on this side instead of the other side so the bull could not push you into the pipe and get you hurt. You manage to always stay in the center of the ring and the bull on the outside towards the fence.

Very seldom did the bull turn on you. But even though you would halter-break and tame him for most of a year, sometimes a bull would act up. If my Dad had a problem with a bull, he would just let 'em go and get behind that guard fence with me until the bull was gone and the vaquero opened the door and out it went. You just get out of the way—that bull is looking for a way to get out. Regardless of how long you work with cattle or how well you know how to do it or whatever, I tell people if once you're inside that ring with that 2,000-pound bull and you tell people you're not afraid, you're lying. Because they're dangerous and you never know what can happen. [My sister] Alicia went to one auction and never went back; she said Dad was too close to the bull he was showing and it scared her.

> The sale made me nervous. I went a time or two; otherwise, no. If Dad was afraid, he didn't let anybody know. But when they dedicated the next sale when he [Librado] was sick [1980], we all went to the sale. We all sat together. I did not stay for Beto to bring the bulls into the ring.
>
> ALICIA MALDONADO

Tio [Kleberg] spoke about Librado's courage while working in the ring:

> He never showed fear. I saw him at one sale get banged up against the arena and the crowd got up—they were alarmed. And he just— all he did was get behind the partition. I mean he got smashed up against the pen. He just kind of gathered himself and got behind the rail and got his composure, and they let the bull out. It could have been disastrous. He was probably hurt, but you wouldn't know it. He never changed expression, he didn't act hurt, he didn't look hurt—but I know he was. The next bull was just like it never happened.
>
> Patience was number one. I never ever saw him, in dealing with cattle, ever get excited. Never. And here he was with a 2,000-pound animal and he was probably five foot four, probably weighed 165, 170; he was towered over by these huge animals. You would have thought he was a man seven feet tall the way he handled them. He talked to them; he'd shake that rope; he'd talk to them. I mean they were like friends to him.

My dad paraded that first bull until Colonel Britten was finished, probably less than maybe three minutes. Then my dad walked the animal to the exit gate on the right and handed the rein to José Silguero and walked back across the ring to greet the next bull. Refugio Rodriguez and José were two of the right-hand men for my dad to bring the bulls in and out of the ring.

One by one, twenty-five animals were presented, and every time, the bulls performed just like we had trained them. That year, the top bull would bring $40,000, four times more than the top price of $10,000 just two years before. One of the reasons was that the bulls had behaved like gentlemen.

Monte Moncrief, DVM, said the way the bulls were presented affected the price they brought:

> The way they [Librado and Beto] handled the cattle made the price go up. I remember back when $25 would last almost a month, and they sold a bull for $52,000. King Ranch employees thought he [the buyer] had lost his mind. We hadn't seen that much written down, much less paid for a bull.

R. P. Marshall agreed that taming the bulls was important. He said, "The behavior of the animal in the ring was important to the ambience of the sale and also affected the price."

THE SILVER LADIES MAKE THEIR DEBUT

> The Silver Ladies, the only foundation cows to be sold at a King Ranch auction sale, were offered on October 2, 1976, at the Ranch's twenty-fifth auction sale, in recognition of the role cows played in the development of the Santa Gertrudis breed. The First Lady of the breed was a cow named Espuma. She bore the foundation sire, Monkey, four sons: Santa Gertrudis I, his finest, as well as Santa Gertrudis II, III, and IV.
>
> For this special occasion, sterling silver buckles were presented to the buyers. (King Ranch, "How the Silver Lady Sale Came About," 1)

Tio Kleberg Speaks of the Master Showmen:

> I may not distinguish between Beto and Librado, but as I saw their role, wherever they went representing the breed—the first American beef breed—it was a very big event because there was no other like it. When Librado and Beto were in front of the public, they were not only representing a breed of cattle; they were also representing the culture and the history of King Ranch. They represented all the people here, all the people who worked here, all the family members here—Beto's family and my family.
>
> When you sent the cattle out, you wanted quality. You wanted the very best people to make that representation. If you ask anybody that's been in the breed forty years, if you ask them who the master showman was of the breed, there'd be no doubt in my mind that they would tell you, "Librado Maldonado." He had everything to do with the promotion of the breed.

When the bulls were sold and we led them to the exit door, the vaqueros took over and tied them to the fence. After about the twenty-third auction sale,

Beto Maldonado (*left*), Tio Kleberg, Bobby Silva, Roberto Mendietta, José Silguero, and R. P. Marshall with heifers to be sold at the Silver Lady Sale in 1976, the only time foundation cows were offered for sale at King Ranch. The average sale price was $7,525. Courtesy of King Ranch.

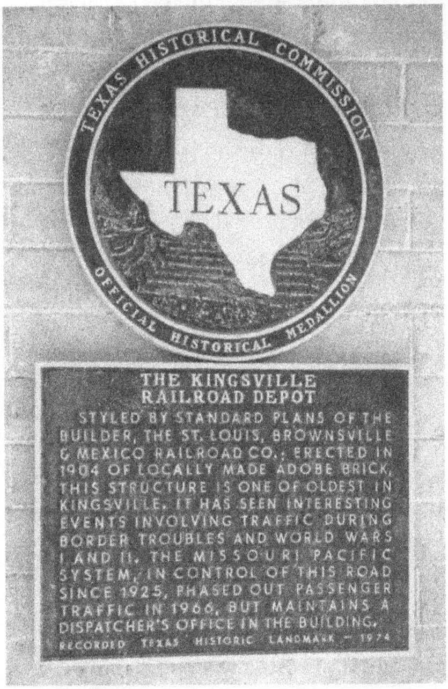

above: Refugio Rodriguez (*left*), Librado Maldonado, Beto Maldonado, and their driver are ready for the gates to open at the Fort Worth Livestock Show, 1956. Courtesy of King Ranch.

left: The Kingsville Railroad Depot was the shipping point of cattle from the Ranch's Caesar Pens, the largest shipping enclosures in the world during the 1920s to 1970s. The depot was built in the early 1900s on land donated by Mrs. Henrietta King to establish the city of Kingsville. Photo by Betty Bailey Colley.

the highest-price bull and his buyer could have their picture taken, like you see in those catalogs, and that picture would go in next year's edition. Usually the Santa Gertrudis Breeders International journal people were there to take pictures, and a few other photographers and newspaper people.

After the sale, we would ship those bulls, and of course they had to have a health paper, a Bang's test to go from one county or one state or country to another. We tested them before the sale. We would have to send the blood by train to San Antonio to have it checked over there. We didn't have enough boxes to send them. I went ahead and ordered a dozen boxes over at the sheet metal works, and I didn't know how much it was gonna cost us. It was a steel box, and in the bottom is where you put ice to keep it cool, and the upper part was where you would put as many as fifty vials. And when I went to pick them up it was 300-some-odd dollars, and I said, "Oh, my goodness, what have I done?"

But it was okay. After that, we had all the boxes in the world. We sent three or four boxes, and it would take three or four days before they came back. We would make a point to go take them to the depot in time for the train from the Valley that would be there at eleven o'clock at night, and it would be in San Antonio by the next morning.

NO CREDIT CARDS

The program specified cash only, but beginning with the twelfth auction sale, checks were accepted. There were no credit cards then. And the program also said that the sold animals were to be removed within ten days, but some were here for a long time. Men from Central or South America would be here for as many as thirty days before they could load their cattle out. The bulls were tested for Bang's disease and what have you, but if their health papers were about to expire, they would have to be bled again and new papers would have to be made after the laboratory results would come. But the local people would take their bulls within two or three days.

THE NEAR DISASTER

It rained so heavy all day Friday of the 1974 auction that people could not fly in, and a lot of other people, some of them key buyers, just could not get to the sale because of the impossible rain. This time a tent just would not work. The animals were ready; a year's preparation for the auction was on the line, and the question had to be answered: should the auction be canceled?

But Ranch management knew that some buyers along with certain notables were driving in anyway. Governor John Connally, who was considering a run for the presidency, was coming, and family member B. K. Johnson would be there, thinking about running for governor of Texas, It promised to be an interesting mix of politics, cattle, and mud. The situation was not a disaster, but it was close. Tio Kleberg recalled:

> The rain came straight down. We had no place to park cars—couldn't get a tricycle in there it was so muddy. We had one option—not to have the sale—and that wasn't gonna happen. We had the animals ready. Whatever people we had here they were gonna get their merchandise, and that's just the way it was.
>
> You know, you work all year for that one day and then—but it happened only once.

Because of the rain, the Ranch moved its, by then, famous auction to the J. K. Northway Coliseum in the Dick Kleberg Park in Kingsville. Fortunately the coliseum was sometimes used for cattle auctions, as well as fairs, concerts, and all kinds of other community affairs, so the auctioneer's stand, folding chairs, cattle pens—most everything needed was already on-site. The sides of the building were open, but the roof and the size of the facility made it a much better choice than a tent when rain was coming down by the bucketful. The vaqueros worked all Friday night, moving panels for a temporary ring, as well as cattle and horses and all of their gear and feed, to the coliseum—all in the soaking rain.

The sale went on, not exactly as planned, but it went on. Because many key buyers could not get to it, the sale averages of the bulls were well below what was expected. King Ranch policy was never to take an animal out of the sale because the bid was not high enough. If an animal walked into the sale ring, whether it brought $10 or $10,000, it was sold; when the auctioneer's hammer went down, that animal had a new owner. Every worker and every family member on the Ranch was disappointed in that 1974 auction because of the less than stellar prices. They all knew that the bulls were as good as ever. And for all the work and all the effort that went into it for most of a year, the outcome, because of the circumstances, was not up to King Ranch standards. Tio Kleberg's face was etched with regret, after all these years, as he recalled that sale.

> I remember it like I'm sitting here with Beto. After the sale was all over, we had people come back to the porch at the Main House for the reception, and I was sitting there with [Librado] and I was crying because I was disappointed that the bulls didn't sell as well. Not for me, but for him, because he had put in a whole year of work.

> He was the master showman, and he was disappointed that his animals didn't bring top price. Wherever it was, whatever sale it was, if we consigned one bull or two bulls—we might not have had the best bull there—but he was disappointed if it didn't win grand champion. That's just the way he was.
>
> TIO KLEBERG

> I remember that sale, of going behind [the ring] and seeing Librado crying.
>
> JANELL KLEBERG

After the 1974 sale, King Ranch management knew that permanent facilities for the auction were a must if the sale was to continue. A modern arena with an auctioneer's booth, auction ring, bleachers, and ample floor space for chairs to accommodate bidders and guests was built in time for the 1975 auction. Today that facility is also used for rodeos, including the annual King Ranch rodeo, which involves owner and employee families competing against each other for coveted belt buckles and trophies. And now there is no more muddy parking either. Caliche parking pads were also constructed just in case of another deluge.

HE DIDN'T KNOW IT WAS HIS LAST AUCTION

He was full of life, strong, and at age eighty-one in 1979, Dad was still walking the bulls back and forth to the ring to get them used to the auctioneer's voice and what have you. Everything went well. He would normally parade every bull for the sale. There were times when I would, but very little, and as I remember, he paraded the whole shebang that day and he was doing okay. He was taking medication for heart problems. Everything went well.

It was about a month after that October sale that my sister Alicia and my mom went into town, and when they came back to the house, Dad was sitting on the porch and he said he had a spell or whatever. So we took him to the doctor in town, and he was sent to Corpus. He was taking that medication and his doctor had pulled him off that medication, and that could be what happened. Anyway, he was sent to Corpus for a pacemaker. He was under observation for so many hours before they would do that, and before they were able to do the pacemaker, he had that stroke. After that, we brought him home, and they prepared a hospital bed for him, installed a phone, and they had an apparatus that over the phone they could check his heart from Corpus. Later they made arrangements to

Librado Maldonado leads a Santa Gertrudis bull into the ring for the last time, at the 1979 sale. He suffered a stroke soon afterward. Courtesy of Beto Maldonado.

take him to Warm Springs in Gonzales, where they work on those cases, and he was doing real well. He could recognize people, but whenever people would visit, he would feel real bad and would cry because he could not communicate with those people.

Dad couldn't talk. And he did everything in the world to try to use his pencil to write . . . but he would understand everything you said. We would shave him with the electric shaver, and he would help you just like he was doing it.

It was hard for Dr. Monte Moncrief to see his friend in this almost helpless condition. He said, "I'd go by there and see him and he couldn't speak at that time, and when he would see me, he would just break into crying and make me feel so bad that I wouldn't go often."

Dad came home, and he was bedridden for three years. My sister Alicia and Mom were right there with him all the time. Alicia was working with the veterinary department, and the Ranch pulled her off to look after Dad. After he died, Alicia continued with my mama, taking care of her, until she died. Now Alicia lives in my dad's house next to mine, and she can live there as long as she lives.

The following year, an article in the *Kingsville Record* described the first auction without Librado:

> At the 1980 sale, the crowd paused for a dedication of the sale to Librado by Stephen J. "Tio" Kleberg. Celebrating not just Librado Maldonado's many years with the Ranch, Kleberg praised him as the greatest showman of them all.
>
> "He's a master with livestock," he said. "He's the finest showman I have ever seen."
>
> To the applause of the crowd, the several generations of the Maldonado family were introduced.
>
> Kleberg noted that when Tom Lea wrote the King Ranch history in 1956 and asked his grandfather R. M. Kleberg to write a preface, he wrote:
>
> "To all these men, King's men for sure, truly King's men, this book is dedicated for recognition of what this Ranch owes them."
>
> Kleberg replied, "This is what we owe this family." (Jones 12)

Martin L. Davey Jr. was a buyer at that first auction after Librado suffered the stroke. In a letter of October 27, 1980, to Tio Kleberg, he expressed appreciation for his purchases of cattle and their safe delivery to his farm in South Carolina. He also wrote poignant words about that sale:

> You people at the King Ranch certainly did a masterful job in employee relations, in honoring the family of Librado Maldonado, and having each member of the family come front and center for personal recognition. It certainly was an emotional event and I imagine every woman in the audience was unashamedly shedding tears as well as probably some of the men.

THAT FIRST SALE BY MYSELF

That next sale in 1980 was my first one by myself. I remember that sale as if it was today. All the responsibility . . . I managed to get it done like if my dad was

Beto Maldonado (*left*) and José Silguero visit in José's home in 2007. The two men carried on the Maldonado tradition in the auction ring until 1986. Photo by Betty Bailey Colley.

there, and everything went well. José Silguero was my dad's right-hand man, and he was my backup in the ring. Of course, I had followed my papa's footsteps since I was a little one, and he taught me a lot of things. If it wasn't because of him . . . He was always telling me, "Never trust a bull, never do it." I would parade the bulls in the ring until the auction sales ended in 1986. During those years, sometimes José would parade the bulls and I would be his backup.

THE MEN WOULDN'T HAVE TIME TO EAT

I started a concession stand at the auction because there was just about an hour between the Quarter Horse sale in the morning and the Santa Gertrudis sale in the early afternoon, and the men would have to go into town to eat something and there was not time. I didn't have the stand at the first sale, maybe at the second or third. Anyway, Dr. Northway gave me permission to set up that concession stand, and I could keep any profit I made. Dr. Northway and Mr. Bob were in charge of the auction for the longest time. I would just set up that stand right across the road from the auction site, and everybody could just get a sandwich and a drink and not have to leave the area. We had a variety of sandwiches, chicken salad, ham and cheese—three or four kinds. They were made for us in Corpus by the Tasty Sandwich Company at 924 South Staples, and I would go pick them up. The sandwiches sold for thirty-five cents, cokes at ten cents. A case of cokes cost me about eighty-five cents at the American Bottling Company in Corpus at that time. Then, of course, Dora [Beto's wife] would brew some coffee and I would have somebody to bring the coffee and the paper cups from the house—that was before Styrofoam, but they made those cups so you could hold them in your hand. Coffee was a dime. Sold candy for that too.

My mama came up with the idea of selling tamales at the concession stand. We would sell three in a little cardboard carton, and people ate them there—we had plastic forks for them. And one year my mama made bonnets to sell. She would make them from bought material because by then they no longer had the nice feed sacks like she made her sheets from. I had that concession stand for about ten years, till 1963. Then, of course, after that, members of the [King Ranch] family had the idea of a barbecue, and the proceeds would go to some charity here in town.

My whole family helped at the stand because I had to be working with the auction. Everybody on the Santa Gertrudis Division was involved in the auctions in some way. When we got started, of all the people who started fifty-eight years ago, I am the only survivor today.

Beto's Children Reminisce about the Auctions

Growing up on the Ranch, I remember all of us kids having a part at the auctions. I remember Sammy and I, at a very young age, handing out programs at a gate close to home. There were so many people around and so much going on that it was exciting to us as kids. As I grew up and ended up on the payroll, I had different duties during auctions. I worked some at the information booth, and then I recorded on a large board all the information about the animals as they were sold. I was close to the actual ring and had a good view of the animals as they were brought in and paraded by my dad and grandfather. I always worried for the safety of them after seeing the size of the animals they were parading around. Thankfully, as far as I can remember, no one ever got hurt. After all, my grandfather spent lots of hours preparing for this day, and his animals were well trained and did their best on this special day.

CATALINA MALDONADO YAKLIN

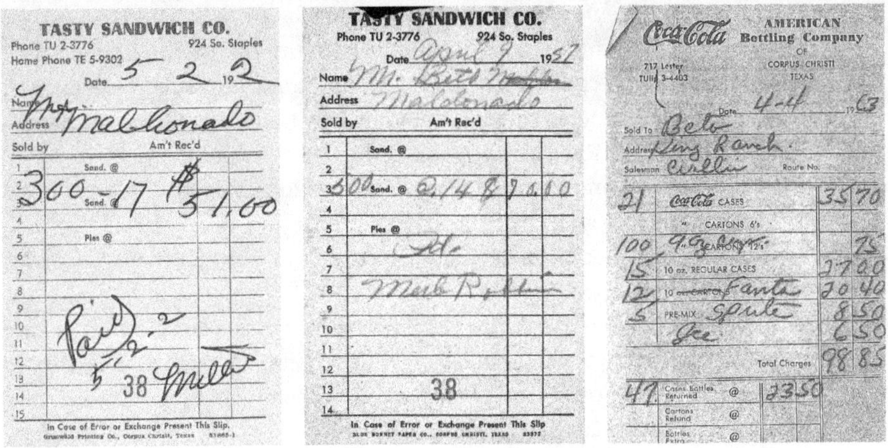

Receipts for soft drinks and sandwiches Beto purchased for the concession stand he started so that people coming to the King Ranch auctions in the early 1950s could have lunch there.

At auction time, there was no school. Auctions were big events. We sold coffee, soda, sandwiches, and grandma's bonnets. I got new boots for auction day, and they would last a year.

SAMMY MALDONADO

When Dad had the auctions back then, she [Ella] would make empanadas days and days ahead, and Dad would sell them in his concession stand. She made these bonnets, and he sold those too. She sat at the machine and sewed and sewed the bonnets. Dad had the concession stand for years and years at the auction sale. He sold soft drinks and sandwiches and coffee and empanadas and bonnets. Dad was the only one who got to do that. This place in Corpus Christi would make the sandwiches for him—chicken salad and others. They came wrapped like you can buy them now. Empanadas—she would beat the yolk or the white of eggs and dampen them with it, and when they were baked, they would have this pretty little color.

DORA MALDONADO GARCIA

TIME PASSES

It was time for the 1975 auction. Private planes began arriving like oversized Texas mosquitoes and parking on the wide prairie paved with King Ranch Bluestem and Kleberg Bluestem grass near the Santa Gertrudis Headquarters. They emptied their noted passengers for the now famed King Ranch auction—passengers like Sid Richardson, Gus Wortham, Governor John Connally, Winthrop Rockefeller, and the du Ponts. Winthrop Rockefeller had been coming since the 1950s; in 1953 he paid the top price of $31,000 for an outstanding bull, later named "The Rock." Beto remembered him as a very nice man who always made a point of speaking to him.

Some dignitaries stayed at the Main House, but most people coming a long way to the auction were housed in Kingsville motels or forty-five miles away in Corpus Christi. All area motels were sold out way ahead of the auction, even in small towns like Alice.

Norman Parish, King Ranch animal physiologist, told a story about airplanes arriving for the occasion:

> Some people flew their airplanes in for the auctions. They landed in the pasture at Headquarters, since there was no county airport. If the airplanes were to land at night, people would line up their cars with headlights on so the pilot could see where to land. One time they didn't take the horses out of the pasture, and the horses chewed the tails of the airplanes. [Winthrop] Rockefeller had an airplane and flew from Petit Jean Mountain, Arkansas. There would be six, seven, or eight airplanes for an auction. Those who flew in stayed at the Big [Main] House.

The auction had grown to premier status, and so had the socializing, as hospitality had always been part of the King Ranch legacy since Captain King first staked his claim on the Wild Horse Desert. At lunch on the day of the auction, buyers, guests, townspeople, Kineños—hundreds of people—feasted at stand-up tables on King Ranch beef, beans, slaw, Spanish rice, and camp bread expertly prepared by Kineños with years of experience in turning out this tantalizing ranch cuisine. These steaming plates of the Ranch's best were washed down with Kool-Aid, iced tea, and coffee. Usually offered at no charge, the plates were sold for $4 that year to benefit the Pan American School in Kingsville. This may have been the first time ever that guests were charged for food at King Ranch.

> The sale got to be a major event. People expected to be invited from Corpus Christi and Kingsville and started showing up. It was so big that the house

King Ranch began charging for its lunch during auctions when the numbers grew. The proceeds were always earmarked for civic or charity causes. Courtesy of Beto Maldonado.

Alicia and Beto Maldonado examine a bonnet made by their mother, Ella Maldonado, like those for sale in Beto's concession stand during King Ranch auctions in the early 1950s. Photo by Betty Bailey Colley.

> guests and buyers could not get lunch and had to go into town to Harrel's drugstore or somewhere else for lunch and could not get back in time for the auction. So I told my dad [Robert J. Kleberg Jr.] that we had to start charging for lunch. He told me that King Ranch had never charged anyone for meals. I told him people were coming for the free food and suggested that we have the money we charged go to the hospital, Boy Scouts, or a charity donation. We still gave the lunch, but for charity.
>
> HELEN KLEBERG GROVES

As was customary, men on the Ranch, whether owners or Kineños, wore King Ranch khaki, but on auction day the Ranch "uniforms" were sure to be freshly starched and pressed. The women from the main office were dressed alike for the occasion, their outfits designed for them each year so they could be easily identified; but whatever their ensemble, it always included a King Ranch bandanna. These competent, knowledgeable employees registered buyers, handed out programs, answered questions, and generally served in whatever capacity they were needed to extend hospitality and facilitate the success of the sale.

By far, the main social event of the weekend was the party at the Main House the night before the auction. Cattle and horse buyers treasured their invitations, and some of their wives treasured their opportunity to shop for "the dress," sometimes during the entire year, for this more formal party. Other women wore more ranchlike outfits, maybe something like a long black skirt with a special shirt, but it was still a dressier affair than the Saturday auction and lunch, when most everybody wore comfortable clothing of cotton and, of course, cowboy boots.

> People dressed up for the Friday night party. One lady wore a see-through plastic dress. Texas chic. There was lots of big hair and diamonds. Generally it was cocktail attire—the men wore coats and King Ranch ties or sport coats with guayaberas or white shirts. I wore denim to the sale on Saturday.
>
> JAMENE TOELKES

Many people considered the Friday party the social event of the year; certainly there was no other like it. At one time a joke circulated that people would spend thousands of dollars at the auction just so they could come to the party the next year.

THE PARTY

The multistyle Main House, with elements of Mexican, Moorish, California Mission, and Long Island, was designed around a courtyard in the concept of a Mexican *casa grande* yet was uniquely suited to the Wild Horse Desert (Lea 572). The house has twenty-five rooms, twenty-six fireplaces, and nineteen baths, with windows in the tower fitted with stained glass designed by Tiffany of New York. On this clear crystal night in 1975, the twenty-fifth anniversary of the auction, the great house was aglow with tiny white lights laced in the oak and mesquite trees. Kineños, dressed in black pants and white guayaberas, met each car as it approached the canopy, opened doors and courteously assisted passengers from the car, then drove the car to a nearby parking space. Flaming torches lit the way for guests, who were greeted by King Ranch chairman of the board, Dick Kleberg Jr.; his wife, Mary Lewis; and Ranch president, James H. Clement, and his wife, Illa.

The veranda was a canvas for lush hanging baskets of flowers trimmed with ribbon streamers in a myriad of colors. Tables covered with brightly colored cloths matching the ribbons filled the porch area and the lawn, providing enough seating for the five hundred buyers, prospective buyers, and guests who would line the sumptuous buffet tables loaded with a wide variety of Mexican dishes served from silver chafing dishes. There was plenty of steaming coffee and an open bar; wine was offered with dinner. A four-piece combo and three *guitareros* furnished music as long as guests cared to dance or just listen (Marshall 50).

Several people shared their recollections of how the Friday night party worked:

> My mother, Mary Lewis [Kleberg], helped run the Main House, and she was in charge of the party, beginning in the early 1960s. Aunt Helen, Uncle Bob's [Kleberg's] wife, managed the affair up until that point. Mary Lewis had in her bedroom a big armoire; it was a large desk that her mother had used in Virginia, and she ran the house from that desk, including the staff and the work.
>
> Leroy Curry, from Pennsylvania, manager of the Main House, helped with the Friday night auction parties. Leroy physically lived in the house in room number five on the bottom floor. He was a bachelor and lived there until he died.
>
> The Friday night party was probably started in the late '50s or early '60s. The Ranch probably started off with a party after the sale for the buyers, Ranch family members, and guests. Then people started coming the day before to look at the cattle and horses, and we had a lot of out-of-country people coming, like from Mexico, Australia, Venezuela, and Argentina, and what were we going to do with them? And so the Friday night party evolved.
>
> In the early '70s, maybe about 100 or 150 people would come for the Friday night party, and the food was prepared by the Kineños under the direction of Mary Lewis, assisted by Leroy Curry. By the time the number grew to 250, Mary Lewis brought caterers from San Antonio, because the staff was busy just taking care of the Main House, filled to capacity with guests.
>
> The house had seventeen rooms for guests, and we'd divide them up. We'd have some "have to's." Mona Holmes would have to be in there; she was a real good friend of Bob Kleberg's and had Santa Gertrudis cattle on Kona, Hawaii. If Mrs. [Robert] Briggs is coming—she's kind of the grand dame of the breed—and everybody loved her; she'll stay here. Then we'd add the seven top cattle buyers and seven top horse buyers from the year before. We'd send them a personal letter that said the sale is October 5 and we want you to be our guest, and we'd ask for a reply. If they declined, we'd go to number eight. That's exactly how it was done.
>
> JANELL AND TIO KLEBERG

A guy named Leroy Curry, the manager, he could set a table for the English elite or he could set a Kineño table, and he was just the most magnificent person along those lines. He was dressed in black pants and a white shirt and a string tie, and he could weave in and out of visiting dignitaries without ever mussing a hair. He really knew how it was done.

MONTE MONCRIEF, DVM

It started with cocktails and dinner at the Main House for about twenty-five to fifty people and grew to well over a hundred. At first people wore western clothes and ranch dresses; it got dressier as it got bigger. We did the food at first, and then we had it catered by Joe Stivers and Tilford Collins out of San Antonio. We planned the menus—we always had King Ranch beef. We had lots of flowers and a florist in Kingsville did it for a while, and then we brought some in from San Antonio later. Mona Holmes always sent beautiful flowers from Hawaii—orchids and other Hawaiian flowers.

MARY LEWIS KLEBERG

The auction parties were the social event of the year. There were lots of people, lots of excitement. It started at seven o'clock, and there were bands on the porch and a dance floor set up. There were hundreds of white chairs and wonderful linens, and tables of eight or ten. There was a board floor in the food tents. Caterer Don Strange from San Antonio was in charge of the food during the 1980s.

JAMENE TOELKES

AN ERA ENDS

Monte Moncrief, came to King Ranch straight out of the school of veterinary medicine at Texas A&M University in 1949. Hired at first as assistant to Ranch veterinarian Dr. J. K. Northway until his death in 1973, Dr. Moncrief was head of the Ranch's veterinary department until 1975. He shared his remembrances of working with Librado and Beto almost every day during those years:

The Maldonados came in first place in getting those livestock gentle. The bulls—it took quite a schedule—and it caused quite a lot of comment and inspection, even in the gentling stage, because at that time there was nothing on the gate. Everybody could come in and drive around, and if they wanted to, they could stop at the gate and get a little number saying where they could go, saying this is the feedlot and this is the horse barn.

It was nearly thirty years that I worked with Don Librado—I called him Don Librado after he turned from young to old. Dr. Northway was head of the department, and I was second in command; Librado and I worked together. He used to come by my house, and we'd drink coffee and I'd drink whiskey. He spilled most of his whiskey.

An era ended in 1986 when Beto Maldonado paraded Santa Gertrudis bulls for the last time at the final King Ranch auction. He would continue working with the Santa Gertrudis A-Herds, keeping careful, accurate records until his retirement in 1990.

3

THE MALDONADOS AND KING RANCH HORSES

Now Assault was the Triple Crown Champion.
Against all odds, he had run and won.

Marjorie Hodgson Parker,
Assault: The Crippled Champion

THE RACE

We would get racing forms from New York or Chicago, but we didn't really keep up with which horses were running where. We were more familiar with the Ranch's Quarter Horses because they were used in the everyday work of the Ranch, and, anyway, there was no easy way to know about the races. But Dr. J. K. Northway, Ranch veterinarian, let us know that Assault was going to run in the Kentucky Derby race. We knew that race was a big one and it was going to be on the first Saturday afternoon in May, so some of us decided to listen and see what would happen. It was in 1946 and I was sixteen years old.

It was raining cats and dogs. My dad, my brother Lee, and I climbed in Dad's black 1942 Ford pickup with our radio and headed for the stables by the dairy barn. We were the only family with a radio in the Dairy Colony, and we operated it with a car battery. Dad bought a wind charger, and it would charge those batteries; we had three, so we would use one while the others were being charged. We drove the pickup right inside the barn, where it was dry, and joined up with Pablo Ochoa and his sons, Pablo Jr. and Miguel. Refugio "Cuco" Rodriguez and Ramón

In the Kentucky Derby winner's circle on May 4, 1946, trainer Max Hirsch (*left*) welcomes jockey Warren Mehrtens and Assault, draped with the traditional blanket of roses. Courtesy of Beto Maldonado.

and Cipriano Garcia were there also to hear the race. It wasn't much of a radio, but we had it as loud as it would go and we were gathered around real close, and we could hear.

When Assault won that race, we were all excited and real happy. We didn't know at that time that he would also win the Preakness and the Belmont and win the Triple Crown. At that time, he was only the seventh horse in seventy years to do that, and he's still the only horse bred in Texas to ever win the Triple Crown.

I HELD ASSAULT

I thought about when I held Assault when he was a baby. He was born in 1943, and I was thirteen years of age. When Thoroughbred mares were to be bred, my dad and my brother Lee would bring the stallions to the breeding barn, and I would help with the mares in season that would be brought across the highway to the collection barn. The mares had to be washed, their tails wrapped, and their harnesses put on and I did that kind of work. When they brought in the mares, they would have an offspring with them already, and we would have to hold them away from the mares. The foal could be young, like six weeks or so, and if the mama came in season, she was bred. And that's when I would hold Assault, when his mama, Igual, was being bred again. There were some foals that it would take two people to hold, but not Assault. I didn't have any problem with him.

I have probably seen Assault more times than any other person because after he was retired in 1950, he came home to the Ranch and he stayed in a little pen right in the corner by the old dairy barn as you go to my house. A lot of other people saw Assault, though, because back then anyone could drive their own cars around the Loop Road and they would go right by him. There was a brick building that was used for something at the dairy, and they actually emptied it out and moved it to the pen and opened the side to Assault so he could go in there when it was cold or whatever. Ramón Rodriguez looked after the stallions, and he was the one that fed Assault and brushed him and checked him out every day.

Assault was in that pen twenty-one years until he died in 1971. Dr. Northway and some of the Kineños spoke at his funeral. He is buried here on the Santa Gertrudis Division, along with Old Sorrel, the foundation horse, and other famous King Ranch horses. They have headstones of Texas granite inscribed, similar to those in any cemetery.

FIFTY YEARS LATER

Fifty years later to the day, on May 4, 1996, King Ranch continued its legacy of hospitality and invited the public to a Kentucky Derby Day Gala to celebrate the fiftieth anniversary of Assault's winning that famous race. Armed guards brought the four trophies from the Main House to the Henrietta Memorial Center in Kingsville for the party. The Derby, Belmont, and Preakness trophies were surrounded with vases of red roses, black-eyed Susans, and white carnations, each representing the traditional flower of the three races that earned Assault the coveted Triple Crown honor. The Triple Crown trophy was on display; it had been presented to King Ranch retroactively in 1956, the first year a trophy was awarded for the Triple Crown. Speakers at the gala were Mary Lewis Kleberg, Dr. Monte Moncrief, Helen Kleberg Groves, and Helen McFarland. The Ranch offered only four hundred tickets, at $30 each or $50 a couple; proceeds from the party were earmarked for the Heart of Kingsville Restoration and Beautification Project, sponsored by the Kingsville Downtown Business Association, to restore Kleberg Avenue in keeping with its historic past.

Southern women wearing fancy hats and guests sipping mint juleps under a tented patio resplendent with roses set the tone for the celebration. The gala lasted from 2:30 to 7:30 p.m. and featured mock pari-mutuel and casino gaming, a sumptuous southern buffet, and jazz played throughout the afternoon by

Plácido, Librado, and Lee Maldonado admire Assault; all three worked with him. Courtesy of Beto Maldonado.

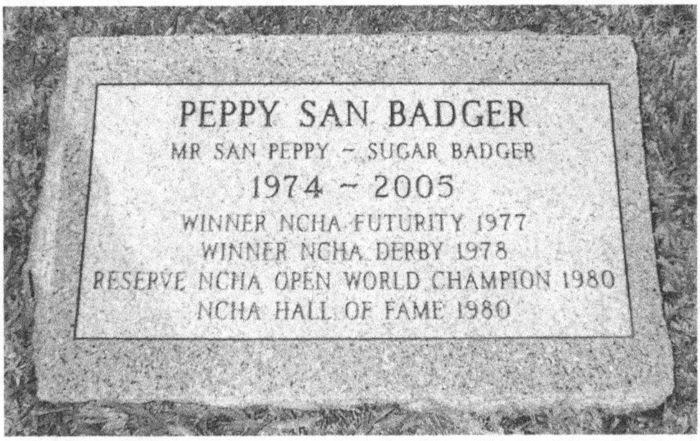

One of the headstones for horses buried on King Ranch.

Old Sorrel
Chestnut Horse
Hickory Bill—Dr. Rose Mare
Foundation Sire
King Ranch Quarter Horse Family

Assault
Chestnut Horse
Bold Venture—Igual
March 26, 1943–Sept. 1, 1971
Triple Crown Winner 1946

the H. M. King High School jazz ensemble. Of course, guests were treated to a TV viewing of the 122nd "Run for the Roses" on four large screens and even to a trumpeter's call to the post. Leslie Gilliam, Mary Lewis Kleberg's secretary, was licensed to take bets for the mock gaming and was hooked up directly to the Derby to know for sure which horses won. There were generous prizes for the winners and door prizes for five lucky guests, as well as for the traditional ladies' hat contest.

Another highlight of the program was an appearance by jockey Warren Mehrtens and his wife, Noreen. He was the jockey who had worn the number 3 on his brown and white silks that day and ridden Assault to win by eight lengths, one of the most impressive wins in Derby history. Riding into the winner's circle that day in 1946, Assault and Mehrtens were met by Mr. and Mrs. Bob Kleberg Jr., who beamed as the coveted blanket of red roses was draped over Assault's shoulders. Just a week later in Baltimore, Mehrtens rode Assault to win the Preakness by only a neck, but that was enough for Assault to win the right to don the blanket of black-eyed Susans, Maryland's state flower. And three weeks later, when Mehrtens eased Assault into the winner's circle of the Belmont Stakes, raised his whip in the traditional salute to the race official, and waited for the Belmont's traditional mantle of white carnations, he could see the gleaming silver Belmont Stakes trophy on a cloth-covered table. They had done it. Assault and Warren Mehrtens brought home to King Ranch that day the first and only Triple Crown title ever won by a Thoroughbred from Texas (Parker 78).

YOU COULD ACTUALLY BET ON THE HORSES

There were a lot of people at that party, and they were having a good time. There were plenty of good things to eat and drink, and it was set up so that you could actually bet on the horses at the party. I didn't bet that day, but I did bet on horses back in Assault's time. We would get racing forms from Chicago or New York, and we could go to the phone and place bets. When they knew we were from King Ranch, they would take our bets and let us settle up later.

But at Assault's anniversary party, I didn't place any bets. I was the guide, or chauffeur or what have you, for Warren Mehrtens. He was the jockey when Assault won the Kentucky Derby, and he came back for the party. I was with him for the whole day, from the time I picked him up at the Main House, and my job was to see that he went where he wanted to go and had what he wanted or needed. He was a quiet, humble man. He wanted to know why I wanted him to autograph some picture postcards of him and Assault. Warren died a couple of years later.

Admit One
KENTUCKY DERBY DAY GALA
A Commemorative Celebration of the 50th Anniversary
of Assault's Triple Crown Win in 1946
RETAIN THIS TICKET
458
Saturday, May 4, 1996
2:30 P.M. – 7:30 P.M.
Henrietta Memorial Center
405 North 6th Street, Kingsville, Texas
$30.00 Individual • $50.00 Couple • Cash Bar
Exhibits, Lectures, TV Coverage of Kentucky Derby 122,
Buffet, Music, Mock Pari-Mutuel and Casino Gaming, Hat Contest
Proceeds Benefit the Heart of Kingsville Restoration and Beautification Project

Ticket for the Kentucky Derby Day Gala on May 4, 1996, celebrating the fiftieth anniversary, to the day, of Assault's Triple Crown win. Courtesy of Beto Maldonado.

Cover of the invitation to the Kentucky Derby Day Gala held on May 4, 1996. Courtesy of Beto Maldonado.

THE QUEST FOR QUALITY IS REWARDED

From the very beginning, Captain King's goal was to have the finest livestock on his ranch. At first he bought the best horses he could find in the area, but still seeking a better animal to work cattle in the rough, hot, dry conditions of South Texas, around 1870 he began bringing in Kentucky mares to cross with his mustangs. The King Ranch horse-breeding success story got a jump start with the purchase of a yearling in 1916 that the Kineños later named Old Sorrel; the Ranch had finally located a horse that had intelligence, athletic ability, and excellent cattle sense and, most important, could pass his remarkable charac-

On behalf of King Ranch, Inc., I take great pleasure in welcoming you to this Kentucky Derby Day Gala and commemorative celebration of the 50th anniversary of Assault's 1946 Triple Crown Championship. The Kentucky Derby is not merely a horse race; it is an event in the lifetime of sport in America, where friends meet in annual reunion at the fiesta of the Thoroughbred. We meet to celebrate fifty years - to the day - the triumph of King Ranch's Assault in the 1946 Kentucky Derby, the first jewel in the Triple Crown.

The story of Assault is one that epitomizes the heart and courage of a race horse, and today we proudly open an exciting, new historical exhibit on this great champion. Indeed, old-timers in Kentucky, Texas and other parts of our nation, still remember the little colt. After his Kentucky Derby victory, Assault, nicknamed by turf writers "The Club-Footed Comet," went on to capture the Preakness and the Belmont and become the seventh Triple Crown champion (and only Texas bred winner) in turf history.

We are especially honored to have as our guests Mr. Warren Mehrtens and his family. Jockey Mehrtens rode Assault to all three victories and brought to King Ranch the Triple Crown, the most coveted, most elusive, and most rewarding prize in American racing. So join us in the spirit of the Kentucky Derby, "the greatest two minutes in sports," and participate in all the time-honored traditions of the first Saturday in May. In addition, all proceeds raised from the mock pari-mutuel and casino gaming events will benefit the Heart of Kingsville Restoration and Beautification Project.

Again, welcome, and make sure to sing along with joy and reverence when the band plays "My Old Kentucky Home."

Bruce S. Cheeseman, Archivist and Historian
King Ranch, Inc.
May 4, 1996

This program is printed on the remaining all-rag paper watermarked with the "Running W" brand, made by the Curtis Paper Company for the original printing of *The King Ranch* by Tom Lea.

The picture of Assault on the cover is from the original pen and ink drawing taken from Lea's *The King Ranch*.

teristics to offspring of the same superior quality or better. Old Sorrel became the foundation sire for the famous King Ranch Quarter Horses; he became to the horse program what Monkey was to the cattle-breeding program. The next step up came in 1930, when Robert J. Kleberg Jr. bought a group of superior Thoroughbred mares with the sole intent of upgrading workhorses to be on a par with cattle in the breeding program. Kleberg designed a carefully orchestrated regimen of breeding these outstanding mares to his Quarter Horses, and this breeding program was wildly successful.

When the American Quarter Horse Association was formed in 1940, the members made the decision that the next year's grand champion stallion of the

KENTUCKY DERBY DAY GALA

A Commemorative Celebration of the
50th Anniversary of Assault's
1946 Triple Crown Championship

Hosted by King Ranch, Inc.

Saturday, May 4, 1996
2:30 p.m. – 7:30 p.m.
Henrietta Memorial Center
405 North Sixth Street
Kingsville, Texas

2:00 – 2:30 ..... Opening Set ..... H.M. King Jazz Ensemble
2:30 ..... Parade to the Post ..... Michael Garcia, Guest Trumpeter
2:30 – 2:35 ..... Welcome ..... Jack Hunt
President and Chief Executive Officer, King Ranch, Inc.
2:35 – 3:00 ..... Opening of Exhibit
"King Ranch and the Sport of Kings"
Introduction of Special Guests ..... Bruce S. Cheeseman
Archivist and Historian, King Ranch, Inc.
3:00 – 3:30 Guest Speakers ... Helen Groves, Mary Lewis Kleberg, Helen McFarland, Warren Mehrtens, and Dr. Monte P. Moncrief
3:30 – 4:30 ..... Pre-Race TV Coverage of Kentucky Derby
Viewing of Exhibits
"Pari-Mutuel" Windows Open
4:15 (time approximate) ..... "My Old Kentucky Home" ..... Guests Join in Singing
4:30 ..... "Pari-Mutuel" Windows Close
4:32 ..... **POST TIME**
4:35 – 5:00 ..... Post-Race TV Coverage
Cash in "Pari-Mutuel" Tickets
Select Prizes for Drawing
5:00 – 5:15 ..... Drawing for "Pari-Mutuel" Prizes
Announce Winner of Hat Contest ..... Mattie Gaston, JoRene Newton, Treba Skipworth, and Susan Webb
5:15 – 7:00 ..... "Casino" Party
7:00 – 7:15 ..... Select Prizes for Drawing
7:15 – 7:30 ..... Drawing for "Casino" Prizes ..... Cynthia Martin, Glenda Webb, and Allen Wilson
Heart of Kingsville Restoration and Beautification Project

Program for the Kentucky Derby Day Gala, May 4, 1996. Courtesy of Beto Maldonado.

Fort Worth Livestock Show would be named the No. 1 registered Quarter Horse in the association's stud and registry book. That stallion was a King Ranch horse named Wimpy. Foaled in 1937 on King Ranch, Wimpy, P-1, sired by Solis and out of Panda, traced back through both his sire and dam to Old Sorrel (Britten 197). The association recorded its two-millionth registry in 1984, and again it was a King Ranch filly, a direct descendant of Old Sorrel and Wimpy (Nixon 29). The Ranch's Mr. San Peppy, twice the world champion cutting horse, was the first to win more than $100,000 in open cutting competition, as well as the youngest horse to be inducted into the National Cutting Horse Association Hall of Fame. His son Peppy San Badger ("Little Peppy") would soon follow. The offspring of Mr. San Peppy and Little Peppy, from breeding Ranch-owned mares and outside mares brought in, would win in excess of $25 million in competition for their owners by the year 2002 (Janell Kleberg 8).

KING RANCH QUARTER HORSES JOIN THE CIRCUS

The Ringling Brothers and Barnum and Bailey Circus purchased King Ranch Quarter Horses for its circus acts. In fact the circus purchased the largest number of horses sold to a single buyer at the 1951 auction sale, when it bought twelve colts. No doubt, it was because of their quickness, intelligence, and speed that these horses could be taught to perform precision drills for the circus's horse acts. At one time during the 1950s and 1960s, the circus used all perfectly matched sorrel King Ranch horses; they were the same size, same shade of reddish brown, and same sex—and they were trained to perform amid the hustle and noise of the circus crowd.

The reason these beautiful horses could be trained to perform the intricate routines seen by generations of circus goers "when the circus came to town" was no doubt due to the way horses were and still are handled at King Ranch. In earlier times some ranchers brutally handled horses as a way to "break" them to the saddle. A full-grown horse on the range, having had little or no human contact, could suddenly find himself hobbled, with a saddle thrown on his back, and as if that was not sufficient insult, a human would mount the saddle and hang on until the horse was totally exhausted from kicking and bucking and could therefore be called "broken." This violent practice could result in injury to the horse's body or worse, to his spirit, and a good animal could be ruined. This type of "bronc busting" has long been forbidden on King Ranch.

Horses begin learning to work on the Ranch when they are foaled. Kept close to their dam, they are continually handled right away by Ranch hands so that when they are grown and ready to be ridden, they have already been gentled. Gradually they have learned to tolerate a bit to the mouth and to hold

Beto Maldonado visits with King Ranch Quarter Horse Peppy San Badger (Little Peppy). Little Peppy was inducted into the National Cutting Horse Association Hall of Fame in 1980. His offspring have won more than $25 million. Courtesy of King Ranch.

still for a saddle on the back, with the cinch tightened around the middle, so that when finally a person mounts the saddle, the horse is ready for that step. There is no violence, only confidence, because the horse has been trained, not broken (Lea 657, 659).

Dr. J. Y. Henderson, the circus's veterinarian, owed his job to King Ranch. Henderson was a good friend of the Klebergs and Dr. Northway. One day John Ringling North called Henderson and said, "We have lost our veterinarian. We need a man to replace him. I've been talking to my friends the Klebergs of King Ranch and their veterinarian, Dr. J. K. Northway. They both recommend you highly." This relationship may be a clue to how King Ranch Quarter Horses came to join the circus. Dr. Henderson said he learned from Dr. Northway that although the circus wanted everything possible done for all their animals, its biggest preoccupation was with its horses, because Ringling Brothers had a fortune tied up in what was undoubtedly the most beautiful collection of horses in the world (Henderson 3, 4).

A COVETED AWARD

On June 10, 1996, the American Quarter Horse Association awarded to King Ranch its eleventh historical marker. For the prestigious award, the association selects recipients who have made significant contributions to American Quarter Horse history through horses, people, and events, and King Ranch had blazed an impressive trail in all three areas. Mr. San Peppy, twenty-eight years old, and Little Peppy, twenty-two, represented King Ranch like the champions they were at the 2 p.m. ceremony that day.

By 1:30 p.m. the stallions, in full regalia, stood at separate stations as their part of the dedication. While Mr. San Peppy with his 1976 World Championship saddle on his back, stayed at the King Ranch Visitor Center, where the marker would be permanently displayed, Little Peppy stood guard at the entry of the Henrietta Memorial Center. Decked out in a prominent Running W saddle blanket, his NCHA 1977 Futurity saddle, and a silver headstall, Little Peppy, the legend, watched as yet another honor was bestowed upon King Ranch (Nettles 4).

I KNEW FAMOUS HORSES

I remember Old Sorrel very well, and I still have a picture of him in my head. We were still hand-breeding him at the age of twenty-six. He was the foundation of the Quarter Horse family here on the Ranch.

And I knew Peppy, grandson of Old Sorrel, sired by Wimpy, who won a blue ribbon at the 1940 Fort Worth Stock Show. I would ride Peppy before Dr. Northway was going to show him to people in the 1940s. He was like riding in a Cadillac or in El Kineño, the Kleberg family hunting car. One time Mr. Dick picked me up on the Ranch road, and I rode in that car. Riding Peppy was like that, with a gentle rock and taking the bumps real easy. Dr. Northway gave peppermint sticks to Peppy, and people found out about it and they sent peppermint sticks from all over. I always loved candy, and I would share with Peppy. He was strong, powerful, and could turn on a dime. At one time there was a twenty-five-pound sack of flour with a picture of Peppy on the side.

THE ULTIMATE HORSE-BREEDING PURSUIT

His success in animal breeding and crossbreeding Quarter Horses with Thoroughbreds, solely for a higher quality of workhorses on the Ranch, fascinated Robert J. Kleberg Jr., and he began to think about developing a stable of Thoroughbreds, the ultimate horse-breeding pursuit. No doubt he wondered whether he had a chance of creating a stable of racehorses bred and raised in semiarid regions of South Texas that could compete with those raised in the cool, bluegrass pastures of Kentucky and the lush green fields of New York (Lea 663). It had never been done before. He had extensive experience in breeding livestock, though, and he astutely decided to draw on this knowledge to design his Thoroughbred program. In 1934 he moved a step up in his breeding venture when he purchased an outstanding stallion named Chicaro, and his quest was under way (Gonzales 9). In 1936 he purchased Bold Venture, the 1936 Kentucky Derby and Preakness Stakes winner, for an astounding $40,000. Bold Venture was the only stallion to win the Kentucky Derby and sire two sons that would also become Kentucky Derby winners, Assault and Middleground.

Bob Kleberg had a sixth sense about animals and could astutely judge the ones that fit the program he had in mind. But fine animals were not enough. Like Captain King, who decided to pursue a ranching venture as a novice and sought highly skilled Mexican vaqueros to teach him, Kleberg sought a person with the expertise and knowledge of the racing industry he lacked. This he found in Max Hirsch, the trainer who would guide Bob Kleberg's Thoroughbred program to, among other feats, Assault's eighteen victories, including the Triple Crown in 1946, still the most coveted prize in turfdom. That year Assault earned $424,195, more than any horse had ever won in a single year, and he had total earnings of $672,500 by his retirement in 1950 (Lea 794, 740). That same year, Middleground won the Kentucky Derby and Belmont Stakes. The Ranch would ultimately produce more than seventy notable Thoroughbreds that would race its brown and white silks to the winner's circle in every major race in the country, and for twenty years it would show a profit in the most exacting and expensive of breeding practices. The Ranch gained a reputation as one of the most consistently successful racing stables in operation at the time (Lea 665).

Not all racing, however, took place in Kentucky and New York.

The Other Race

Once we had our own race, and Plácido [Maldonado] was involved with that. Plácido was a very good horseman. The racetrack was still in Kingsville and was not being used at the time. We took our ponies, buckets, sacks of oats, and various equipment to the stables, which were empty, and arranged our horses there. We led our "racing" horses and rode our other horses. We were late getting home that night, so my mother was very mad at me.

We invited the adults to come to our race the next day. Someone took me into town to buy the prize, which was a box of Whitman's candy. The jockeys were Plácido, "Chino" [José Gonzales Jr.], "Chancle" [José Angel Gonzales], and maybe [Alberto "Lolo"] Treviño. We held the race. B Johnson's horse came in first, Alice's horse came in second, B Johnson's horse came in third, and mine came in fourth and fifth.

HELEN KLEBERG GROVES

I GOT TO HELP WITH THE THOROUGHBREDS

When I was working with Dr. Northway at the vet department in the '40s, we were right next door to the Thoroughbred barn. One of my jobs was to take medications like 6X Liniment or Forest Liniment No. 2 to the grooms working with the horses so they could treat a hurt foot or leg. And anything that they needed in the Thoroughbred operation besides medicine, I managed to get it. One time they had a horse that was sick and they had an air fan put on him so he'd be cool, and that fan would stay on day and night, day and night. Eventually that fan just wore out. Mr. Egan, William Egan [King Ranch trainer], said, "Beto, the fan played out, so why don't you get us another one?" So I went ahead and went into town and got another fan. They were going to throw away the fan that was no longer in service, so I worked on that fan and oiled it and worked on it and worked on it until it worked. It was our first fan, because at that time we didn't have a fan in our house.

THROUGH THE NOSE

Dr. Northway and Dr. Moncrief had to worm those horses and I would help them. They would actually have to insert a hose through the nose, I guess all the way to the stomach, and make sure that it was at the right place before we poured that medication in to kill the worms. People who do that kind of work, they actually need to know what they are doing. Once they got that hose in there, they needed me to put that funnel on that hose and pour that medication in. It was kind of hot, and if I got it on my hand, it kind of burned. It took just a small amount of medicine to pour in there, but it worked. Once the medication was poured in, they would pull out the hose and it was done.

You know, at the very beginning they had the racetrack here in town right where the Javelina Stadium [at Texas A&M–Kingsville] is today. I would ride with Dr. Northway, and we would go there. A whole bunch of people worked there and they had a kitchen, and the people that worked there could eat breakfast, lunch, and, I think, dinner—I know breakfast and lunch. And they had coffee there all day. They also had a blacksmith shop and a full-time farrier by the name of S. K. "Kid" Hall at the racetrack, and he made horseshoes and trimmed the hooves of the horses and shoed them. In 1948 or '49 they [the Ranch] built new brick homes, buildings, and stables at the Headquarters, and that's when they built a racetrack near where we live, and you can still see where it was today.

> I worked with the Thoroughbreds. I cleaned the horses and got them ready to go to exercise every morning by around six o'clock. I started [work] about four thirty in the morning. Around 1965 I started working with Librado and the bulls.
>
> JOSÉ SILGUERO

NEW YORK, NEW YORK

Max Hirsch was the expert trainer of King Ranch Thoroughbreds in New York. Of course, he had all the help in the world, but he was actually the trainer. There were a lot of times I would go pick him up at the airport [in Corpus Christi] and take him back when he visited the Ranch. He was a very, very intelligent man, very nice, and I remember he had a real hoarse voice. His son, Buddy Hirsch, also trained horses for King Ranch in California.

Max Hirsch and Mr. Bob, Dr. Northway, and William Egan would get on that grandstand, and they would time those horses and pick the ones that they had an idea that they were gonna be winners. Of course, you send a whole bunch of horses and you hope they'll all be winners, but you actually don't know they are winners until they win a race.

Mr. Bob knew a lot about livestock. We would line up those racehorses, maybe twelve or fifteen of them, for Mr. Bob, and he was able to point out defects on those horses or a problem that they had that had to be corrected. He would have Dr. Northway with him and, a lot of times, the trainer, and he would tell Dr. Northway just what to do with the horses. Dr. Northway would write down what needed to be done, and Mr. Bob would come back a month or two later and he knew whether or not they had been treated and were like he wanted them to be.

Dr. Northway was the head Ranch veterinarian from 1916 until his death in 1973, and he would always do everything for the animals to get them cured. I remember snakebites and cases of sleeping sickness, screwworm cases—he would do everything in the world for them. After Assault hurt his foot on the surveyor's stake in the pasture, he was put aside until Dr. Northway actually worked on him and wrapped his foot with a thin cloth with medicine on it. He would tell the farrier what to do, how much of the hoof to keep on or take off, or to put on some kind of a special shoe until he got him to the shape that he would have a fairly normal hoof and was able to run.

I broke Assault. When Assault was a colt, his mother was in bad shape. We were told to kill both. Then Mr. Bob [Kleberg] came, and Assault was weaned and we began to work to straighten out his bad foot. Dr. Northway and I took the loose stuff off his hoof, used ointment, and wrapped it with a thin cloth. He began to improve.

ALBERTO "LOLO" TREVIÑO *(quoted in Monday and Colley 77)*

The Heart Break

Assault was always a story. They blew that foot problem way out of context—way out of context. He was a cripple and Max Hirsch actually said he had an impediment in his walk, and he couldn't walk very good, but he was hell on running.

I knew about Assault. Well, we'd try to breed that animal in the breeding shed and they had chosen prime Quarter Horse mares to put with him, and they'd put him out as a stallion with these thirty mares and invariably he was infertile. And they never would accept the fact, and then they'd make the mistake—this is hind thought—instead of losing the whole season, they'd put a stallion with those mares and the horse that they put in there was fertile, obviously, because there were two or three of the mares that cycled and got pregnant. And Uncle Doc [Northway], he kept saying, "I'm sure that it was Assault . . ." And I was the one looking down the microscope at the semen samples, and I said to Tio, "Tio, you're just fooling yourself." That horse was sterile and he stayed sterile, and it was the heartbreak of all time.

MONTE MONCRIEF, DVM

I GOT TO TRAVEL

I think I asked Dr. Northway if I could ride with the horses and visit New York, where King Ranch had a racing operation. I actually got to go and stay there, oh goodness, for a good ten days.

What they would do, they would load the horses in those express cars attached to the passenger trains. They would load them over at the Caesar Pens, then move them to the depot here in town, and there would be maybe three or four cars full of horses. It took about forty-eight hours from here to New York; if you sent them in boxcars, it would take a week. A lot of the exercise boys and

NEW YORK RACING
RACE TRACK
IDENTIFICATION
1957
GNYA
DISPLAY FOR ADMIS

NEW YORK RACING ASSOCIATION
1954 Temporary Track Identification Card No. 1497

NAME OF HOLDER Alberto Maldonado #55934
SIGNATURE OF HOLDER Alberto Maldonado
EMPLOYER Max Hirsch TRACK Belmont
DEPT. Groom BARN 1-2 T.R.P.B. 83694
ISSUED 6-29-54 EXPIRATION DATE 7-10-54 195_

This Card is issued to the above person only, is non-transferable, is the property of Pinkerton's National Detective Agency, Inc., and must be surrendered upon demand
J. V. O'GRADY,
SPECIAL ASS'T TO PRESIDENT P.N.D.A.

Beto used these New York Racing Association passes to get into Belmont Park while visiting the Ranch's racehorse operations in New York. Courtesy of Beto Maldonado.

some of the grooms would go along and would stay there at Belmont for a length of time and work with the horses. When I went, I just went for the ride to visit New York. I got to see Times Square, Jack Dempsey's restaurant, Radio City, Empire State Building, Rockefeller Plaza, and I had a pass to go to any of those racetracks around the area. When we left from Belmont Park to go to the Queens, we would ride the bus; I think they charged us a dime for a ride.

I stayed at the stable with the grooms and the jockeys, and that's the first time I played Monopoly and I don't know how I managed to do it, but I won. There was a luncheonette right across the street where we would go eat breakfast ,and there was an Italian restaurant by the name of Luna. That's where Billy Anderson—we were good buddies—and I would have a big ol' pizza for a dollar. Billy and I actually went to Yankee Stadium and saw the Washington Senators play there. When I went home, I rode all the way to Grand Central Station to get the train, so I got to see that too.

KENTUCKY WAS BEAUTIFUL

The first time I went to Kentucky was in 1948, and Dr. Northway went with us to take a load of mares. The Ranch had a farm in Kentucky, and when the foals were weaned, they would ship the offspring back here to Texas by rail for Bill Egan to begin training them for the races. Then they would send them to New York, where Mr. Max Hirsch would be in charge of the rest of their training, or to California, where Mr. Hirsch's son, Buddy, was the trainer. Of course, every time I eat jellyrolls, I remember that trip because we had a big ol' box of jellyrolls, I don't think we ever got to eat all of them, because there were so many.

The express car was just like a passenger train—it went at that speed. We took canned goods and something to eat, and of course the express cars had running water. We wouldn't drink that water, but we could give the animals that water. The train had a restroom with a commode; it was like a passenger car, and that's how I traveled. We did a lot of traveling on the train at that time. We spent three days after we got there. They took us on a tour of the horse farms, and of all the farms, I liked the Calumet Farm best; it was very neatly kept and was painted red and white. They had a man there who did nothing but shine the brass on those doors, and the bluegrass—it was just beautiful. One day we drove by a cemetery where they buried the horses.

Anyway, on this trip were Dr. Northway, George Mayorga, and Martín Mendietta Jr., cowboys who were working with the Thoroughbreds at that time. We took off at eleven o'clock at night, and Martín had married that day or the day before, but he went with us anyway.

HE LOST ASSAULT AND THE JOCKEY

Dr. Monte Moncrief arrived at King Ranch fresh out of the Texas A&M school of veterinary medicine in 1949, following a stint on the Aggie line that earned him All American football honors his senior year. In his nearly thirty years as a King Ranch veterinarian, he and the Maldonados worked closely together with cattle and horses. He told of Librado's being the "head honcho," as he and his son Lee took care of stallions, including Bold Venture, sire of Assault, and others such as Wimpy, Wimpy Jr., and Columpio, while Beto worked with the mare side of the operation. Librado was an expert handler of horses as well as bulls, and for that reason he was chosen to bring the prized stallions to the breeding barn, where Dr. Northway and Monte were in charge of hand-breeding the racehorses. This could be a rambunctious, somewhat dangerous activity, and Librado's gift of calming the horses was critical. During a visit with Beto and the authors, Monte told a story that surprised even Beto.

> The only time I had anything to do with him [Assault] was the time I lost him on the train—oh, yes, the Triple Crown Winner—and I lost my jockey too. I lost José [Garcia]. I think we need to call this "Don't Get Off the Train."

After Assault didn't show up well in the breeding shed, we had an old trainer named Bill Egan, and Uncle Bob decided he wanted to put Assault back in training. Bill Egan started training him, and they started shooting for the Hollywood Gold Cup, naturally at Hollywood Park in California. After he got there, he didn't do too well—won four or five or something like that, but he didn't win the Gold Cup.

Anyway, to tell about the fateful trip, Pastel [José's nickname] and I took Assault to San Antonio and put him on a Pullman horsecar, and we took off for Arcadia, California. We were going to Santa Anita. We plodded along and looked out at the antelope as we went through Sanderson country in West Texas, and we finally got to El Paso.

I had just started at the King Ranch, and I had a dear friend named Robert Butchofsky that was also a veterinarian and he was in practice in Ysleta, about nineteen or twenty miles from El Paso. He had played on our Orange Bowl football team—and I was so proud of being a Kineño that I wanted to talk to him on the phone. I went in to call and in the interim, when I stopped, I found the yard foreman and I said, "I want to use the telephone. How long is the train gonna be here?" He said, "Oh, we're gonna spot your horsecar on the far track over there, but we're gonna be here about forty-five minutes." And I said, "Well, good. That'll give me time to make my call."

So I went in and called Butchofsky, and he and his wife, Jackie, were up in the mountains skiing and it took a while longer than I anticipated being in there, trying to get him on the phone. Anyhow, I came out, and the train was gone. My horse train was gone, my jockey was gone, and I was left standing there!

Pastel probably didn't have any money and didn't know what he was going to do. I chartered a private plane and managed to get there a day earlier than the horse and Pastel got there, and I found out when that train was coming in. And when Pastel saw me, he said, "Compadre!" He was real glad to see me. We got to Santa Anita, and Citation was in the barn and I got to go in the stall with him. Citation had won the Triple Crown in 1948, and it made me so proud to see that horse—big bay scoundrel. He must have weighed 1,400 pounds, and Assault probably didn't weigh more than 900. Anyway, I brought a three-crown winner and I walked in and saw another, and there have been eleven of them in all these years.

Dr. Moncrief's story reminded Beto of another story.

You know, compadre, about leaving your train . . . You know, when my daddy was traveling with those Jerseys, there were times that they would run out of what they had to eat, and he'd run to the nearest grocery store or what have you and buy something to eat. One time, by the time he was getting back, the train was pulling away, so he ran and climbed that ladder and rode on top of the train for the longest time until the train came to another stop.

WORKING WITH QUARTER HORSES

Back when I was working at the veterinary clinic as a young man after my brother Plácido went to the service, King Ranch had an abundance of horses. That was when it took a lot of horsepower to get the work done. I vaccinated as many as 2,500 or 3,000 Quarter Horses, cow ponies, mares, and mules, and at that time we still had mules that were mean like the dickens. We actually had to run those mules through a chute to vaccinate them.

We went to the horses in pens located all over the Ranch. Cowboys helped us a lot by roping the horses and getting them to the pens. The horses were usually gentle. We vaccinated on the neck. We clipped the hair, rubbed the spot with cotton soaked in alcohol, pinched the skin, and gave the shot with a tiny little quarter-inch needle. A little ball built up if it was a good shot; if there was no little ball, I would have to vaccinate again.

Cipriano Mendietta, a vaquero, would help me here at Headquarters; and over at Laureles, Rogerio Silva and some of the other vaqueros would do the clipping for me. That was the time that we had vials that held only a couple of cc's, and the horse got one cc, so I could vaccinate two horses with one vial. We would end up with a big ol' tub full of those [empty] vials. It was a lot of work. We had to vaccinate horses for encephalomyelitis, or sleeping sickness. There were two strains of the virus, called eastern and western encephalomyelitis, and we gave four series of shots in those days: eastern, then western, then eastern, then western, and we had to wait seven to fifteen days apart, and it would take a long time to get all the horses vaccinated. By the time I got around to all the horses, it was time to start again. I vaccinated here at Headquarters, and at Laureles, Norias—about fifty miles away—and Encino. That would put me on the road quite a bit; at that time I knew almost every pasture of the Ranch.

Driving on the roads at that time could be a problem because the Ranch had just started paving the roads and there were still plenty of dirt roads. Tire chains were very popular; most every Ranch vehicle had a set of tire chains because when there was nothing but dirt roads and it rained a lot, you could get stuck in the mud real easy. Of course, the sandy country in Encino and Norias was a whole lot different, and if you didn't know what you were doing, you could get

Beto Maldonado (*left*) and Dr. Monte P. Moncrief share a laugh about the time when, as the new King Ranch veterinarian, Dr. Moncrief lost the Triple Crown winner Assault on the way to California. The two men have been friends since 1949. Photo by Betty Bailey Colley.

stuck very easy. You would actually have to let half of the air out of your tires, from about thirty-five pounds to fifteen pounds to widen them, drive to the gate, get that gate open, drive through that sand, then air the tires up again and take off. Otherwise, you could get stuck.

THAT TRIP TO CALIFORNIA

One time I took a Quarter Horse to California. There would be buyers that would come and buy horses, and the ones that were out of town or out of state, Dr. Northway would send the horses by train and he would send someone with them. This time he had a horse buyer from Chicago and a buyer from Santa Ana, California, and he said, "Beto, I have two horses to send to these people. Find me somebody to do it." I had been to Chicago, so I went to California. Alfredo Cortez took the other horse to Chicago and back before I got to Santa Ana.

That was a big ol' car, and the horse was at one end and I had my bed at the other end—a straw mattress—and I had a flashlight and a radio and reading material and canned goods to eat and the whole shebang. My dad was an expert as far as preparing those boxcars to hold cattle or livestock, so he prepared mine. One of the doors was shut completely, and the other one was left open just wide enough for maybe to stick your head out and that was as far as you could go, so nobody could come in.

In El Paso a man that was working the tracks asked me, "What you got there?" I said, "A horse." And he said, "Who's with you?" I told him, "Nobody. I am by myself." And he said, "Well, don't let anybody in. Even if they work for the railroad, don't let anybody in that car. Not too long ago there was some people come through here with livestock, and they found that man dead—they had killed him." I rode in that boxcar four nights and five days, and I never got off. And when I got to Santa Ana, I still didn't want to get out.

KING RANCH QUARTER HORSES AT AUCTION

Superior King Ranch Quarter Horses, bred to work cattle on the open range, were offered in every King Ranch auction, beginning in 1950 and ending in the late 1980s. The horse auction was usually held in midmorning, and the Santa Gertrudis bull auction in the early afternoon.

Tio Kleberg, vice president for agribusiness from 1980 to 1998, was in charge of operations in Florida, Kentucky, Brazil, Australia, and South Texas, and he grew up learning about livestock from the best. Tio's father, Richard M. "Dick" Kleberg Jr. came home to work on the Ranch in 1940 to assist his father, Richard M. Kleberg Sr., and his Uncle Bob [Kleberg], who ran the Ranch. Mr. Dick became familiar with all phases of Ranch work and became manager of horses and cattle on the Laureles and Santa Gertrudis divisions. He served as chairman of the board from 1968 until his death in 1979.

When Tio's military service ended and he wanted to return to the Ranch to work, his dad told him he would have to apply for a job with his Uncle Bob, who agreed to hire him and assigned him to Mr. Dick. His dad astutely assigned Tio to work for Emert Crocker, foreman of the Santa Gertrudis Division, and Tio found himself learning to mend fences and windmills, move cattle, work the roundups—do every phase of Ranch work. Kineños taught basic ranching skills to Tio, and King Ranch family members taught him their vast knowledge of livestock. He worked with Librado and Beto for many years, and he and Beto remain good friends today.

During a delightful day visiting with Tio and his wife, Janell, in February 2007, the authors and Beto listened to firsthand experiences of work with the Quarter Horses. With infectious enthusiasm for the subject, Tio and Janell shared fascinating stories of working with some of the finest animals in the world.

After buying a house in Kingsville over the phone, Tio moved Janell and their baby to King Ranch in 1971. Although Tio had spent most of his life on King Ranch except for the years at Texas Tech and in the U.S. Army, Janell was relatively new to ranch life. She met a steep learning curve almost immediately, as it soon became obvious that this was not just being married to somebody on a ranch; she had a job, and she would have responsibilities as a working member of the Ranch family. Right away, she faced a huge challenge. Janell arrived at her new home on King Ranch with almost no knowledge of horsemanship, the hub of Ranch work.

> I was twenty-three years old and I got here and I mean it was like—I'd had a Shetland pony as a child. I knew nothing. I went up there every day after Buster and Sheila [Welch] got here, and I would go help rope horses, wash, and show sheen, and oil saddles, and I'd go just help any way I could. Sheila was a wonderful horsewoman and teacher, and she took the time to teach me everything, from putting the saddle on to polishing the silver [on bridles]. And I learned a lot of what I saw that Librado had—Librado could walk up to a bull and touch it, and there was just a sense of a symbiotic relationship. Sheila and Buster had that, and they taught that to me, as much as you can teach that to anyone. Buster was an expert horse trainer, and what Buster had to teach me was to step up, to have the courage just to be able to ride through that one, two, or three seconds that made a difference whether the horse could really perform or not, and trust the horse to be able to do it.
>
> On Friday afternoon before the sale, the cattle were available for viewing, and then starting at two or three o'clock we would have a horse demonstration, not with the sale horses but horses whose pedigree would be represented in the sale. It was kind of the event of the afternoon, and I would ride fillies that were going back to the breed band, so they weren't for sale, and a lot of them were smaller fillies that a grown man couldn't show.

YOU JUST NEVER KNEW WHAT WAS GOING TO HAPPEN

> Helenita [Helen Kleberg Groves], Tio's cousin, bought, sold, and showed a lot of King Ranch horses. Tio's cousin Leslie Clement rode and showed horses also. They'd try to divvy up the horses to be shown at the demonstration, and they might put me on a horse I'd never ridden before. You just never knew what was going to happen. I'll never forget one of the most terrifying things.
>
> Helenita had this wonderful mare, Tot O' Gin, and sometimes she showed her and sometimes she didn't. For some reason she wasn't going to show this mare that day, and this mare was so big and strong and she turned so hard and she also was unusual. Most all King Ranch horses

you could walk up to and they were like pets—they were like Librado's bulls. But this mare—you had to be really careful. I just remember when they told me, "You're gonna show Tot O' Gin," I went, "I'm the mother of three children. I cannot ride that . . . I can't show that mare." They said, "Don't worry about it." People who came to watch the horse demonstration couldn't see, but they had about four people holding this mare and the others were pushing me up there on her. Tio said it was like trying to put a cat in a bathtub. I got on her and did okay, but it was a Hail Mary ride.

JANELL KLEBERG

I sold Tot O' Gin to King Ranch, and Tio showed her. I also showed Miss Peppy, acquired from Buster Welch, and Tot O' Gin's mother and sisters. I showed Miss Peppy without a bridle before the King Ranch sale, and Buster showed Little Peppy, and Tio, Mr. San Peppy. A great sale followed the next day.

HELEN KLEBERG GROVES

SALE DAY

On the day of the sale, I would go up at daylight and we'd start loping horses, and every one of those horses had to be ridden ten minutes to an hour, depending on the age. And if we had twelve [in the sale], I'd probably take three or four. The old racetrack back there was plowed, so I'd go first thing and saddle a horse, ride it to the racetrack, ride it thirty minutes to an hour, hand it off, and get another one. We'd get them back and have them all tied up out there by the hose, and we'd shampoo them just like Librado did the bulls, scrape the water off with a scraper, and spray them with show sheen.

At the sale we felt a responsibility to make sure that people had what they needed, like water, and knew where the restrooms were, about a motel in town—anything they might need. Family members and Kineños watched the crowd closely and were there to help. Also, we set up in the Quarter Horse barn during lunch so buyers wouldn't be mixed in, standing at tables eating. Leslie Clement and I would go in the crowd and find those buyers and take them over. We had a bar and some hors d'oeuvres set up for them so they would have a place to sit down and rest and have a glass of wine if they wanted a drink.

JANELL KLEBERG

Beto checks out his Winchester rifle that Dick Kleberg Jr. gave him to use for killing snakes and coyotes. When Mr. Dick died, his son and then-Ranch manager, Tio Kleberg, insisted that Beto keep the rifle, which remains a prized possession. Photo by Betty Bailey Colley.

SELECTING THE HORSES

Janell and Tio described how Susan Cude, Quarter Horse secretary, kept scrupulously accurate records on every horse. This information was critical to the breeding program, as well as to evaluating horses for the auction sale. As with the Santa Gertrudis bulls after they were selected for auction, the horses were placed in what was judged to be the proper order for securing the optimum price. Janell assisted in the record-keeping process:

> Twice a year they would bring all the mares in with their foals. Susan would get those books in order, and we would spread them out on that rough wooden table in that tiny space and Susan would match the mare with the registry. The foal would always get behind the mare, so we'd have to kind of turn the mare to get a good look at the foal. Susan had a big chart up in her office, and those mares would be listed under the stallion where they were bred. At first Tio, and then Tio, Buster [Welch], and Joe Stiles, would look at those mares and their foals, and they would grade the foals. Everything was documented.
>
> So the breeding was intermingled with record keeping and then selection for the sale, just like the bulls. Tio, Buster, and Joe, but especially Buster, would make comments—say, on a stud colt—and they would kind of grade them because we had to set the sale order. A sale has almost a bell curve, so you know statistically and by feel what slot in the sale is going to bring the highest price, so Buster would grade them where he thought they would sell the best. I learned so much from him because he was always

very specific about the conformation, and I would write down what he said in my little spiral notebook. A lot of times people would want me to sit next to them in the sale and consult with them. It was an art rather than a science of knowing your buyers and knowing what they were looking for and also having that little spiral notebook in my pocket to know what the comments were.

Tio talked about the value of the auction to marketing the Ranch's prize animals all year:

The cattle would be out in the morning. But when we sent out the invitations, we'd say the livestock showing is at one o'clock [on Friday]. It would give them time to come in, get lunch in Kingsville, and then come out. But they'd be there by seven o'clock in the morning; they [the cattle] were ready to go.

The auction was an opportunity to bring people to your location and show them, but the primary reason, besides marketing, was to establish the value of those animals for the next year. It established the price, so it was important that we had the best we could offer in that sale. Everything we did for twelve months culminated in that one day, and that's why it was so critical.

We did a little bit of advertising in magazines, but the marketing piece was the sale catalog. It wasn't your typical deal where, when the sale was over, they left them on the bench. People took them home with them because the photographs and the copy—I mean, they were pieces.

I RESPECTED THEM

Tio and I were close. We were as close as we are today. Always a lot younger a man than I am, but I have always respected any member of the family, regardless of the age or what have you. We got along very well. Of course, Tio managed the Ranch for twenty-some-odd years and had to do with the whole shebang, and we would communicate by radio or in person. And he was the kind of a person who could understand and help you any way that he could. Same thing with his papa. Anything that I needed, he was willing. I needed something related to my house. He went ahead and added a room and covered the porch and the whole shebang. Mr. Dick Jr. told me that I should have a rifle to kill coyotes and snakes and what have you, and I carried that Winchester rifle all of the time. When he died, I told Tio that I'd return that rifle, and he said, "Beto, you go ahead and keep that rifle."

4

WHEN BETO WASN'T SHOWING CATTLE

He had immaculate records.

Tio Kleberg

I have been on the King Ranch payroll since I was ten years old, when I made $5 a month working around the Jersey barn with my dad. While I learned how to take care of cattle and how to tame and show Santa Gertrudis bulls, I did a lot of other jobs too. I was always willing to go where the Ranch needed me.

> The most amazing thing, at one time in his [Beto's] career, of which he had several, he was assigned the job of taking the birth weights of the single herds. There were several single herds that they watched after. Beto did it faithfully. He had to register the birth weight of a new baby, and if you've ever grabbed a new baby from a Santa Gertrudis cow and you didn't have your Achilles tendon on, you'd better hook up, because that was what they expected Beto to do and he did it. He had a history of everything. We had to use all that kind of information that Beto kept all the time on those herds because when they [the vaqueros] took them in to brand them, they had to know the sire and the dam.
>
> MONTE MONCRIEF, DVM

TWENTY-EIGHT YEARS OF METICULOUS RECORDS

I actually worked with the A-Herds [single-sire herds] for twenty-eight years, showing and keeping records. When we had the auctions, about two months ahead of the shows in October, I would work with my dad showing the bulls, and after the auctions, I would go back to working with the A-Herds. After the auctions ended in 1986, I worked only with the A-Herds until I retired in 1990.

We had about eighteen single-sire herds. We were four men, and we would go into those herds early in the morning and then in the afternoon, seven days a week, especially if we saw a cow that she looked like she was gonna drop a calf in the afternoon. We would stay right on top of them when they were dropping calves to make sure they were okay. And once they dropped a calf on the ground, a lot of times the calves were still wet when we got to them, but we didn't dry them off unless it was winter. But if it was real cold, we'd dry them with a tow sack or something like that. We'd tie 'em down, get a birth weight, and put a tattoo number, at first in the ear and later on the horns, with indelible ink, and that was their number for the rest of their lives. Later they came out with ear tags, and that was a miracle for us because when the numbers were in the ears or horns, they [calves] would play in the dirt and cover those numbers and we were lost; we had a hard time getting the number.

Sometimes the mamas didn't like us fooling with the calves. The older cows are good mothers, and they don't want their babies to be harmed in any way. There were times that we went underneath the vehicle or on top of the pickup or in the bed or top of the cab to get away from them. There were times when the mama was that bad that we would let the calf go and catch it at a later time, but we liked to get a birth weight on those calves soon after they were dropped.

We weighed them with what we called a cotton scale that would weigh up to two hundred pounds. The average birth weight was seventy-nine pounds; that's what we wanted. What we would do, we would tie the feet of the calf to a position so we could put that scale on that rope and we would lift it up and weigh him. It took just a second; then we would untie him and let him go with his mama. With the younger cows dropping calves, we would really have to do it in a hurry before they got away, because once they got away, they had a hard time coming back to find their baby calf. The older cows wouldn't go away, but if they did, they knew more or less where the calf was dropped. But if a younger cow started to leave, we would have to make a point to actually push her back to that calf so she would mother up, or it could be that she would walk off to the other end of the pasture, which could be a mile or two away.

I had a little book that I kept the date, pasture, birth weight, the dam's number, and the sire those cattle were bred to. I put this information on a pad and

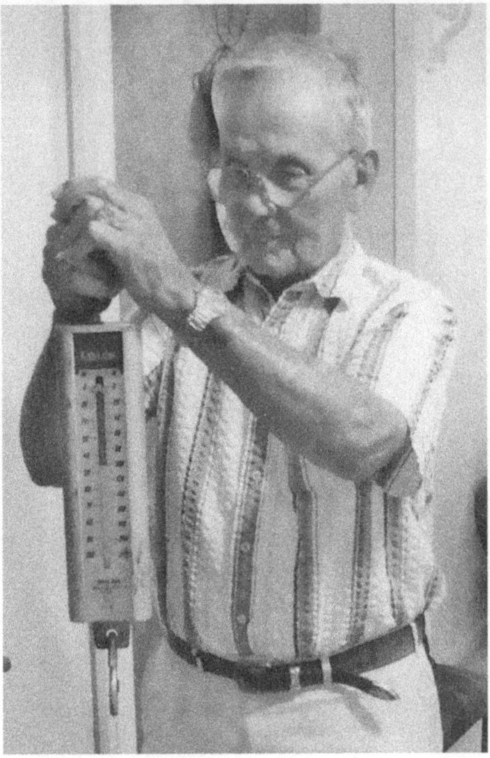

Beto Maldonado demonstrates the use of the scale with which he weighed Santa Gertrudis calves at birth. Beto recorded the weights and kept meticulous records on the Santa Gertrudis herd for twenty-eight years. Photo by Betty Bailey Colley.

turned it in to the office every day, and the secretary would record it into three ledger books. I actually kept three records, one in my little book, one for the office, and one for Mr. Dick so he could have it when he drove through the pastures.

> He [Beto] had immaculate records. Beto and Leonard Stiles are the only two people I know that kept everything.
>
> TIO KLEBERG

I do the same thing with my possessions too, even my clothes. I put the date, put the percentage of cotton and polyester. I am now wearing some pants that are dated back in the mid-'90s.

I'm a funny person, but I came up with the idea that I'm particular. I never did learn that much about mechanics where carpentry is concerned, but I have a whole set of tools for carpentry and of course I use the pliers and wrenches and what have you. So I got me a marker to mark the steel pliers. We were cleaning out the garage at my dad's one time, and I ran into a screwdriver and I said, "Here it is, I've been missing it." "No, no," he said. So I showed him my name, and he said, "You, Beto, you're a smart rascal." It had no date, but it had my name on it. I say if they steal anything from you, you probably can't find it, but you can always find it if you have your name on it.

BRANDING THOSE CALVES

Captain King probably branded cattle with the Running W for the first time in late 1867 or early 1868 (Lea 257).

When calves were old enough to be put away from their mamas—I would say from seven to nine months of age—it was time to brand them. I would look at the records, and I would know the mama and papa and the cowboys would use this information to brand the calves. Single-sire cattle were forty cows and one bull to one pen, and they were branded by known sire and dam. On the left hip was the Running W, under that the year it was dropped—like "06" if it was dropped in 2006—and under that its number. The sire is branded on the left butt, and the dam's ID number or letter on the right butt. There are no single-sire herds today.

Multiple sire are hundreds of cows in with bulls in one pasture—no more than one bull to twenty cows—and they usually have the number and year because there is no way to tell the papa. For the longest time, the Running W was put on the ribs of the cattle, but then if that animal ended up at slaughter, people would claim that the brand ruined a lot of the hides when they tanned them, so the Ranch moved the brand from the ribs to the hip.

The cowboys would rope those calves and pull them off, tie them down, brand, and vaccinate them in just a few minutes and put them with the steers. Some of the older Longhorn steers played a big part in working cattle at one time, and we would normally have a group of them set aside when we were working cattle out in the open. They were halter-broken and taught to lead. At the end of the day, the cowboys would turn the keeper cows back in the pasture and bring those steers to the pens, and they would actually lead the barren cows and the calves to pens without any problem.

And that's how it was done at one time in those big roundups in the middle of nowhere.

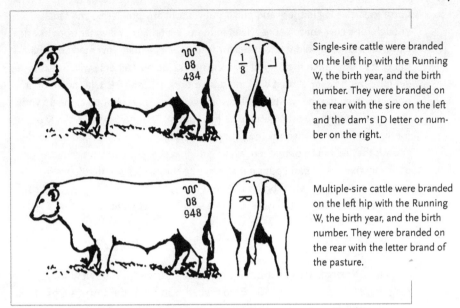

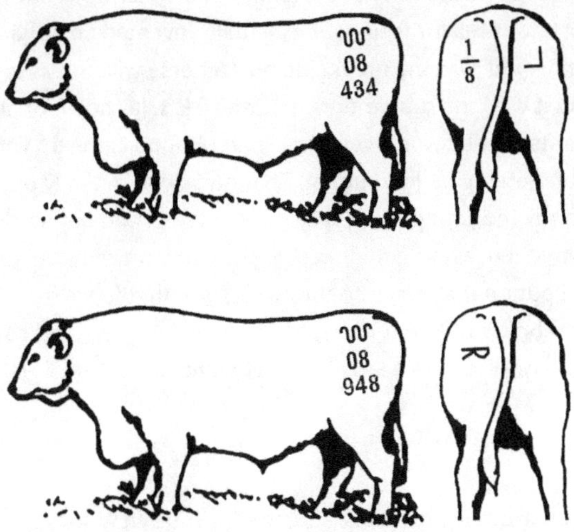

Single-sire cattle were branded on the left hip with the Running W, the birth year, and the birth number. They were branded on the rear with the sire on the left and the dam's ID letter or number on the right.

Multiple-sire cattle were branded on the left hip with the Running W, the birth year, and the birth number. They were branded on the rear with the letter brand of the pasture.

Single-sire and multiple-sire brands. Courtesy of Beto Maldonado.

MR. BOB CARED ABOUT US AND THE ANIMALS

You know, I was interviewed for a write-up about the Ranch, and I went ahead and said that I considered Mr. Bob a genius. He was the type of man that would listen to the smallest people on earth or the tallest people on earth, and he had ideas that nobody else did—big dreams that the good Lord granted those dreams. He had a sharp eye for livestock.

Mr. Bob was the type of a man that cared about his people, about his animals—the cattle and horses. He would tell the cowboys that they might not get tired, but the horse will, so you take care of that horse and be reasonable. That's why a cowboy would have as many as fifteen horses. Whenever the cowboy saw that horse getting tired, he pulled the saddle and got onto another one.

Mrs. Helen, Mr. Bob's wife, was nice too. I would get to see Mrs. Helen quite often by coming by and bringing some things that Dr. Northway would send Mr. Bob at the house, or whenever I would go by and drop Mr. Bob at the house and we would be riding with Dr. Northway. Mrs. Helen was a nice lady. So was Helenita, Mr. Bob's daughter. Helenita and I grew up together.

Anyway, he [Mr. Bob] would do everything in the world to keep the livestock from getting hurt—like that fence he designed with squares big enough for a horse to stick a leg in there and pull it out without any problems, and small enough for a cow not to get her head in there. He built round water troughs and came up with using old tractor tires for feeding. He actually invented an apparatus here at the Ranch that would turn the tire inside out. A horse will find a way to get hurt, but he cannot do it with the rubber tire—he can kick it, lay down on it, or do anything that he wants, but he won't get hurt. Then Mr. Bob came up with the idea of putting up that metal band [on fences]. That metal was actually put up for the racehorses. Especially the young ones, they go to playing, and before they know it they're on top of that fence and get injured. So he came up with the idea of having that metal band put on that fence so they would see that fence from a distance and slow down or take a different route. Mr. Bob died in 1974, and some of those fences you see today were here a long time before he died.

When Norman Parish, animal physiologist, came to interview for a job at King Ranch in December 1961, Beto picked him up at the Corpus Christi airport, the first time they met. Parish went to work for the Ranch in January 1962 to do an artificial insemination project and worked there for twenty-six years. His responsibilities included the single-sire herd, and Beto worked for him part of the time. Parish recalled:

> Beto was a good employee. He was always right there and he helped me a lot. He was always good-natured and always looked starched and clean like he stepped out of a bandbox. I wondered how he did it. Even when he was doing the same work I was, he always looked clean.
>
> Beto kept meticulous records, and I think he learned that on his own.

Norman Parish's wife, Seba, worked for the Santa Gertrudis Breeders International, headquartered near the entrance to King Ranch. She was a statistical analyst and also worked with insurance, investments, and accounts payable. The Parishes are retired and live in Wimberley, Texas.

THERE WERE ALWAYS CHALLENGES

Soon after Santa Gertrudis was designated as a breed, King Ranch began participating in cattle shows in the United States and abroad to introduce its new breed to other cattle breeders and the public. Taking cattle out of the county, state, or nation was often complicated. Dr. Monte Moncrief, one of the King Ranch veterinarians, was in charge of vaccinations necessary for papers certify-

Beto Maldonado, age seventeen, poses with the Willys Jeep and cattle sprayer assigned to him when Bob Kleberg Jr. taught him how to spray the herd for ticks in 1947. Courtesy of King Ranch.

ing that the animals were healthy and could travel. He worked with Librado and Beto for nearly thirty years, getting the cattle ready to travel. Different countries had different requirements. For instance, to take cattle into Brazil or Argentina, the animals had to be tested, but there was also a requirement that no animal could have a spleen. Dr. Moncrief took the spleen out of about a hundred steers. He learned to complete the procedure in about twenty minutes, and there was almost no death from this surgery.

However, the biggest local problem in those days was the screwworm. Dr. Moncrief said that if an animal had any kind of a *yaga* (sore), it had to be taken care of immediately or else the screwworms would devour the animal; it would eat right through until something like a vein ruptured. He explained that the screwworm is the larval stage of a fly, looks like a maggot, and is plainly visible. It lives off of live flesh, then grows up and flies away and makes more screwworms. It was a challenge that demanded a solution.

I LEARNED TO MAKE FORMULA 62

For the longest time, because of the screwworm, we could only bring cows in to breed once a year, and we would breed them to where they would drop calves the latter part of December and through January and February. Any calf that was dropped during the summer on a hot day would develop screwworm by the third day on the navel. Screwworm eggs are laid by flies. Any open wound they would go to, and there was at one time nothing you could do for that. That's why we were keeping those horns, the tip of the horns, cut for the longest time because the sharp point—if an animal is playing with the other one and the horn makes any scratch that draws blood, the fly goes to that one, and that was the main cause of death years ago. Some of those cows would get a lot of ticks in their ears and would have screwworm cases, and the cowboys would have to cut part of that ear and keep on and would have to cut so much, those cows would have no ears.

Then the U.S. government developed a treatment for screwworm called Formula 62. We used to make our own Formula 62 medication when I worked in the veterinary department. Formula 62 was made of benzene, lampblack, and Turkey-red oil. I learned to make it, and I would go in to town and buy jars at T Jacs Stand to hold that formula. T Jacs Stand was close to the campus [Texas A&I University, now a Texas A&M branch], and back in the early days when the students would come to school without a vehicle, T Jacs is where they would find most everything that they needed, like school supplies, things to eat, and what have you. I remember T Jacs had booths of telephones there—maybe three or four of them, the wooden kind—and they [students] would call their mama and papa from those pay phones. I knew the owner. He was armless and yet he had an apparatus and you would go there to pay and he would work that register and give you the change with that wire. Anyway, I would buy those big empty jars of pickles and mayo and what have you, and that's what I would fill up with Formula 62 for treating those screwworm cases.

The screwworm medicine was like a paste. Smear the wound, and it would kill the worm and heal the wound. Most of the time one treatment would do it. The cowboys would notice the screwworm cases, and those cattle were brought in or tied down at the middle of the pasture. The cowboys had at one time in their saddle bags, in one side, an extra rope to tie 'em down and, in the other, the screwworm medication, and they would treat those cases right there. It was a lot of hard work. You could treat livestock, goats, and whatever with Formula 62, but deer would die with the screwworm. It was the main cause of deer death during that time.

Now we don't have screwworm. They [U.S. Department of Agriculture] eliminated that problem in the late '50s with sterile flies. There was some kind of radioactive material that they came up with to sterilize flies, and what they would do, they would drop boxes of those sterile flies to the ground and they spread around. They were flown over here and dropped by air.

MR. BOB TAUGHT ME HOW

I grew up working with my dad, but when my brother Plácido went to the service in World War II, I kind of took his place working in the veterinary department with Dr. Northway. I was about thirteen or fourteen years of age. I was in charge of keeping up with medications that were lacking, and I would have a list for the salesmen from the laboratories when they came to check our shelves and make sure of what we needed. Most of the time we ordered medication on the phone from local pharmacies when we needed special formulas like 4X liniment or 6X liniment. Anyway, I would keep up with medications, sweep the floors, and help the doctors around the operating tables. Then in the late '40s, when I was about seventeen, the Ranch purchased a high-pressure sprayer to spray the cattle with insecticides to kill as many flies as possible. Mr. Bob was working cattle at the Norias Division, and he was the one who actually taught me how to spray a big herd of cattle.

The Ranch had purchased a fleet of brand-new Willys Jeeps, and I was assigned one of them. The Jeeps had a power takeoff on their rear so they could be used like a small tractor to harvest hay or do anything that would require a power takeoff to make the rest of the equipment work. We used it with the sprayer. It was a piece of round metal with openings, and it made the motor build up pressure for the sprayer. Mr. Bob actually got in the Jeep and showed me how he wanted it done. He also told me that I should get in the middle of the herd of, I would estimate, eight hundred to a thousand head of cattle, and the cowboys would make them circle around into two or four circles and they would circle and circle until all the cows and calves were sprayed, so that's what we did. We sprayed in favor of the wind and the cowboys; there would normally be twenty-five cowboys on horseback keeping the herd moving.

After I learned how, I would spray here at Headquarters, then go to Laureles and Norias, fifty miles south of Kingsville. I remember spending a week at Norias and a week at Laureles when they first purchased the machine. Later I could do all three of those divisions in one day. That was during the time that I was also vaccinating thousands of horses.

5

GROWING UP A MALDONADO

Everybody had the authority to discipline children.

Sammy Maldonado

THE TRADITION

Well, here he comes. I can hear him tamping his cane as he walks down the covered porch that runs along the front of the schoolhouse toward the auditorium. The "ho-ho-ho's," and the horn honks get louder as he gets closer. It must be Santa Claus.

The kids are laughing and talking as their parents try to calm them down from the excitement. They know what is coming later and they are having a hard time sitting still. A murmur runs around the room as Santa's "tamp, tamp, tamp" gets near the door and the crowd calms beginning from the right corner of the room where we hear him first, then it spreads around the room as everyone begins to notice the quiet. Nick Diaz, the coordinator of this magical event calls out, "Oye! Oyete! Aquí viene Santa Claus."

Santa seems always to be the same age no matter what year it is. Maybe it is because of his annual special night job. This is our Santa, Librado Maldonado. He's dressed in his oversized red and white suit with white-trimmed coat that falls below his knees. The pants have extra red wool fabric that gathers generously at the top of his black rubber Wellington boots—all of this punctuated with the exaggerated stoop and syncopated gait of a gimpy legged beggar tapping his inevitable cane and calling "Ho, Ho, Ho" in a decided Mexican accent.

We have a world class Santa. Librado Maldonado, former manager of the dairy herd now in charge of grooming and gentling the purebred Santa Gertrudis bulls for the annual cattle auction on the Ranch. . . . I am years older before I figure out that Santa Claus and Librado are one and the same. He is the only Santa most of us ever knew at King Ranch. (Sally Kleberg 55, 57)

MY DAD PLAYED SANTA CLAUS FOR MOST OF HIS LIFE

I remember those Christmas parties that the Ranch gave. When I was a kid, we would all get together and meet at the commissary for Christmas presents and what have you. Lauro Cavazos would be in charge of the program and members of the [Kleberg] family would come to the party. Of course, B [B. K. Johnson] and Bobby [Shelton, nephews of Bob Kleberg,] were reared with Mr. Bob at his house, and they would make a point to be at those Christmas parties and they and other Ranch family kids would actually hand out the treats. They were maybe a couple of years older than I was. That is where I got to know, or got to see or meet, Alice King Kleberg, the youngest daughter of Captain King. She died in 1944 when I was fourteen years of age. Mr. Bob and Mr. Bob's wife, Helen, and their daughter Helenita would come. And Mr. Dick and his wife, Mamie, and children would come. Mr. Dick was in Congress at that time, and he would make a point to be with us at the Christmas party. I remember him saying that he would come from a big city—Washington, I guess—where there were a lot of people, and he just wanted to come be with us at that time. Mr. Dick—he spoke excellent Spanish—would come to thank the men for their work and things like that. Mr. Bob would speak and Lauro Cavazos would speak also, and they would make a point to let the people [Kineños] know that they appreciated what they were doing for them.

We would get in line as a family and shake hands with Santa Claus, and they would pass out presents for the kids and bags of goodies—apples and oranges and candies and pecans and what have you. Employees' wives would get a present along with the employees. The wives would get sheets or blankets or something like that for the house, and employees usually got a wool jacket. After they passed out the presents, and we finished shaking hands and visiting, we would walk across the road to the school building and have a *baile*. It was a pretty good-sized building that could be converted into a dance hall. They would split the building in two for school, but there were doors that could fold back and have the whole building for the dance. That's where [there was] a big giant pit with barbecue and dinner was served, barbecue and all the trimmings. They would play the music with a guitar and the *guitarrones* with the big fat back.

I never did learn to dance, but my dad was a good dancer. They would play music till about midnight and then everybody would head home.

When we were about five years old, we used to believe in Santa Claus. I remember one time that he brought me a little coin purse with a nickel in it, and I was so happy because I had a little purse and Santa Claus had brought me a nickel.

One of my nephews, my sister's son, Joe Henry Perez, used to go every time they had a Christmas. At first he believed that it was Santa Claus. Then one time he said, "Oh, now I know who is Santa Claus. It's my granddaddy 'cause I notice his ears." He was about six or seven.

One time Daddy wore his suit so the kids would see him at home, and then the kids started crying because they were afraid of Santa Claus. They were tiny little kids. They were about three or four years old.

ALICIA MALDONADO

LA PATRONA

The tradition of the King family celebrating Christmas with the Kineños trailed back to the time of Captain King and his wife, Henrietta. Armed with a solid moral arsenal from her Presbyterian upbringing, Henrietta King evidently embraced the Mexican culture from the time she came to Brownsville with her missionary father in 1850, three years before Captain King bought the first acre on the Wild Horse Desert. From all accounts, when Henrietta arrived on the desert as a brand-new bride, she almost immediately turned her attention to the welfare of the vaqueros and their families, and this would undergird her remarkable leadership during the forty years following her husband's death as she, with the help of Robert J. Kleberg Sr., built King Ranch to legendary status. She became known as La Patrona, a Mexican term translated variously as "protector," "employer," "saint," or "boss," and she was most likely all of these.

According to Tom Lea in his two-volume history, *The King Ranch*, she was the Kineños' advocate and defender. She nursed them when they were sick and tended to their needs with an abiding spirit of respect for them and their culture. She became fluent in Spanish as it became the language of the Ranch and Mexican food became the daily diet. No doubt it was in this same spirit that she established the Christmas tradition at the Ranch as a time of celebration, the sharing of gifts, visiting, special food, and music. She even grew to allow dancing—but only at Christmas.

Librado Maldonado, holding Hipolito Silguero Jr. and with Ella Alvarado Bustami beside him in 1968. Librado played Santa Claus at the Ranch Christmas parties for years and was the only Santa most Kineño children ever knew. Courtesy of Beto Maldonado.

> Once a year Mrs. King allowed her disapproval of dancing to be overruled to attend with all her family the festive Christmas Baile *Kineños* held at their quarters "beyond the stables." At this holiday celebration, La Madama made presents for everyone; for the grownups, gifts of "clothes, petticoats, jackets," for the children, bright red tarlatan stockings bulging with candy and fruit. A prominent part of the preparations for Christmas at the big house each year was the cutting and sewing and filling of the many stockings made from red tarlatan always ordered from Alkemeyer's in Houston. (Lea 521, 522)

This era of the traditional King Ranch Christmas party ended around 1968 (Sally Kleberg 15). Too many people with no connection to the Ranch began coming for the free gifts and food, and the event became unwieldy. By this time the party had been moved to the auditorium of the new school building, which was completed around 1950. Tomás Rodriguez, Steve Cavazos, and Beto Maldonado had the unhappy task of identifying these uninvited "guests" who lined up to receive the gifts intended for the Kineño families. Security became a problem at the *baile*, which sometimes became overcrowded with too many unruly people nobody at the Ranch knew, and Alejos Gutierrez, a cowboy who "knew everybody," was stationed at the door to try to discourage these party crashers from interfering with the event, usually unsuccessfully. So the traditional celebration, the one time a year that all the people on the Santa Gertrudis Division had the opportunity to gather, the King Ranch Christmas Party instituted by Captain and Mrs. King a hundred years or so before, ended.

Still clinging to shreds of the King Ranch Christmas tradition, Ranch trucks began delivering the traditional gifts and bags of goodies to the homes, and this practice would continue until around 1980, when the Ranch began giving bonuses so the families could buy what they needed or wished. By the time Beto's children came along, Ranch trucks had already begun delivering the children's Christmas toys and bags of goodies and the wives' gifts to their home. The men's jackets were not delivered; the men went to the commissary and tried on their jackets to be sure of a proper fit. The jackets were of different design from year to year; sometimes the jacket might have fur on the collar or they might be black wool jackets with leather patches on the sleeves.

The Maldonados, starting with Librado and Ella and continuing with Beto and Dora, early on established their own Christmas tradition of gifts and plenty of good food shared with family celebrating together on Christmas Day. Even the days following were a kind of gift, as there was almost no work on the Ranch between Christmas and New Year's Day, the only time of year that the men could spend a weeklong holiday with their families. Christmas was a special, happy time for the Maldonados, just as it was for all the King Ranch family.

I BELIEVED IN SANTA CLAUS FOR THE LONGEST TIME

At the house I remember my dad buying a Christmas tree for us. We didn't have electricity, and they would decorate the tree with icicles and bulbs and what have you. And they would have some kind of a clamp deal that would hold a little candle like birthday candles for children, and they would light those candles once in a while, and they would have them on for maybe five or ten minutes and then they would blow them out.

There was very little exchange where Christmas presents were concerned. Of course my dad was the kind of man who would do everything for us, or everything that he could, and he would manage to buy us a little toy or whatever for Christmas. I believed in Santa Claus for the longest time. One time I wanted one of those Red Flyer wagons, a red wagon, and was talking about it. My dad made an effort to buy one for me and he actually put it in the garage, and a day or two before Christmas I happened to go into the garage and saw that little red wagon. So after that, I didn't say anything. I said to myself, "Oh my goodness, I know who Santa Claus is!" Of course, my dad played Santa Claus dressed up in his Santa Claus suit for most of his life.

In 2007 Sammy Maldonado could still quick-draw his U.S. marshal Matt Dillon *Gunsmoke* pistol set, a Christmas gift he received from King Ranch as a small boy. Photo by Betty Bailey Colley.

The holidays were spent at my grandparents' home. My aunts, uncles, and cousins would all gather. Christmas was extra special. We would look forward to the Ranch truck coming to see what we would be getting. We would see the truck drive up; there was one item for each one of us. I don't know how they determined who got what. Mom got something also—things like blankets, pillowcases, or sheets.

Most of our toys were saved, and some are still at my parents' house. I have some of my Barbie dolls. I particularly remember one doll because it still has the original clothes.

My grandmother Ella would get brand-new one-dollar bills from the bank and would fold them in the corner so they would not stick and then would fix Christmas envelopes for all the grandchildren. This continued until the family grew, and then each family would celebrate at their homes.

Everybody also came at Thanksgiving, my aunts and cousins. We ate outside if weather permitted. My grandmother would cook turkey and dressing homemade from scratch, and pumpkin pies and salads. I called her Welita [Grandmother]. My mother got a lot of her recipes from my grandmother.

At Thanksgiving and Christmas it was us, just immediate family members. That's why we've always been close. We were always together.

NORMA MALDONADO QUINTANILLA

Alicia received a twelve-piece set of aluminum children's cookware complete with measuring cups and percolator with glass top and basket inside. She has saved it as her favorite gift. She was seven years of age when she took it home [in 1930]. When Beto showed it to me at his interview in 1998, Alicia was seventy-four and working at my brother's [Tio's] home on the Ranch at the time. I noticed there wasn't a dent in the cooking set, although it looked very well used. She took very good care of it. (Sally Kleberg 64)

The holidays were a lot of fun. Even though we didn't have a whole lot of money, we had lots of love to give to one another. We all got a little something, all the boys, girls, and grown-ups. Back then any little gift was greatly appreciated because they were few and far between. We were always happy with what little we got. We usually had lots of good food. The grown-ups got to eat first and then the younger ones. Lots of good times had by all.

CATALINA MALDONADO YAKLIN

I would cook Thanksgiving and Christmas dinner at my home. We would all gather and enjoy all the fixings—we always had turkey at Thanksgiving, along with all the other goodies that went along with it, like pumpkin pie, salad, and rolls. At Christmastime we would have a ham, tamales, and other kinds of beef, along with potatoes and salads and things like that. I enjoyed cooking for everyone.

DORA MALDONADO

THE MALDONADO HOUSEHOLD

Every person in the Maldonado family knew exactly what his or her role was and what was expected in that role. The children understood very well the importance of their chores to the welfare of the family, just as they grew up understanding the importance of their father's work to the smooth operation of the Ranch. There was a lot of work to be done in the home, and every family member, even at age five or six, contributed to making the family function in an orderly manner. Four generations of Maldonados grew up learning to take pride in their work.

Alicia Maldonado has kept this Christmas gift from King Ranch she received in 1930, when she was seven years old. Though well worn from play, the cook set is still in excellent condition. Photo by Betty Bailey Colley.

MAMA WOULD BUILD A FIRE AND LET 'EM BOIL

When we were old enough to help around the house, we all helped my mama. The girls did a lot of the washing, and, of course, that was the time when you would have to do it on a washing board. We got running water in the house in the early '30s, and my mama would fill up special No. 3 galvanized tubs to do the washing, and she would have one particular tub for the white clothing, the white shirts, bedsheets, and whatever. She would build a fire and let 'em boil there, and that bluing was very popular to make the clothes white; that was before we got electricity at my dad's house in the early '40s. I remember two soaps that Mom would use were Crystal White and a kind of brown Octagon soap. Most of the sheets she would make herself. We had some of the feed that was sacked in some kind of white material, one-hundred-pound feed sacks. Mama would wash them good and then sew some of those sacks together and make it into a bedsheet. She would do a lot of sewing. She had a Singer sewing machine, the pedal kind, and she would make dresses for the girls and later, when she was up in age, she still had that sewing machine and she would make all kinds of things with that machine.

The girls helped inside the house, and boys worked outside. Everything was cooked on a woodstove, and we boys would make a point to go cut wood before the day was over and bring it into the house for cooking the next morning. We would clean around the yard and also help fill up the kerosene lanterns for light at night.

My mama had hens, and she would feed them and let them out to roam during the day and pen them up at night from coyotes or whatever. One of our chores was collecting eggs. We would go with a basket and maybe get a dozen a day or something like that.

I remember in my time we would use crayons to color [Easter] eggs. Mama would start collecting eggs way ahead of time, and she would empty the eggs. We made *cascarones* [empty eggshells filled with bits of festive colored paper], and they would hide them at Easter. I don't remember baskets; maybe we used those brown paper bags.

Sonia [Garcia Due, my granddaughter], when she was a little one, she was over at the other grandparents at the Ranch, and they had hens. She was walking around and she saw a hen lay an egg, and after that she didn't want nooo eggs, because she said she knew where they came from.

> We did what our mother did. Scrubbed floors. The floors were always clean. We scrubbed them with a broom and soapy water and swept the water out the door, every other day. We bathed every day in a tub. We had running water, and it was heated on the stove.
>
> ALICIA MALDONADO

It was not unusual for Kineño children and King Ranch family children to play together. Ranch owners' children were expected to be fluent in Spanish before they started school, and playing together was not only fun but a natural daily laboratory for the acquisition and practice of the language of the Ranch. Beto remembered playing with the Jersey calves with Helenita (Helen Kleberg Groves) when they were children, and Helenita would ask his dad, "What's the name of the mama of that little calf?" However, before Kineño children played, they were expected to complete jobs assigned to them by their parents.

> The boys did their chores, and then they had time to play with us or to play on their own. The girls did not have time to play. They worked with their mothers from before sunup until after sundown. They washed the clothes, cleaned the floors, made masa. All the diapers were cloth and had to be boiled with soap and hung on a clothesline [to dry].

Plácido and I played together as children. We would play cops and robbers together. We would chase each other on horseback along the creek. We would choose sides as bandits and cowboys. We would break swords over each other's heads when we fought; the men in the shop would make them for us. No one cried when they fell off their horse, fell on a cactus, or got hit with a sword. The only time they cried was when they broke the rules of the game, because it was not right to break the rules!

HELEN KLEBERG GROVES

NOT MANY TOYS, BUT LOTS OF PLAY

We had dolls to play with. We did not have many toys. We played jacks all the time—Mama would get mad. We did jump rope, made mud pies and little houses, and caught lightning bugs to put [in jars] in the house for light.

ALICIA MALDONADO

We had very little toys to play with. We would all get together at the end of the day or late in the evening, and the girls would play jacks with the other girls and, of course, we played marbles while the girls played jacks. We also played tops. We would actually make a longer peak on those tops and sharpen them good to where we could break the others' tops in pieces and be the champions. We would play all kinds of games, girls and boys together, like *veve leche* [hopscotch]. We would draw on the ground with a sharp piece of glass or something, and we would all have our own piece of heavy glass that we would use to play that game. We would also play what we called Red Rover Come Over, and we had jumping ropes. We played hide-and-seek, and boys would—on windy days at the time of the kite—we would make our own kites. We would use the brown bags that the beans and rice and other items were sacked in and the pieces of string [from them]. We would tie one string to the other until we had enough strings to fly a kite. We used bamboo to make the shape of the kite, and we would actually use flour [mixed with water] to make paste to glue them together. We would use some old clothing strips for the tail of the kite.

Some of us would play with car tires. And there was a wheel that would come off of some of the farm equipment that was about ten or twelve inches in diameter and about one and a half inch wide, and we would make a handle with a heavy-gauge wire. The handle must have been thirty-six inches long, and at the end was the square of metal that would hold that wheel and keep it running.

My children did not make toys like I did when I was small, but they played marbles and jacks and jump-the-rope and things like that also. And they would play with the toys that they got at Christmas. I got them a swing and slide and a *sub-ibaja* [seesaw]. They would be sitting there, and then when one went to the swing, the rest wanted to use that swing or the slide or whatever the first one wanted.

MOVIES WERE A BIG PART OF OUR LIVES

We would go to town on Saturdays, and my brother Lee and I would get to see a cowboy movie when we were maybe six and eight, and they had a serial each week that would end with something exciting that was going to happen next week, so we would want to go back and see it. The Saturday morning movie was in English. My dad would give us a quarter each, and we would go to the movie, get a hamburger and a soda pop with the twenty-five cents. At that time we would see Hopalong Cassidy, Roy Rogers, and Gene Autry at the Rex Rio Realito Theater, and then on Sunday we would saddle up and try to do some of those tricks that the cowboys did, and we would run into a problem!

When we got older, I'd say beginning when I was about twelve and Lee was ten, we would walk to Kingsville, four or five miles from where we lived, and we would normally go to see a Mexican movie at the Teatro Carpa, located at Alice and Twelfth Street. Families from the Ranch would go in their cars, but there were a lot of us that didn't have a car, so we got together and walked; it was about a thirty- or forty-five-minute walk. The man at the Teatro Carpa was a gentleman by the name of Stout Jackson. There was a Teatro Carpa in Robstown and one in Falfurrias.

We would actually get three or four or five boys together, some from Rancho Plomo, and we'd take off into town and we'd all wind up on Richard Street before we went to the Teatro Carpa. The girls didn't go unless their parents went. There was a café called Royal Café at the bottom and a dance hall on the second floor on weekends. We would stop there and eat a bowl of chili with a soda pop. It would cost us thirty-five cents for a big bowl of chili and a nickel for an RC Cola, so we would be pretty well full when we got to the Carpa. The cook at the Royal Café was Daniel Acevedo, and he worked at the cowboy camps on King Ranch for many years. When he retired, he actually opened a business of his own at the Royal Café.

On Tuesday they would have a new movie. People would line up maybe half a block to buy a ticket. I think it cost fifteen cents to go in, and of course they would walk around in between the chairs and sell Chiclets, popcorn, chewing gum, and peanuts at a nickel a bag. It was under a tent; it had a dirt floor and wooden folding chairs. After the movie was over, there was a gentleman we called El Maestro selling *taquitos* for a nickel as you exited the Carpa. He would make super *taquitos* with or without hot chili and I think they had little potatoes

Young children, including Beto and Lee Maldonado, lined up to see the Saturday morning movie at the Rialto Theater in Kingsville, at Kleberg and Sixth Street. On Sunday the boys tried—with little success—to emulate the tricks they'd seen Hopalong Cassidy, Roy Rogers, and Gene Autry perform the day before. Courtesy of Beto Maldonado.

and spices, and we would buy a *taquito* or two and then head back to the Salazar Store and get in a group and head back to the Ranch.

Serafin "Pepiño" Mendietta drove a bobtail [truck], and he would always go to the Carpa. He would make a point of driving by Richards Street to Salazar Store and picking up as many of us as were there ready for a ride. He had plenty of space for twenty or thirty people on the back of that bobtail. He lived near the Headquarters, a mile before my house, but he was a very nice gentleman and he would bring us all the way and drop us off near the dairy, where we lived. There were times we would hitchhike, and at Lauro's Hill he would drop us there and we would walk through the pastures, not thinking about rattlesnakes and what have you. But most of the time we had to walk all the way home.

It got to the point that the tent was ripped and there was a hole in that tent, and you were actually seeing the movie under the moon and stars. I remember being there when it rained, and water was coming in and we would walk in the mud. Later they did away with the old tent and built a very neat building, but still without air-conditioning. They would have the sides open so air could come inside the building when it was hot, and canvas sides that could be let down to keep the cold out. The building is still there today, but they did away with the movies there a long time ago [1963].

WE PLAYED AS A FAMILY

At night when I was a kid, the family would get together and play some kind of game. Of course, we didn't have any light. No electricity. Later my dad was able to buy a radio operated by a car battery or a plain battery, and he also bought a wind charger that would charge those batteries.

One of those games we played at night was a little apparatus that's made in Mexico. It's called *quita y pone*. It's got a little deal that you swivel around like a top, and then whatever number it lands on the top, whatever it says, that's what you do. You have to add more money to the pot or you take it all or you split it or whatever. And we also had *lotería* [Mexican bingo].

There was a big hole where we lived that I guess was used to do barbecue at one time, and the older men and boys would play baseball after work. Of course, some of the families almost had a full team to play against others, like Samuel Garcia Sr. There were seven in the family with Samuel Jr., Lupe, Jesus, Juan, Manuel, and Cipriano. With Pablo Ochoa Sr., there were eight boys and one girl: Pablo Jr., Miguel, José, Avelino, Gilberto, Olidio, Preseliano, Pedro, and Juanita. We would actually play baseball at the end of the day, and Pablo and his kids would make a baseball team, so we actually didn't have much of a problem getting a baseball game going.

AND THERE WERE PRAIRIE TREATS

When the mesquite beans were ripened, they were sweet and we would chew them. When we chewed mesquite beans, we did not swallow, just chewed and got the juice out and threw the rest away. There were plenty of them around! You could tell when the bean was ripe by the looks; it was a more brownish or reddish color when it was ripe. And there was some kind of grass or weeds called *grahitos* that we would pick from the ground and they were kind of sour.

What I remember more than anything else was those berries we called *morras*. There were a lot of *morras* most everywhere we went, and I remember we would get on top of the hog pen and harvest those *morras* and eat 'em. They were about a couple of inches long. They had little bitty things and what we would do, we would pick 'em and put 'em in the mouth and pull the centerpiece out and leave all the juice. They were sweet and a purple color.

There was a palm tree near the dairy barn, and that palm bore pretty good-sized dates. We would get on top of the dairy barn and throw rocks and then go down and pick 'em up and eat 'em. They were very sweet; we ate 'em the minute we picked 'em up. I don't remember washing them or anything. The palms Mrs. King had planted from the gate to the house—she actually had those palms planted to harvest the dates for the employees, but they didn't turn out that way because they bear little bitty dates, and it's more bone than anything else. I don't remember anybody harvesting those dates.

THERE WAS PLENTY OF GOOD FOOD

We had all the fresh milk in the world. Of course, we never did sell any of the milk at that time; I think we used every bit of it at the Ranch. When I was a kid and my dad was in charge of the dairy, he and the men would milk ninety-six Jerseys twice a day, at two o'clock in the morning and two o'clock in the afternoon. We would take our cans the night before, and everybody had a different-shaped can. They would fill them up, and in the morning we would pick that can up. Manuel Amaya would be the one who would fill up all those cans for those people over at the Headquarters. They would do the same thing for the people at Lauro's Hill; there were not many houses over there, but they would deliver milk there, and Miguel Muñiz would fill their cans. They would take another big ten-gallon can at the Plomo Ranch; there were fifteen or twenty families over there, and Roberto Mendietta would be the one to fill up all those cans early in the morning. Then late in the afternoon Manuel Amaya would do it over at the commissary.

When automation took over, they went into bottling. They would process the milk to a cooler and bottle it in quart bottles, and they would deliver the milk to the doorsteps early in the morning and late in the evening. They would also deliver milk for the Main House residents and members of the Kleberg family that lived here on the Ranch. Lorenzo Salinas was the man in charge of the deliveries. There were times I would ride with Lorenzo and keep a list of the deliveries that were done on the Ranch and some [to Ranch employees] in town.

But Mr. Bob had the idea he wanted milk from the Santa Gertrudis instead of the Jerseys. What they would do, they would bring some wet Santa Gertrudis cows into the dairy pens. Valentín Quintanilla Sr. lived in the Rancho Plomo, a good couple of miles south of where we had the dairy, and he and his son-in-law Ramón Moreno would get up early in the morning at Rancho Plomo and would come by horseback all the way to the dairy pen to milk those cows so Mr. Bob would have the milk.

THE BUTTER RACE

We all churned butter. I still have my grandmama's churn. It's a square glass deal with an apparatus on top, and you turn it. I think my grandmama died in the '50s, and they gave her churn to my mama. Before that, the way we would do it, the milk was in molasses glass jars, and mama would put so much in mine and so much in Lee's and we would shake it and shake it. It was a race; no reward, just fun. The fun about it was who made the butter first. And then, of course, we liked butter. Mama would make hot cakes and use butter and syrup, that Brer Rabbit syrup. I remember a big ol' jar cost forty-five cents. That was on the weekend, because that was something you didn't have every day. We made butter every other day or three times a week.

Jersey milk is very rich. You put a quart of milk in a glass bottle jar and leave it in the refrigerator for a day or two and half will be cream and half milk.

Kineño children were not the only ones who made butter. Sally Kleberg said that Librado taught the kids to milk, and they would get the cream and make butterballs with wooden pallets. She said that Clement and Kleberg kids would sit in the kitchen and make butter balls that looked like golf balls.

NO DAYS WITHOUT MEAT

In the early days they [the Ranch] would deliver meat whenever they would slaughter a cow, a bull, or calf; that was when we would get meat. We would get veal more often because we had all those Jersey calves at the Dairy Colony where I was raised—there were about fifteen houses there and my dad was in charge of the dairy. He would make a point that you get some meat this time and other people get it another time. Two or three people [families] would get meat at one time. I don't remember days without meat. That's how cholesterol built up through the years. I tell people we would eat beef and freshly made tortillas and freshly made butter, and we didn't know all of this then.

Rice and beans were popular. We got a ration per month. We got flour and sugar and coffee, beans and rice, and, I think, baking powder. We bought tomatoes and tomato sauce, all charged. We bought cornmeal, onions, and potatoes at the commissary. I think she [Beto's mother, Ella] bought spices in town. We would buy kerosene at the commissary and charge it to the account; it didn't come with the ration. I remember that a gallon of kerosene would cost eight cents, and we would use it to get the fire started in the morning for cooking. There was no electricity then in my dad's time.

There were times that Dad would take us, Lee and I, on a jackrabbit hunt. In less than thirty minutes he would kill three or four, and we would go home and he would clean them. Then my mother would cut them in pieces, soak them in salt water, and the next day we would have fried rabbit. It tasted like fried chicken.

> My grandfather [Librado] fixed the meat—even fried turtle, which tasted like chicken. Jackrabbit, cottontails, armadillos with chili powder all made

Beto Maldonado with his grandmama's churn. Before Beto's family inherited the churn in the 1950s, he and his brother Lee raced to see who could make butter first by shaking the rich Jersey milk in glass bottles. Photo by Catalina Maldonado Yaklin.

it to the oven and to the table. They [employees] were not allowed to shoot birds or deer on the Ranch.

My grandfather would tell tales of when he was little, and he told stories about Morocco when he went there in 1969. He brought cameos and lace mantillas back from there.

My grandfather said that one day people would go to the moon, but he wouldn't be here, but they would go.

DORA MALDONADO GARCIA

DORA'S TAMALES ALMOST WON

My mama sometimes made tamales for the auction concession stand, but not every year. She made some for the family, and my dad had friends that he would pass out tamales to. There were three girls in my family, and they would help mama make tamales. Before the machines in town, they would have to do it with the metate and grind the corn, but in my time I didn't see that done. My dad would go into town and buy the masa, and mama and the girls would actually put it on the shucks with their hands. Today Dora and I make tamales, and we have a machine that puts that masa on there and we can go real quick like.

They actually didn't make that many types of tamale's in the early days because they didn't have a way to keep 'em. That was when my dad would have to go to town and buy a block of ice to keep things cool. But they would make tamales often. And, of course, Christmas was a big event, and they would make plenty. If anybody came, we would have tamales to serve and even have some to give to friends as gifts. She [Ella] never did sell any tamales; it was my Dora that started to sell them. She learned to make tamales from my mama.

One time a visiting nurse was over here visiting Dora because of a problem with the circulation in her legs, and she liked her tamales a lot. She encouraged Dora to send some tamales over to Channel 3 TV station in Corpus for a contest. There were five picked and Dora was one of the five, and then they had to pick the winner. Freddy Fender, the singer—he was the judge and he had a compadre in the contest, and his compadre won. Dora was a good sport, and of course everybody said to her, "We know that your tamales were the best."

The last twenty years, the girls [daughters Dora and Catalina] took some tamales to the [Ranch] office, and the rest of the girls there liked them so much that they said, "Would your mama sell me a dozen tamales?" That's when Dora started selling tamales. She doesn't publicize herself; she doesn't call anybody. They come looking for her this time of the year [Christmas holidays]. She loves to do that. At one time she made them out of beef, beans, and turkey, but now she makes them only with beef. If the people like them hot, she makes them spicier.

Now I'm against her doing that so much because of problems with her legs, because sitting down all day—what she does, she wants to make a whole bunch in one day, then continue the next day, and that's not good for her circulation in her legs. This year she didn't know whether I was gonna give her permission or not, but just to make her happy, I told her that we would make them, but not so many. I told her if we make any, maybe it'll be fifteen dozen a week or something like that. She loves to make those tamales.

I DATE THE CANNED GOODS

In my time, I got twice as much rations [from the commissary] as my dad. We would go pick it up at a certain time of the month. Lots of times, the next day or so we would buy the rest of what we needed, and we wouldn't have to go to the commissary for the rest of the month. Also, I had a charge account for food at the grocery store named Red and White Store [in Kingsville]. I bought fruit and vegetables and cold cuts and things like that that they didn't have at the commissary.

I actually take the time to put canned goods in the cabinets for Dora, pull all the old cans to the front so they will be used first; they would be used faster back then than now. I didn't label them with dates back then, but I do now; I number them by month and year. What Dora does, she buys them by the bargain, and that's why I date them.

Dora Maldonado makes dozens of her famous tamales with her tamale machine at Christmas, one of her favorite things to do. Photo by Beto Maldonado.

DISCIPLINE WAS THE RULE

Discipline was a way of life on the Ranch, whether the work was at roundup in the midst of hundreds of milling red cattle, branding a bawling calf, repairing some of the miles of fence, or gentling bulls for the auction. Every person on King Ranch, young or old, knew what the rules were and was expected to follow them.

Firm discipline of Kineño children prepared them for their life's work on the Ranch. They were assigned age-appropriate chores very early, and there was never any discussion concerning whether they would do them. They just did as they were told. If they did not, there were reasonable but firm consequences. Following instructions was a critical habit, as boys began following their dads for on-the-job training that might involve dangerous work with a cantankerous bull, an irate bucking horse, heavy brush-clearing equipment, or a red-hot branding iron. The boy usually followed his dad and learned his dad's job, not by being told about it but by actually helping to do it. This practice created a true apprenticeship system critical to the Ranch's quest to become a superior ranch and make cutting-edge contributions to the development of the ranching industry to feed the nation.

Likewise, girls learned household skills from their mothers. The Kineño family was the support system for the men who were responsible for the work of the Ranch all year round except for Christmas holidays. This was an unusual arrangement. By the 1870s all but a few cowboys worked only part of the year, making it difficult, if not impossible, to establish a stable family life. Especially on large spreads, cowboys were more often seasonal workers who were paid off after the fall cattle drives and left to fend for themselves during long winters. Captain King developed a distinct and different relationship with his employees, perhaps because he needed them as much as they needed him, and a unique culture of interdependence was born (Monday and Colley xx).

But for this mutually beneficial culture to develop and endure, discipline was critical, and Kineño families, including the Maldonados, took on that responsibility. However, discipline was not limited to parents in the home. Any adult on the Ranch was entitled to correct a young person, whether a relative or not. As Sammy Maldonado told us, "Everybody had the authority to discipline children."

> Beto was a nice boy. None of us got spoiled. Plácido was always very quiet. Beto was quiet, but he joked a lot. But Plácido was Mama's pet. We would ask her which was the favorite, and she would say she liked us all. But she would finally say, "Plácido. Why did you ask me?"
>
> ALICIA MALDONADO

I know that there were a lot of people that helped guide me in the right way besides my dad, because at that time if my dad wasn't around, there was somebody else there that was going to tell me what to do. And you were supposed to do what you were told, not do it just because you wanted to do it a different way. And most of those people would say those things to you because they wanted for you to go the right way and be somebody one of these days.

My brother Lee got in trouble for climbing windmills. A lot of times he got in trouble, and my dad would straighten him out. I didn't get in trouble climbing the windmills—I was always afraid of heights—but sometimes I got in trouble. Riding the Jersey calves was strictly forbidden. The dairy barn was not far from where we lived, and we would get together and go to the barn and ride some of those calves. And we tried to be as quiet as we could so nobody could hear and find out what we were doing. One day it got out of hand, and the south wind was blowing towards my dad's house and my dad could hear us. So he came over to the barn and ran all the kids to their homes. I got a spanking after that happened.

> Sometimes they [Ella and Librado] spanked when we did something wrong. I think it was just once or twice, not much. He would just talk to us; they wouldn't spank us.
>
> ALICIA MALDONADO

Beto Maldonado stands next to the last wooden-frame windmill on King Ranch. The windmill was relocated from the Alto del Burro pasture to the home of Tio and Janell Kleberg, where this photograph was made in 2004. Photo by Janell Kleberg.

> Children were taught to respect and obey. They [parents] would spank Beto and Lee, but not the girls. One time Librado was spanking Beto and he broke his belt, and Beto laughed. The parents taught the kids what no and yes meant.
>
> AURORA MALDONADO PEREZ

IF I DIDN'T LOVE YOU . . .

When we got older, we didn't get spanked. He [Librado] would just tell us what we did wrong and not to do it again. I did the same thing with my kids. They would do something wrong, and when they were young, I would use that whip lightly, and later I would let it pile up and I would take them to one side all by myself and tell them what they did wrong and not to do it again. They would sit there and listen to what I had to say, and it seemed like it worked every time. I would tell them if I didn't love them that much, I wouldn't do that to them, but I love them too much and I didn't want them to be doing things that are wrong or they are not supposed to do. But the good Lord has blessed us, and there've hardly been any problems of any kind, and, of course, being all by ourselves living right next door to my dad, I think that had a lot to do with it.

Our family and my grandparents and Aunt Alicia were the only families on this part of the Ranch [Dairy]. The Colony was a few miles away; therefore, we only played with our siblings or relatives when they came by to visit.

My grandparents, Librado and Ella, were the best grandparents anyone could ever have. They were very kind, loving, giving people. It is such an honor to have grown up next door to them. We spent many hours sitting outside on their porch, listening to stories about them when they were growing up. It was great!

CATALINA MALDONADO YAKLIN

Mama kept a record of who misbehaved. Dad came home; he knew what we had done. He spanked, but now I look back, I'm grateful for the way we were brought up with discipline. He spanked until we were old enough. Then he talked to us and wouldn't let us go anywhere, maybe for a week. We would go to Mama; she would back Dad. Things would pile up, and Dad would say, "Let's go for a ride." Dad would talk to you about why you shouldn't be doing what you were doing. In high school, when I was doing something wrong, he would say, "I don't feel comfortable with this."

Mom had a list taped to the wall. She took care of discipline when Dad was sometimes gone two or three weeks, and she could be Mom and Dad when Dad was gone. She didn't do punishment unless she had to. She spanked behind the knee with a quirt.

I wouldn't do anything wrong because Librado would find out. I learned to mind, to listen to older folks. I learned respect—wished I could be in his [Librado's] place in the ring. He was king of the family.

You'd better behave at the dinner table. No laughing, kicking, joking. But if you did something wrong, when it was done, it was over.

We keep in touch with each other. Anything I'm going to do, I let him [Beto] know—like buying a house or car. He uses discipline with nieces and nephews. He sits down and talks things out.

SAMMY MALDONADO

Dad was strict. No was no. I stressed out two months wanting to go to a valentine dance. He gave me permission! Boys couldn't go to the Ranch to pick me up. Dad brought me to Dora's [in Kingsville], the boy would pick

Beto Maldonado talks with granddaughter Sonia Garcia. Her married name is Due. He keeps in touch with grandchildren, nieces, and nephews, sometimes offering advice and counsel. Courtesy of Beto Maldonado.

me up, and Dad would wait for me at my sister Dora's. Dad took the time to explain things instead of arguing or yelling. One time Dad said he would appreciate it if I didn't go to this movie. I went anyway and was acting out the movie for Albert and Sammy. They were laughing because Dad was standing behind me!

I was called "square" sometimes because I couldn't go to weekend parties.

CATALINA MALDONADO YAKLIN

I was spoiled because I was the only child and grandchild until I was six years old. But I was taught to mind. My grandmother [Dora] had a belt hanging behind the door, and that belt was to keep me in line. The last time I was in that house, I noticed that the belt was still there.

SONIA GARCIA DUE

IT ALL BEGAN OVER A HUNDRED YEARS AGO

Lasater Ranch, a spread of 107,030 acres located south of Falfurrias, was known as a premier breeder of Jersey cattle. On June 30, 1924, King Ranch purchased Lasater Ranch for $547,619.19, and the Lasater property created a whole new division of King Ranch. It became known as the Encino (Lea 598, 599).

My father, Librado Maldonado Sr., was born and raised in Realitos, Duval County, on Lasater Ranch located near Benavides, Hebbronville, and Alice, Texas. He was born April 3, 1898. Later he moved to La Mota, another ranch on Lasater, eighteen or twenty miles south of Falfurrias, and he was reared with his grandpapa Plácido in that location in Brooks County. He grew up there as a vaquero helping his granddad, halter-breaking some Brahman bulls and steers and what have you. Lasater, at that time, was another big ranch in South Texas and had a lot of Brahmans, Herefords, and Jerseys. As a matter of fact, Mr. Ed Lasater had one of the biggest Jersey milk cowherds in the world.

My dad started riding when he was a young kid. One day he was on the back of a bucking mule and Mr. Lasater happened to be at the pen where it was going on, and my dad, one way or the other, managed to stay on that mule. At the end of the ride, he got off the mule, and Mr. Lasater told my dad that he was considered as a vaquero and he was going to get paid like one. So my dad continued to work on horseback at Lasater Ranch, working cattle. I've forgotten the age at which Mr. Lasater put him off the saddle and got him on the show circuit, because Mr. Lasater, along with other Jersey breeders here in Texas, showed these cattle all over the country, and he needed my dad.

My dad didn't like the idea of not being a vaquero so much, because it was gonna keep him from a lot of fun when they were saddle-breaking and herding cattle up. He liked being a cowboy, and he was going to miss being out there with the cowboys and roping. But he also began thinking about traveling and maybe going to some cities. He said, "I heard some people saying they had been to San Antonio. In those days that was like going to New York is now." So, anyway, Lasater got him on the show circuit, and one of the first livestock shows he attended was the International Exposition in Chicago back in 1918, where he showed the grand champion cow; he was nineteen years old. My dad showed Jerseys all the way from Mexico City to Canada.

The Jerseys were probably the reason that my dad came to King Ranch. There was a time when Lasater, King Ranch, and Taft Ranch were the largest Jersey breeders in the state. My dad was showing Jersey cattle for Lasater at the time

Librado Maldonado (on the horse) and his grandfather, who raised him on Lasater Ranch in Falfurrias. Born in 1898, Librado went to work for King Ranch in 1925. Courtesy of Beto Maldonado.

King Ranch was also showing Jersey cattle. Oscar Anderson, or somebody, saw my papa's ability showing cattle. Anyway, they offered him a job, and in 1925 he went to work for King Ranch when he was twenty-seven years old.

We [sons] were not vaqueros. Plácido worked most of his life at the veterinary department, and Lee worked mostly with the Thoroughbreds in New York because that's what he wanted to do. I did a lot of jobs, but I think the one I liked best was working with the Jerseys. Maybe it's because it was the first job I had, but I really enjoyed that time. Of course, if I hadn't traveled with Dad and those Santa Gertrudis bulls, I never would have seen all those places, and if I didn't work with the tourism department leading those tours, I never would have met all those people that I got to know.

DON'T BE MAKING CHICKEN FACES

My dad loved dances, so he would get permission from his grandpapa and go to Falfurrias to a dance, and he would ride horses that knew the way around very well. From Falfurrias back to Dad's home was eighteen or twenty miles, and he said after the dance was over after midnight or so, there were times when he would fall asleep and the horses knew their way very well and they would stop at a gate until my dad would wake up and open the gate and go through. Back in those times, a good horse and a good pair of boots and a hat were just like riding in a Cadillac car today.

There was a time when my dad would come home and his granddad would ask the time, and my dad said. "It's maybe twelve o'clock" or something like that, and his granddad would look through the window and say, "No, I think it's later than that, so we better milk the cows." He [his granddad] would get up and get dressed and head to the pen to milk the cows, and his granddad would have all kinds of talk and kept on talking, and my dad would be half asleep. In a day or so or the next weekend, my dad would ask his granddad to go to a dance. [He'd say:] "You can go to the dance, but next morning don't be making chicken faces at me."

I STILL HAVE TO WEAR THE FLANNEL PAJAMAS

After many trips to Falfurrias, eventually my dad finally met a pretty girl by the name of Ella Byington, probably at a dance, and later, in 1920, he married my mama. She was born in Wallace County south of Falfurrias on a ranch and later moved to Falfurrias. After their wedding, they actually rode to the Lasater Ranch, and that's where my mama spent some time newly wed to my dad. My mama had an aunt by the name of Barula Williams. She was a midwife. The first children, Plácido and Alicia , were born in Falfurrias [in 1921 and 1923, respectively,] and then later when my dad went to work for King Ranch in 1925, my mama had twin girls, Amelia and Aurora, but she actually went back to Falfurrias and got her aunt to help her. My younger brother Lee [born in 1932] and I were the only ones born on King Ranch, and she [Barula] would come over and help my mama when she was going to have a baby.

Actually, I was born on January 16, 1930. I tell people the temperature was down to eighteen degrees. We had a wood-frame house, no electricity, no natural gas. We had a wood-burning heater in the room that kept us warm. According to records, it stayed cold for the longest time, and so now I still have to wear the flannel pajamas when I go to bed.

When Librado was gone for weeks or months at a time showing cattle, Ella was strictly in charge of the Maldonado household. He had been going on these trips since they were married, and she was well accustomed to managing the children and the house.

Ella rarely shopped. Librado stocked the house very well with Ranch rations supplemented with food purchased at the commissary before these trips, as Beto would later do for his family. Neither Ella nor Dora learned to drive and never went to the commissary; the men did most of the shopping, as Beto still does today. Dora Maldonado Garcia said, "Dad did the money—he always did the bills and buying. He keeps all the records. Mom has had her name on the bank account for thirty years and she's never written a check."

OUR MOTHER COPED

> Dad traveled a lot with the bulls. Some of the men would shop for her [Ella] when dad was gone for two or three months.
>
> ALICIA MALDONADO

My dad showed Jersey cattle for Lasater Ranch at the State Fair in Dallas in 1921. The people liked the show so much that some people from Mexico asked if the exhibit could go to Mexico. Dad ended up being in Mexico for three months. My oldest brother, Plácido, was born at that time, and he was already two months of age before my dad got to see him for the first time

I remember my mom as a very good mother, but she was extra careful. I never learned to swim; my mama didn't even want us in a No. 3 tub of water. She never would let us have a bicycle; she'd say, "Oh no, it's too dangerous for you." But she raised six children, was a very good cook, kept the house, and helped us with our homework. She always wore an apron, and she would bake the best lemon pies, yeast bread, and *pan dulce* [sweet bread] in the woodstove. I remember her putting the bread in one of those tin cans, and it would stay good for the longest time. She would also make Brer Rabbit syrup cookies, sugar tortillas, and candy made of syrup; she would add other ingredients like a little butter and vanilla and boil that Brer Rabbit syrup until it was thick; then she would let it cool. Before it was hard, she would work it with her hands, like they do today with saltwater candy machines, until it came to a pretty blond color. Later, all of us would help do the same thing.

Alicia told about her mother's talent for sewing:

> My mother used to make our clothes. She would buy material from the store in town and she just cut them. She could see a dress and she could make it. If you showed her a picture in a magazine, she could copy it.

Dora Maldonado Garcia's eyes twinkled as she talked of her grandparents:

Granddad [Librado] would come home for lunch, take a quick siesta, and go back to work at one o'clock. I remember they had *merienda* [snacks] at 3 p.m. when they had coffee and sweets, and he could come home for that because he worked right there. They made coffee, bought at the commissary, by boiling the grounds and sugar together—that's how they all drank it. Cookies were made of molasses, and they had yellow cake with pineapple preserves and coconut, my favorite. Chocolate was Granddad's favorite. Cakes were three or four layers. My grandmother also made empanadas with pumpkin, pineapple, and jams in homemade crust

My mom and dad actually started out with a four-room house, three bedrooms and one living room. Before my time they [the Ranch] moved another small house near the four-room house, and that was converted into a kitchen and dining room and my mama would do all the cooking with firewood in that part of the building. The two houses were connected with a covered porch so if it was raining, you didn't have to go to the ground.

When I was growing up, we had no fireplaces, just one wood heater. That heater was one of those long steel heaters that had an apparatus that you could actually bake tortillas on top. It had a tube that would let all of that smoke out [the ceiling], and it had an apparatus that would let part of it go out and you could control it.

The girls were in one room and we boys in the other. If there were any closets, it was probably in the late '30s or '40s.

LIBRADO KNEW EVERYBODY'S SIZE

When I was little, my mama would order our clothing from catalogs from Sears Roebuck, Montgomery Ward, and Spiegel, and that's the way she would buy clothing for us boys and the girls. Those catalogs would stay good for the longest time. Years after we would receive the catalogs, the prices were still the same, and of course when we would get new catalogs, we would actually fold the old ones sheet by sheet into some kind of a shape, like a bullet-head shape, and we would use those as door stoppers. They were heavy enough to keep the doors from being shut from the wind. And then, of course, a lot of them would wind up at the outside toilet. We got our first inside toilet in the late '40s when my house was built.

My dad would go to Salazar Store for the rest of our clothes. He knew everybody's size, and he was the one who would keep us with clothing. My dad was very sharp at knowing the style, the color, the size of all the girls. What he would do, he would bring so many dresses in a size, and pants and socks for us. They would make a list of what he would bring, and whatever he took back they wouldn't charge him for those, and he would have those [we kept] charged on a charge account.

Of course, we didn't have that many clothes; like myself, I remember having just three pants and three shirts, and you actually didn't hang 'em. I mean my mama would iron 'em, fold 'em, and put 'em in that box. Everybody had a wood box until later when they built a closet or two. I don't know about the girls, but I had one pair of shoes when I was a kid and that pair of shoes was to go to school, go to work, go to church, go to town. We had an abundance of shoe shining to keep them clean; we shined them very often. We would get them all smeared up at work and we would have to clean them, and then whenever they were dried up, we would shine them. Whenever the sole or heel wore out, my dad would take them into town and have a half sole put on for a dollar, or less than a dollar, until toes came out.

When we were maybe ten or twelve, my dad would bring Lee and me to a shop right behind Salazar Store and there was a boot maker there, and that's where our boots were made. Chapita was his last name, and that's what we called him. He was on Sixth Street. When we grew up we bought them at the Saddle Shop, maybe in the '50s.

> And we used to go to school about a mile away, and we used to rest under a tree and one time—he [Librado] used to buy all the clothes. He'd just go to the store and buy us shoes, dresses, and everything. One time he bought me shoes that I liked very much. And he said, "Be sure they're not too tight." And I said, "Nooo, I like them," but they were kinda tight. So I went to school and wore them and I had to take them off, and Daddy got real upset at me. He said, "You told me that they were just right for you." I said, "Yes, I'm sorry, but I can't wear them anymore."
>
> ALICIA MALDONADO

Most of the employees at King Ranch from Laureles and Santa Gertrudis all shopped at Salazar Store, located at Richard and Sixth Street. Salazar Store originally started in Falfurrias when my mom and dad were living there and they shopped at that store. Vicente Salazar moved to Kingsville in 1927, two years after my dad, and had a business going there for the longest time. Vicente's sons continued to manage the store. José was the manager and his brothers Nicolas and Eduardo helped José around the store. The building is still standing; it's an antique store.

THE ONLY TWO HOUSES AT THE DAIRY

In the late 1940s, they [King Ranch] built what we called the Colony—a little over a hundred homes, brick buildings. All of those people from the Dairy, Lauro's Hill, Rancho Plomo, and the Headquarters were all combined at one location. Mr. Bob and Mrs. Helen had to do with the building and how they assigned the houses and how they wanted them built. They were built almost like a cowboy camp house.

I think it was a little later that Mr. Bob told my dad, "Librado, I'm going to build you a house close to your work so you can be near work." My dad was already maybe a hundred steps from the dairy barn if that house would be there today. And I tell people he [Bob Kleberg] was just like a jet pilot, always thinking ahead, always thinking ahead. He said, "Librado is going to be there by himself. When he gets up in age, he's not going to have a neighbor." So King Ranch built me a house right next door soon after my dad's house was built. Those were the only two houses at the dairy near the stables.

In Dora's and my house at the very beginning we got an electric washer, and it was kept in the bathroom. Wash day, we would put it out of the bathroom onto the porch; the porch was not covered at that time. We also had two tubs that were welded together and had casters, I think. We would keep those on the front porch and that's where Dora would do the washing, and she would have clotheslines behind the house, not that close. She said, "You have those lines at Premont [a town about twenty-five miles away]; I have to walk all the way to Premont to hang those clothes." The funny thing about it is that when we had those more modern washers and dryers, she wanted a clothesline for sure. There is one there today, a slip wire from one tree to another. I fixed it to where it can be adjusted with a spring, and you can use it and it will go back. From time to time Dora uses it to dry bedsheets and what have you; she says that she loves the smell of the sun. And there are times in winter when we take out the jackets and sweaters and hang them on the line to air them out.

Our house had two bedrooms, a living room, and a kitchen. When Dora and I got our own house, some furniture was given to us. The kitchen/dining room my dad gave to us, and the bedroom set was given to us. We still have it; Sammy has it in the first room of his house. When the family got bigger, they [King Ranch] added on another room and another bathroom; it took them maybe a couple of months. That was the first time the bathrooms were inside. The boys were in one bedroom and girls in another. We had bunk beds for the boys, and I think the girls had a double bed and a single bed. The children shared one bathroom. They did not fight, because I guess they got to the point that they knew who had to go first, got to know who needed it when. Dora and I still live in

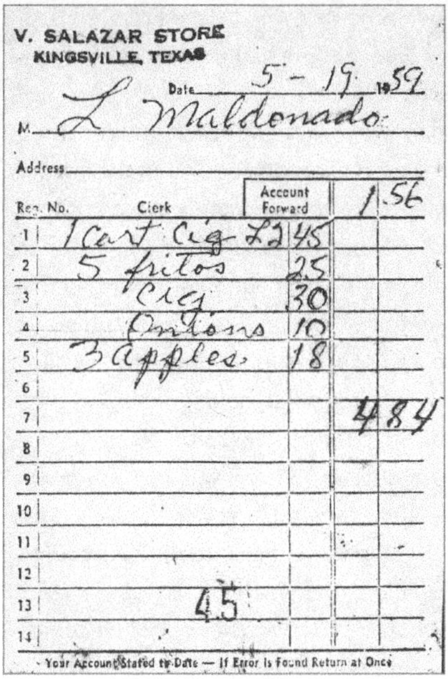

V. SALAZAR STORE
KINGSVILLE, TEXAS

Date 5-19 1959

M. L Maldonado

Address

Reg. No.	Clerk	Account Forward	1.56
1	1 cart cig L2	45	
2	5 fritos	25	
3	cig	30	
4	Onions	10	
5	3 apples	18	
6			
7			4.84
8			
9			
10			
11			
12			
13	45		
14			

Your Account Stated to Date — If Error Is Found Return at Once

Like many Kineño families, Librado had a charge account at the Salazar Store in Kingsville, where he bought grocery and personal items for the family. Librado knew everyone's size and would take several dresses, shoes, or pants home to be selected and fitted and then return the rest to Salazar's. Courtesy of Beto Maldonado.

that house today, and my sister Alicia still lives next door in my dad and mom's house, and she can live there as long as she lives.

> Mama raised kids. She washed on Monday using a roller washer and two bins, one for prewash, one for rinsing. Bluing would be used in one tub to make the white clothes look whiter. We hung clothes on the clothesline way away from the house; we had to lug them. She cooked starch on top of the stove and starched blue jeans and shirts. We used a Coke bottle with a cork with holes to sprinkle the clothes. Then we put them in the refrigerator in a plastic bag. We ironed on Tuesday and Wednesday. We did not have a steam iron. She used leaves from a plant that grew by the back door to run the hot iron over to make the bottom slick.
>
> DORA MALDONADO GARCIA

MY DAD AND I HAD CARS

My dad had a car at the very beginning. He had a Ranch vehicle in the early '40s, but I think he had his own personal car when he went to work [for King Ranch] in the '20s. He actually had enough money to buy a personal car.

Dad knew how to manage money. At one time he owned eleven rent houses, and he left an estate in six figures when he died, and he had no education. I have four rent houses, and my children live in two of them.

I remember visiting relatives in Falfurrias. We would go see my grandmama—my mama's mama, Catalina. We all got in the car, Librado and Ella in the front and six kids in the backseat. Maybe Lee and I were younger, and we would sit on Alicia or Plácido's lap. It was just an hour's drive. I know that there was a [Ranch] road that would go, and I remember people would point out, "This is a road that would take us to Falfurrias," but I don't remember driving through pastures. I think we always went the long way around on Highway 141. I remember my dad would carry patches and an air pump, and if we had a flat, he'd jack her up, take that wheel off, repair the tire, air it up, and put it back and keep on going.

There were only a few times we went out of town. When I was real young, the brother of my dad was living in Harlingen, and I remember very well that I didn't like their water and that's how I remember going there. I also remember going to Laredo, Texas, one time. A brother of Emiliano, the weaver, had worked here, and he was heading back to Mexico. He asked my dad whether or not he could take him to the border in Laredo, and as a kid I remember spending the night at some lady's house and coming back the next day.

Like my dad, I was able to have plenty of money to give the down payment on a car when I got my first one in 1955 or '56 for $795, and then I would pay $30 a month. Dad may have done that. Before I bought my personal car, I could take the family in a Ranch vehicle into town. We would go to the drive-in movie in a Ranch vehicle and use Ranch gas. If we were in the Ranch vehicle, we used Ranch gasoline. If we were in our personal vehicle, we had to drive into town to buy gas.

I got a Ranch vehicle to drive when I was about seventeen years old, a brand-new Willys Jeep. I used it to take that high-pressure spraying machine when I started spraying thousands of cattle in the mid-'40s after Plácido came back from the service. I liked to drive that Jeep over those terraces Mr. Bob had built to hold some of that rainwater.

EMILIANO CUT MY HAIR FOR TEN CENTS

Emiliano Garcia wove saddle blankets, and he was also a barber. He did haircuts for ten cents, and I remember when I was a kid, I would go to Emiliano for a haircut. He lived not far from where we lived. His house faced an alley where they [the cowboys] would drive cattle through there from one spot to the other, and I remember cowboys coming from other parts of the Ranch, from Rancho Plomo, Headquarters, Lauro's Hill—they would come to have their hair cut—and I remember they would come on horseback and tie their horses along the fence.

Emiliano came from Mexico in the early 1900s and came to work for King Ranch building fences. Later they found out he was a weaver. In the mid-'30s the price of cattle was down, and the Ranch was in the sheep and goat business—we had as many as 50,000 head—so we had all the wool in the world and the right combination of colors of wool to go on those blankets. The combination of colors of the saddle blankets was brown and white. Those were Mr. Bob's racing colors when he would have those horses racing.

So in the mid-'30s, Emiliano and a carpenter, Juan Zapata, actually built a loom and a spinning wheel out of a Model T wheel, and Emiliano made his own baskets [to hold yarn] out of bamboo. He was a very knowledgeable man.

Emiliano would do all the processing of the wool. Once he had everything on the loom, he worked very fast. He said that at one time he could make a dozen in six weeks, and later, with three assistants, they could make forty in a year. Later his brother learned the trade, and other members of his family. At one time he had as many as three looms going full blast, and he would make as many as six saddle blankets a week. He would make all kinds of designs that were very pretty, and the Running W in every corner of the saddle blanket.

King Ranch never did sell a saddle blanket like the ones that Emiliano would make. The cowboys and members of the King family would use them for their saddles whenever they saddled up.

MARRIED NEARLY SIX DECADES

People ask me, "Where's your wife from? Is she from town? Is she from the Ranch?" I tell them, "No, she's a city gal." I met her when I used to hang around with her uncle, Johnny Marroquin, and she would come from Corpus to visit her grandma, Manuela Marroquin, at 711 Richard Street [in Kingsville]. And after so long a time I said to myself, "I'm gonna bring my lariat next time I come and put a lasso on that filly." She's still beautiful—that's why I married her almost sixty years ago.

What they would do at St. Martin's Church in town on the day for weddings, they would start having weddings at six o'clock. Our wedding was at six o'clock in the morning on February 6, 1949, and Johnny Marroquin and his bride were married at seven o'clock. My uncle Alfredo Byington and his wife, Anna Belle, stood up with me, and Dora's father, Reynaldo Ruiz, stood up with her.

A funny thing happened. My mom had a person who would come help her with the housework and whatever. Well, for that wedding, Mom was all dressed up and had been to the beauty shop and had her hair all fixed up, and the lady that helped her didn't even recognize her when she saw her all dressed up. We always laughed a lot about that.

Anyway, after the wedding, Dora and I went to her Aunt Lillie's house for chocolate and cake, and then at noon members of the family came to my dad's and mom's house at the Ranch for a big lunch of things like *carne guisada*, rice, and beans. After that, we went to San Antonio and stayed at the Bluebonnet Hotel for our honeymoon. Johnny and his wife went there too and stayed at the same hotel but, of course, in a different room.

When Dora and I married, we lived with my mama and papa for a while. Dora actually would call mom and dad "Mama" and "Papa" or "Father" and "Mother." She was very close to them.

I wore a long white dress with a short veil. It was a silk dress. Beto wore a suit and shoes—no boots. The bridesmaids were my half sister and my cousin, just two. They wore long pink dresses.

We lived with my mother-in-law and my father-in-law when we first married, and Beto's sister Alicia and her daughter, Mally, lived there also. Mally was maybe a year old, and I took care of her because Alicia was working in the vet's office. We lived with them four months. It was a year after I married that I had my first child, Dora.

Ella was a very pretty lady, not so tall, just medium, and she had a fair complexion and her eyes were green. Her hair was gray and black, and she wore it in a *moño* [bun]. She wore simple dresses, no pants.

Alicia is kind of like a sister. My father-in-law and my mother-in-law were like a father and mother to me because I didn't have any mother. My mother went away [died] when I was born and my sister, Josephine "Chepa," was a year old. My father couldn't take care of us, so one of his sisters, Angelita, raised me, and his other sister, Petra, raised my sister, Chepa. Librado and Ella were the best in-laws and the best grandparents to our children.

DORA MALDONADO

THE FAITH OF THE MALDONADOS

This land, called the Wild Horse Desert between the Rio Grande and Nueces River, has been the scene of many disrupting forces, including droughts, hurricanes, floods, and epidemics of yellow fever and cholera. This desert has also suffered many wars and conflicts, including the Texas Revolution, the Mexican-American War, the Civil War, and endless bandit raids from both sides of the Rio Grande. Since the time that the conquistadors and priests first set foot on this land in the early 1500s, there has been one constant force that has remained steady, and that has been the influence of the Roman Catholic Church.

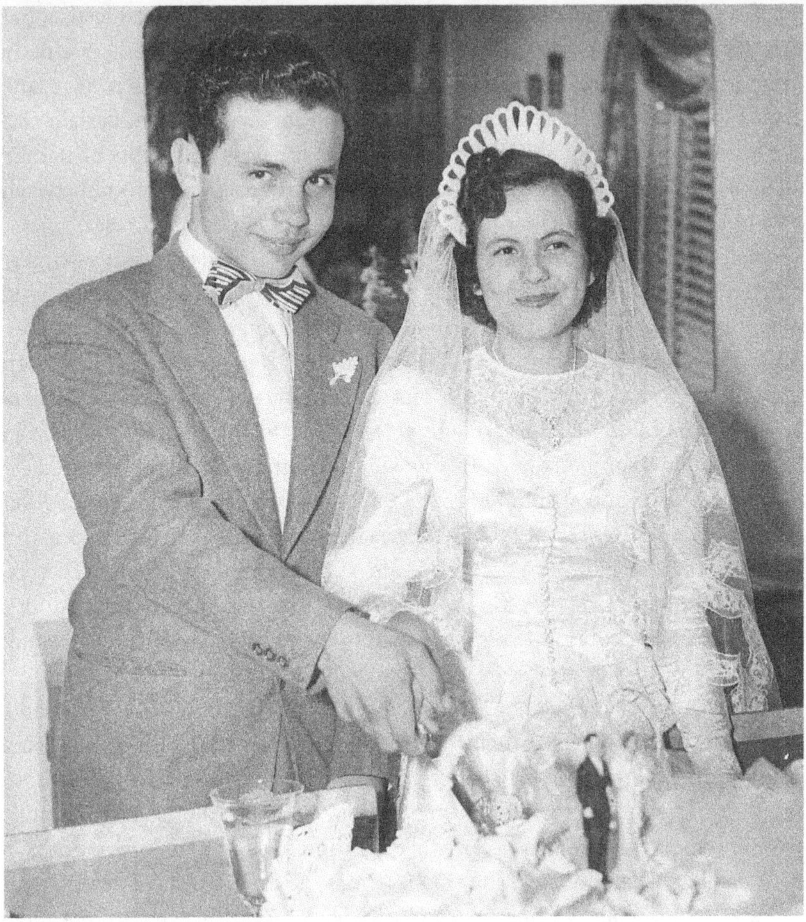

Beto and Dora Maldonado cut their wedding cake at their reception at the home of Dora's aunt, Lillie Marroquin, on February 6, 1949. Photo by J. A. Dodd.

The early settlers from Mexico obtained land grants north of the Rio Grande and settled in a land that was inhabited by Indians, had little available water, and was full of dangerous rattlers swarming among a sea of prickly pear cactus. Despite these challenges, the Catholic faith managed to survive the loneliness and remoteness of these frontier settlements, bringing hope and comfort to its members in life and death. Priests rode long distances to reach the isolated ranchos where they said Mass, solemnized weddings, conducted baptisms, and heard confessions a few times a year. Among the people they served were the Kineño families of King Ranch.

Henrietta Chamberlain King came from a devout Christian ethic also, but of a quite different orientation. Her father was Rev. Hiram Chamberlain, an ordained Presbyterian minister who brought his family to Texas in 1850 and established the first Protestant church on the Rio Grande. Chamberlain was a missionary dedicated to bringing to attention the evils and errors of Roman Catholicism, thus beginning what could be referred to as a tug-of-war between Catholics and Protestants for the souls of the settlers in South Texas.

Henrietta was close to her father. The missionary carried on a loving, lengthy correspondence with his daughter, beginning when she was a fourteen-year-old attending a girls' boarding school in Mississippi. Even though most of his letters were destroyed over time, twenty-two of them remain. Bruce Cheeseman in his book *My Dear Henrietta* wrote that "in spite of such loss, the extant letters reveal the moral foundation, unfailing Presbyterianism, missionary zeal, and love of family Chamberlain instilled in young Henrietta."

Richard King and Mifflin Kenedy of the Kenedy Ranch, which adjoins King Ranch, were business associates as early as 1847, when they ran their successful steamboating business on the Rio Grande, and became close, lifelong friends. In 1850, Kenedy introduced King to Henrietta Chamberlain (Monday and Vick 7). Richard King courted Henrietta for four years, finally winning her hand, and on December 9, 1854, they were married, with her father conducting the wedding ceremony. They honeymooned on King's fledgling Santa Gertrudis rancho. By then, King had convinced most of the citizens of Cruillas, Mexico, to come with him and bring their expertise to help him establish his ranch. Those families brought the traditions of the Roman Catholic Church with them as well, and their traditions have remained on King Ranch for six generations.

Henrietta Chamberlain King was mistress of King Ranch for seventy-one years and, surviving her husband by forty years, built it into one of the most successful enterprises led by any woman in American history. She was a generous benefactress as well as an astute businesswoman, donating land for the city of Kingsville and building churches, schools, hospitals, and libraries (Cheeseman 9). She also had an ecumenical bent when that was anything but the order of the day and arguably was contradictory to her upbringing. She saw that an abandoned chapel was moved to the Ranch for the use of the Roman Catholic Kineños as their first church building on the Ranch, and she gave land to any church denomination that wanted to build a church in Kingsville (Nixon 19).

Kineño families would often designate a special place for an altar in their homes. In the early days, mothers were usually in charge of the religious education of the children, including the learning of the rosary by age eight to ten, so they would be prepared when the visiting priest came. Later, when no visiting priests were available to travel to the Ranch and transportation became more available, Kineño families, including the Maldonados, began going into Kingsville to attend church.

When I was young, we had a chapel here on the Ranch, and we had Masses every Sunday for the longest time. That building was moved here from Laureles in the early '70s. Mr. Bob died in '74, and it was a number of years before that when it came. It was actually a two-piece building that was put together and they sided it, and it was air-conditioned with window units. When they first had the dedication, the priest from Corpus came over, and there was a big turnout. Mr. Bob was there also. My dad went there often, and all of a sudden they were short of priests available to come to do Masses at the Ranch and we had to come to St. Gertrude's in town.

> He [Librado] was a good Catholic. On Sunday morning he and his wife were going you know where. He wasn't going to be deterred from that.
>
> MONTE MONCRIEF, DVM

SHE TOOK THAT KNIFE AND PRAYED AND SWUNG THAT KNIFE

When we were kids, Lee and I would come with my dad to hear what were called missionaries. Missionaries would come from some other parts of the country, and they would do that kind of work for a whole week at night, and we would come with Dad for that. They came about once a year and let everybody know ahead of time. It would be at St. Martin's Church [in Kingsville].

Mom was a big believer. When those dark clouds came, she went outside and took a knife and prayed and swung that knife and "cut" the clouds. It worked. We were never hit by a tornado.

My dad was also a big believer in praying, and he called everybody's name out when we were at the International Fair in Casablanca. He was a big believer in Mary. He and my mom said prayers every night. They would actually do it at the bed; they wouldn't go to the altar or anything like that, but they would pray every night. They would not pray a rosary. What prayer they would say, it was quiet, and I think it was just a personal prayer. The altar was in the corner, high off the floor to keep children from bothering it. It had pictures and figurines, mainly the Virgin of Guadalupe, Virgin Mary, and Jesus Christ. Mom had a lot of faith in those figures, and she would light little candles for them, and later the larger ones. She would put some kind of a flower there. Of course, back in those days, there were very little artificial flowers, so she used fresh and artificial.

I saw Mom pray at the altar at moments when she had a particular problem, especially when Plácido went into the service. We would hear from him at least twice a month or something like that. What he would do, he would say he was somewhere in North Africa or somewhere in Italy or whatever. Plácido was a medic, and when he was in Italy after the war was over, he was checking soldiers to send them back home. In the line there was a friend of his named Andres Gonzales that lived right here on King Ranch, and they were good friends and had grown up together. Of all things and all parts of the world, they met there and were so glad to see each other.

Dora prays at night. In a way, Dora has an altar. It's actually on top of a chiffonier, a chest. She's got a Jesus Christ figure and St. Jude; I think she has about three figures, and she puts artificial flowers there. She does candles. What she does with the candles, she actually puts them on her stove, like Sammy [their son] does, to be on the safe side as far as fire is concerned.

THE NUNS TAUGHT US

When I was a kid, we prepared for our first Communion when the nuns would teach a group of us after school. We would have to come to St. Martin's in town for our first Communion. I would say I was seven years old when I did my first Communion. We wore nothing special, didn't have them [dress clothes]. No celebration that I can remember, but my mama would probably bake a cake and have chocolate for the *padrinos* ([godparents], and they would come to the house for a while. My *padrinos* were my aunt and uncle Allie Byington and Samuel Byington [Ella's brother]. He was named for his papa, Samuel Byington, and we named our son, Sammy, after his grandpapa. Sammy still goes to church at St. Martin's.

There were no gifts. They would tell us, "Go shake hands with your *padrinos* or give them a hug," and we knew what we were supposed to do, actually be nicer to them than the rest of the people or the family. They [*padrinos*] showed us favor too, very much so.

Our children also did first Communions in town at St. Martín's. They would do classes to get ready by age seven or eight. They would get a *padrino* or *madrina*. Normally in our race we did members of the family for *padrinos* and *madrinas*. There were times when they would pick other people to do it, but most of the time they would pick uncles and aunts. That's what we did.

The girls would dress up in a nicely made white dress, and boys would wear black pants with white shirts. We would normally have some kind of a feast after

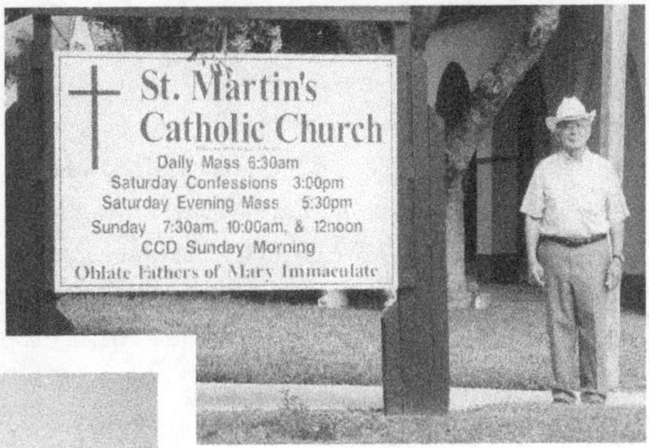

Members of the Maldonado family, including Beto, took their first Communion and attended church at St. Martin's Catholic Church in Kingsville. Photo by Betty Bailey Colley.

Dora Maldonado, as was customary with Kineño women, still maintains an altar in her home. In the early days, the women were responsible for the children's religious education in preparation for an occasional visit by a priest, and the home altar was an important teaching tool. Photo by Catalina Maldonado Yaklin.

it with cocoa and cookies or cakes or whatever. Not everyone would do it, but some would go to that extent to have a little get-together afterwards. We did that at the house with our family.

Norma Maldonado Quintanilla remembers going to church:

Aunt Alicia would drop us off at St. Martin's. I always went to church with my grandmother, but my grandmother would like to go to church early at five or six on Saturday evening because she would pray the rosary before the Mass started. Alicia would drop us off. Then on Sunday morning she would come with Plácido's daughters. My grandfather went by himself.

DÍA DE LOS MUERTOS

We celebrated Día de los Muertos (All Saints' Day) and it's still a big deal today. We still buy flowers for my mama and papa, now more than ever, artificial flowers. Over at the cemetery, if you take fresh flowers, in a couple of days they pick them up and throw them away. Artificial flowers, you can let them sit there as long as they look okay. We clean up the graves. Alicia, for the longest time, would visit those graves every day, clean the stones, and take flowers; she doesn't do it that often today. We do it too from time to time, especially Father's Day, Mother's Day, and Día de los Muertos.

Tio [Kleberg] told me about being in Mexico for Día de los Muertos, and he was amazed how those people celebrate that day. They have all kinds of goodies today. They do or take what that person liked a lot in their lifetime, and they take that food to the grave and spend the whole day. He said it was something to see.

WHEN WE WERE SICK

During the seven-plus years that the authors conducted oral histories with more than sixty Kineños for earlier books, they were struck by the few times that family members mentioned being sick or hurt. Either these mishaps rarely occurred, or these people did not believe in giving in to them, for very few serious accidents were reported, a surprise on a sprawling expanse where men and animals often competed to see who was the toughest. The animals definitely had the size advantage, given that some weighed more than two thousand pounds. When probed, interviewees did admit to cuts and bruises, both to limb and pride, but to amazingly few critical injuries and deaths while they worked dog-tired, sometimes twelve- to fourteen-hour days at nail-hard, back-wrenching jobs vaccinating livestock, building fences, branding calves, and doing countless other jobs. The Kineños even tamed those huge, fifty-two-ton twin D-8 Caterpillars that replaced hand clearing of prairie brush in the early 1900s without many injuries (Nixon 21).

Despite the many poisonous snakes that called the Wild Horse Desert home, the Kineños reported few snakebites, no doubt partially thanks to the Ranch "uniform" of khaki pants tucked into cowboy boots and long-sleeved jackets made of thick, sturdy cotton. Of course, the main reason for the lack of bites was the moxie of the vaqueros as well as the men who worked boot to dirt amid cactus, oak mottes, and knee-high grass. They were smart—they knew where to look and they knew how to listen for that tinny rattle that warned, "Snake!" But when the occasional snakebite did occur, a member of the crew cut an X on the wound to let the poison out, then poured on kerosene (Monday and Colley 154).

Obviously, clean fresh air, exercise through work in the outdoors, and a stable, high-protein diet served the Kineño families well, though sometimes they had the usual childhood maladies such as chicken pox, mumps, colds, and flulike illnesses. Especially in the early days, when the men or their families needed medical care they used *curanderos* (folk healers) or their own home remedies handed down for generations. Folk medicine is still in common use on King Ranch today. "Most people try home remedies based on folk medicine first and seek help through professionals when they have been unsuccessful," according to Cecelia Rhoades, a professor at Texas A&M University–Kingsville who teaches a class in *curanderismo* (Manning B1–2).

CURANDEROS

In the early days when clinics and hospitals were available only in population centers, pioneers had to depend on themselves for treatment of their ailments. This situation gave rise to the seeking of cures by a group of people in South Texas called *curanderos,* who became proficient in treating illnesses with natural materials that were available to them. Some of them planted plants and herbs right in their front yards and over time developed a remedy for almost every kind of sickness and pain their family and neighbors endured (*Corpus Christi Caller-Times* 105). *Curanderos* can be either male or female and may even specialize. The *curandero* heals on two levels, a rational level using herbs and amulets (charms) and a spiritual level using religion, God, saints, and prayers to heal a patient.

Pedrito Jaramillo, one of the most famous *curanderos* of all time, was born in Mexico. In 1881, when he was fifty-two years old, it is said that he asked God to heal his sick mother and promised God that if that didn't happen, he would leave Mexico. When his mother died, he came to Texas and spent the rest of his life in Falfurrias, where his shrine at Los Olmos (the Elms) remains a famous South Texas pilgrimage today. The walls of Los Olmos are covered with written testimonials of people who have been cured by the spirit of Don Pedrito, and stowed in the rafters are crutches left by pilgrims whose crippling conditions evidently vanished. Don Pedrito is not a canonical saint of the church but is recognized as one by the people. The State of Texas appointed the charismatic Don Pedrito to serve as a welfare agent for the people of South Texas during the great drought of 1893, and he had hundreds of followers (Torres 36–41).

Stories have it that Don Pedrito learned of his unusual gift of healing when he fell from a horse, landed on his nose, and was in excruciating pain. For reasons unknown he went to a muddy bog and dabbed the mud all over the injury; then he experienced relief and was finally able to sleep. During that sleep, he said God spoke to him and told him to spend the rest of his life healing the sick and injured, and this he did until his death in 1907.

Most of Don Pedrito's cures involved bathing and poultices of one kind or another. He also prescribed drinking lots of water, often in ritualistic patterns of a certain number of days, usually intervals of three or nine, so-called mystical numbers. He may have had psychic powers, for there were reports that he could read minds and could detect nonbelievers. It was said that sometimes when someone came to him suffering from *susto* (fright), he could discern the traumatic event causing the *susto* without being told what it was; the *susto* might have been something such as trauma from seeing a ghost or a black cat. The cure was to lay the patient on a bed, cover the patient with a bedsheet, and hit the sheet with a broom or bunches of leaves, such as sage. Don Pedrito said that he could not cure anyone, but that patients could be cured by their faith in God, and like other healers, he used Catholic symbols such as crucifixes, rosaries, and holy pictures. His patients included many Anglos (Torres).

My parents and a lot of people used *curanderos* while they were young and still living in Falfurrias, and after they came to King Ranch in 1925, they would go back to Don Pedrito's shrine from time to time for treatment because they had a lot of faith in that *curandero*. Don Pedrito was very famous, and many, many people would come from miles and miles around in buggies and on horseback to find a cure because they believed in Don Pedrito so much.

One time after I was married and had children, I hurt my back lifting something heavy. I went to see a *curandero*, a lady in Kingsville. It was cold and rainy, and she said she would work on my back, but I would have to go back home because I should not go out in the weather after the treatment. So we actually came home, and she worked on me. She had a candle, and she would light it and place it on a folded rag, then cover it with a clear drinking glass and move the whole thing from place to place on my back and when she was finished, my back was okay. One of her treatments for colds was to heat up a tub of hot water and put your feet in there wrapped in a rag or towel to get your feet real warm. You could not go out after that in the weather until the next day.

Curanderos did not charge a fee, but people sometimes brought gifts, maybe *pan dulce* or some other gift of food, or they might give money.

Our families had our own treatments also. Some of our treatment for coughs and fever were *yerba buena* and sage tea, also kerosene mixed with sugar. Very early we could buy Vicks and Mentholatum for colds at the commissary and Mercurochrome for cuts and scrapes and even sores in the mouth. Dr. Collier Sublett in town would say, "Oh, you Kineños—you have to stop treating yourselves." Also available over the counter at the commissary was paregoric, a very popular medicine for babies' colic, earache, upset stomach—any number of things.

> Rice water was given to babies. They [parents] boiled sugar and rice for stomach problems, *manzanilla*. They also gave them chamomile tea with honey, and *comino* seeds were boiled, sifted, and drained and the water sweetened with honey for colic or upset stomach.
>
> DORA MALDONADO GARCIA

Some medicines were used for both people and animals. That 6X liniment we made here on the Ranch, White liniment, and Phemer-Nite were used for cuts. Bigeloil liniment was good for aches and bruised bones. Pynotal Blue lotion was used only on animals, no people.

I had measles and chicken pox when I was little, but I had mumps when I was a mature man. What happened, Sammy had mumps and he used to sleep with me, and I got 'em from Sammy, I remember, in '61 or '62. The doctor told me to go lie down and stay in bed. I came over to the commissary to buy groceries to make sure there would be something to eat, and I stayed in bed for two weeks with high fever. We already had TV at that time, and any little noise would bother me. For two weeks I went through a lot. I got up and tried to make the Loop Road, and when I got home, I thought I had a new case of the mumps, so I went to the doctor and he said, "You stay home another week sitting down or lying down, one of the two," so it was a three-week deal.

The Good Lord has been real good to me. I go to the clinic once a year, and they find my cholesterol a little high and they get me scared for a few weeks, and then I go right back to that red beef. I can eat chicken and I stay hungry, but a hamburger will do it—I've gotta have that beef. Mama wouldn't cook beef on Fridays during Lent, and I would develop a headache by Saturday. I've gotta have beef.

Until 1976 the Ranch had its own clinic in Kingsville, staffed by experienced physicians who took care of owners and Kineños alike. Kineños used a Ranch form authorizing treatment at the clinic. A doctor would treat them or refer them to the Kleberg County Hospital or Spohn Hospital in Corpus Christi, depending on the severity of the case. Now the Ranch furnishes health insurance for its employees.

> When I moved here in '71, the Ranch had a clinic [in Kingsville]. And everybody—like if I had a sick child or was sick, I would go down and sit in the clinic in the waiting room, and all the Ranch people would come.
>
> JANELL KLEBERG

> You would get an order. Beto would go to Dr. Northway, and he would write an order out with Beto's name on it and he would go down and present that to the receptionist, and he'd see the doctor and leave. At the end of the month the clinic would send King Ranch a statement—here's who we've seen—and we'd pay the bill.
>
> TIO KLEBERG

> Most people that lived on the Ranch didn't have cars, so there was a bus that went around, and if anybody was sick, they would get a ride to town. It was like a little van. They'd come to the commissary and pick you up there. You knew who the driver was, and you'd see him and you'd say, "I need to go to the clinic tomorrow," and he would either come by and pick you up or you'd say, "I'll be at the commissary in the morning," and he'd go by at nine o'clock and whoever was there, he'd pick them up and take them. He also made the mail run; he would take them to pay a bill. He did everything.
>
> TIO AND JANELL KLEBERG

The commissary was the hub of Ranch life on the Santa Gertrudis Division. Besides being the center for monthly disbursement of food rations and stocking of clothing and supplies like kerosene for lamps, it also served as a meeting point for all kinds of purposes, even elections. It also served as the Ranch pharmacy.

The clinic doctors wrote prescriptions in quantity so the commissary could have on hand medicines readily available for men who would not think of missing work to go see a doctor just because they were sick. These prescription medicines were probably antibiotics like tetracycline or penicillin (Janell Kleberg interview 2/2/07). Beto told about having capsules there "in little bottles," as well as over-the-counter medicines for common maladies such as cold, flu, and stomach upset. All he and his dad had to do was go by and pick up what they needed. This was especially important when they were to be gone for weeks on the show circuit. Beto said one day they were in another state and one of the men was very sick, and Librado gave him some of those capsules. The next day that man wanted to go to work.

Librado and Ella's children were birthed at home with the help of midwives, as was the custom and often a necessity in those days. The first Kleberg County Hospital opened on January 12, 1912, and many babies were born there under the care of a physician, including all of Beto and Dora Maldonado's children. A new Kleberg County Hospital opened in 1980, and Beto's granddaughter, Veronica Maldonado Garcia, was one of the first babies to be born there. Dora Maldonado said, "My kids were born in the hospital. I stayed at the hospital two or three days. No problems."

When the men were gone for extended periods, their wives, with the help of family, were accustomed to coping with any emergencies, including illness. Dora Maldonado told of a time when one of their children became very sick while Beto was away showing cattle. It was the only time she could remember anyone having a serious illness while Beto was gone.

> Cata [Catalina] got sick one time when he was gone. She was two years old. She had a lot of fever and she was shaking, and Beto's brother, Plácido, came home, and his wife, and they brought us to the doctor in town. He gave us some medicine. My sister-in-law [Alicia] stayed with the children while we brought Cata to town.
>
> DORA MALDONADO

Naming our kids was not a problem. Dora was named for Dora, Albert Jr. for me, Norma "for your girlfriend," Dora says, Sammy for my grandpapa on my mama's side, and Catalina for my grandmama on my papa's side.

WHEN FRESH AIR AND A GOOD LIFE WERE NOT ENOUGH

When a person died in the early days of the Ranch, the family prepared the body, which was kept at home until time for the burial. Sometimes during extreme heat, ice was placed beneath the body to help with preservation until time for the funeral. Dora Maldonado recounted this practice at the death of her parents. In both the Kineño and King Ranch families, it was customary for family members and sometimes friends to sit up all night with the body, and often friends and relatives brought food to the house. Sometime around 1909 a funeral home was established in one side of the Allen Furniture Store to serve both Anglos and Mexicans. Allen Furniture Store, which had been in business in Kingsville since 1926, was owned by Clyde M. Allen Sr. and then by his son, Clyde M. Allen Jr. C. Bernard Kennedy worked for the senior Allen and was interested in the mortuary business, so he serviced that side of the business, though both he and Allen earned embalming licenses. When time permitted, Kennedy sold furniture on the other side of the store.

A chapel and embalming room were set up, and the business sold caskets and other burial supplies. Employees working in the furniture store also dug graves and drove the hearses (Monday and Colley 158, 159).

Librado "Lee" Maldonado Jr., Beto's younger brother, was the first in his family to die, unfortunately at a very early age, in 1971. One of Lee's sons, Librado Maldonado III, also died prematurely in 2004 at age forty-one.

> Lee was the youngest. He died when he was thirty-nine. He's been dead for thirty-two years. It was not unexpected. He used to work with the horses in New York, and he got sick. He came home to die. He had been home about a month. They took him to the hospital and he passed away.
>
> ALICIA MALDONADO

The entire King Ranch family was devastated when Librado had a stroke in 1979, just a month after the October auction, and remained partially paralyzed and unable to speak. He was bedridden for three years before his death in 1983.

> He was in the hospital three months in Corpus Christi. I was there all the time. Then they brought him here [Kleberg County Hospital], and then we took him home and the doctor said to take him to Gonzales because they were going to give him speech therapy and everything. At first he was very bright, and they'd come and get him three times [a day]. So he got tired, and in the third week he wouldn't go to the therapy, so we brought him home. My sisters [Aurora and Amelia] used to come and help me at night. Sometimes one would stay there one night and the other one stay there the next night. And he stayed home three years and three months.
>
> A month or so [before he died] I used to tell him, "Give me your hand, Daddy." And he would put his hand on my hand, his left hand; he was paralyzed on the right side. And then I said, "Give me a little kiss." And when he got real sick, when he passed away, I asked him and I could feel his hand, that his hand was kinda heavy, you know, and he wouldn't give me a kiss. And I got him in my arms and let him go. I held him in my arms while he died. I did my mother too.
>
> ALICIA MALDONADO

Dora and Beto Maldonado at home in February 2008, a year from their sixtieth wedding anniversary, on February 6, 2009. Photo by Catalina Maldonado Yaklin.

RESPECT FOR DON LIBRADO

Dad died at home. He is buried at the Resthaven Cemetery, a newer one, probably the second one in Kingsville, located south of town on land donated by Mrs. King. We buried Mom side by side there three years later. My dad never went to school a day in is life and he couldn't even write his name, but he was so smart and learned so much. He learned English by traveling around and hearing it, and he spoke very good English and could talk to anybody. And his cattle expertise he learned at Lasater. He learned to shape the animals' horns like he wanted them by using a nut and bolt and a welded piece so he could adjust the tension with a leather strap.

When my dad died, Leonard Stiles was in charge of the *corrida* group. He actually sent the two cooks and the chuck wagon and parked the King Ranch chuck wagon at my dad's house, and there was plenty of food for family and friends to have all day long. Coffee too.

A lot of people came for his funeral. He was at the Turcotte Funeral Home. The funeral Mass was at St. Gertrude's Catholic Church. He was buried in his suit. When those ties with the Running W came out, Tio Kleberg had a box of them in his car, and he came over to the area where I was working one day and he said, "Beto, every time y'all go show cattle or have to do anything, I want y'all to wear a brown and white tie with the Running W and a Santa Gertrudis tie clip," so we put a King Ranch tie on Dad with the suit. Tio [Kleberg] represented the King Ranch family at the funeral, and he brought medallions to Alicia, Plácido, and me. They were bronze King Ranch medallions. Not many people have them.

> If it were not for the people, King Ranch would be a name; it wouldn't be an enterprise. Captain King had a vision, but without that *entrada*, it would never have happened. If he hadn't had the legacy, he never would have convinced Librado Maldonado to leave the Lasater family to come over here and be responsible for the Jersey herd, which was renowned in its time. And without Librado . . . he never would have had the notoriety . . . Somebody else could have done it, there would have been somebody . . . but not to the class, certainly not to the notoriety of Librado.
>
> TIO KLEBERG

> Don Librado—I called him Don Librado after he turned from young to old as a sign of respect—was the finest gentleman you ever saw in your life. He was more intelligent than most scientists, and he had no formal education that I knew of at all. He just knew the ways of the world; he had been down the trail. He was the perfect gentleman, and he knew a lot about cattle. I worked with him nearly every day.
>
> MONTE MONCRIEF, DVM

On a crisp autumn day with the sky painted that clear blue as it can only be in the Wild Horse Desert, Beto stood with the authors at the foot of his parents' graves and talked about his mother dying three years after his dad and about the burials of Librado and Ella. His brother Plácido's wife, Lillie, had been buried the week before in the Maldonado family plot. The flowers were still fresh and beautiful, and a peace seemed to settle over him as he wistfully remembered.

She [Ella] was hospitalized and she actually died of complications from the hospital instead of why she was ill. I don't remember what she had. She didn't have cancer for sure. I don't think it was her heart. She did not have an operation. I'm sure you've heard of people being hospitalized for sickness and winding up dying with complications of what they do at the hospital. Anyway, she was hospitalized for a sickness, and she wound up dying of what they did at the hospital.

Normally a rosary would be said the night before people were buried. I forgot what time they [Librado and Ella] died. If they had time enough to work on them, they would have the rosary at night. If not, a day would go by, and it would be a couple of days before they were buried. The bodies were taken to the funeral home at the chapel.

DORA PLANS AHEAD

Dora Maldonado has already made detailed funeral plans for herself, much to the dismay of Beto. He says she talks about cemetery plots and funeral homes, and he says, "Why don't we talk about weddings or birthday parties or something like that?" But Dora keeps telling Beto and her girls exactly what she wants to happen when she dies.

> We've been married fifty-nine years. I don't know how to write checks—I don't pay bills. The only thing I enjoy doing is going grocery shopping. I tell Beto that he's going to go after me. And he says no, no, no—let's not talk about that. He doesn't like to talk about dying. I want to make all the arrangements, and he refuses. I want everything taken care of before I die.
>
> And I've already told my girls, "No makeup and no lipstick. Just make sure I have on my black-and-white dress, and fix my hair. That's all. Not so much, I tell them.
>
> DORA MALDONADO

6

REALIZING A DREAM

I used to dream about being
back there in school.

Beto Maldonado

FINALLY, AFTER FORTY YEARS—GRADUATION

The long black gown was just a bit tight, but it felt just real good. The flat-topped, square black cap was a lot different from the cream-colored straw cowboy hat I usually wore this time of year, but I was proud to wear it. Finally, in 1984 at age fifty-four, after forty years of feeling sorry about turning in the books and checking out of Henrietta King High School in Kingsville, Texas, in the ninth grade, the regret was finally put away. The dreams of being back in school kept coming and coming over the years. One day I opened the paper [*Kingsville Record*], and there was that ad saying that they were going to offer night classes at the old high school where I started and that you could get your high school diploma [general equivalency diploma, or GED]. I said to myself, "This is what I've been waiting for." I attended classes for the longest time, at least two years. It was not every night, but I think two or three nights a week that high school teachers would teach us at the old Henrietta King High School. The books and everything were free.

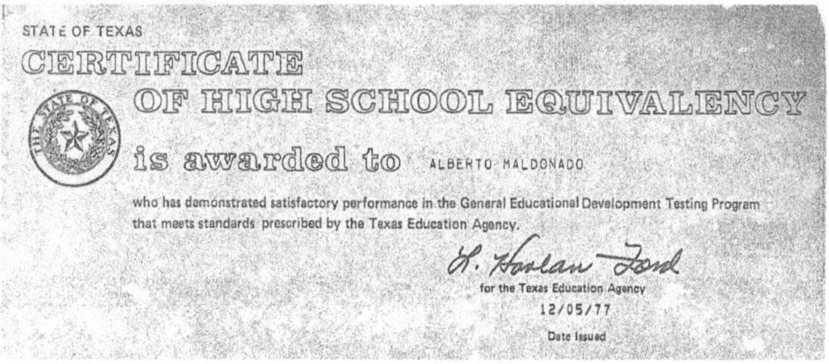
STATE OF TEXAS
CERTIFICATE
OF HIGH SCHOOL EQUIVALENCY
is awarded to ALBERTO MALDONADO
who has demonstrated satisfactory performance in the General Educational Development Testing Program that meets standards prescribed by the Texas Education Agency.
for the Texas Education Agency
12/05/77
Date Issued

Beto Maldonado's children gathered to celebrate when their father earned a general equivalency diploma (GED) in 1977, more than forty years after he dropped out of school in the ninth grade. Pictured are Catalina (*left*), Sammy, Beto, Norma, Alberto Jr., and Dora. Courtesy of Beto Maldonado.

Beto Maldonado reached a longtime goal when he received a certificate of high school equivalency from the State of Texas. Courtesy of Beto Maldonado.

There were probably twenty of us. I remember some guys were as old as I was, and some were younger. The younger ones that had attended school were probably seniors, eighteen or nineteen years old. They just needed a credit or two to finish high school, and they didn't stay very long, maybe a few weeks. When I decided to enroll, I started at the eighth grade and went on and on until I was ready to have a test at the A&I University [now Texas A&M University–Kingsville]. My biggest problem was mathematics. I passed mathematics and all the classes the first time except for English. I had to take that test for the second time.

We celebrated at a family party at home after the graduation ceremony. All five of my children were there, and my sisters Alicia and Aurora and my nephews.

My family was very proud. They prepared hot chocolate and cookies and cakes and what have you. My daughter Dora had already graduated from high school, and I actually wore her cap and gown to have some pictures made, because we didn't wear caps and gowns to get the GED certificate. I wore khaki pants and a white shirt—that was my favorite—and we walked across that stage and they called out names and we were handed a certificate, just like regular high school grads. I actually knew some of the school board members. One was Minnie Rangel Henderson, the sister of Irma Mae Rangel, who was a state representative for many years [1977–2003], and they named the pharmacy building [Irma Lerma Rangel College of Pharmacy] at Texas A&M University–Kingsville after her. She was the first Hispanic American woman elected to the legislature.

It made me feel real good about getting the GED. You have something in mind, and when you accomplish what you have in mind, it makes you feel real good.

THAT FIRST DAY AT SCHOOL

I will never forget my first day when I entered school at the Santa Gertrudis Headquarters [in 1936]. We always spoke Spanish at home, and Spanish was the language of the Ranch. Ranch owners' children were expected to speak Spanish before they started school, so they spoke our language when we played together. Spanish was strictly forbidden on school premises, even during lunch and recess, but of course we sneaked conversations in our native language at those times when we thought the teacher couldn't hear. I was luckier than most of the Kineño children because I knew a few words of English from hearing my dad speak it away from the house, but I didn't know much English. We had no television at that time, radio, or newspapers [at home], so there was little or no opportunity to learn or practice English. The teacher spoke no Spanish. This may have been one reason why students were not allowed to speak Spanish, because she wouldn't know what we were saying. There were ways we would let the teacher know what we wanted to do, what we needed to do. Of course, we had outdoor toilets. We would go outside, and we had to wait and ask permission to go to the restrooms.

> I remember playing with Spanish-speaking Kineño children, and I actually had to learn English when I went to school, just like they did.
>
> SALLY KLEBERG

I still remember the title of the first book I got. It was *Spot and the Mother Cat*, and I also remember the name of the young man who helped me cover that book. His nickname was Sambo, but his real name was Ambroso Cantu. I always remember Ambroso from time to time because I didn't know what to do and he helped me. I remember the first writing tablets I used. There was a picture of an Indian head on the tablet, a Big Chief or something like that. The school was a frame building, and there were folding doors that would split the big room into two rooms. That's where all grades were taught. Ambroso was probably in the seventh grade or something like that. My teacher was Mrs. Gary Ellis, and another one was Mrs. Delia Embruck. Mr. Oliver Nanny was the principal—he was here for many years.

We would play games of all kinds. We would take marbles and tops—we were not allowed to do it—but we would take marbles and tops to school, and play baseball and volleyball and have all kinds of games. We would go in at eight o'clock, and we would have a recess and then lunch between twelve and one in the afternoon, then go home around three.

Besides being away from home all day for the first time, a new language made being at school even more uncomfortable. At that time, my dad was doing a lot of traveling, showing cattle around the country, and he would stay gone for a week or two or three. There were times when my dad was gone that we actually didn't want to go to school that bad, so my mom had a little problem getting us on the road to school. There were times we were walking to school early in the morning on that dirt road from the house to the road that leads to the Calera Barn and heads back to the Headquarters, and I would look at that sand and I could just feel that sand, how it would be so nice and soft to just lay down and go to sleep there. But I didn't do it; I just kept walking. When we were not in the mood to go to school and didn't want to go to school, my mom would say, "If y'all don't get on the road and go to school, I'm gonna call Dr. Northway and tell him to come over here." So after she would say that, we would go ahead and get back on the road and go to school.

At first we would all walk to school together. In the early days, because of a lack of transportation, there were what they would call ranchos—a group of people, four or five families in one location, five or six in the other. These people would do most of the work on horseback and mules pulling the wagons. They would have a location to look after their cattle and repair fences and check the windmills, water troughs, and what have you. There were several of these locations on the Ranch [Santa Gertrudis Division], and I would say in the '20s they started to bring these people to one location at Headquarters near the commissary, near the maintenance department, near the Main House. Later, in the late 1940s they built what we called the Colony—a little over a hundred homes—and those people from La Lechera [the Dairy], Lauro's Hill, Rancho Plomo, and the Headquarters, they were all combined at one location.

EVERYTHING ON KING RANCH HAS A NAME

Every ranchero, every pasture, every windmill, and every set of pens here on King Ranch has a name. From here at La Lechera, where we lived, there were fifteen homes, and out of the fifteen homes there were at least twenty or more attending school at the Headquarters [Santa Gertrudis Division]. We were a mile away from the school, and we would walk back and forth to school, and so would the people at Lauro's Hill and Rancho Plomo—they were about a mile away also. They would walk on the roads, and the ones at Rancho Plomo would come to the middle part of the pasture and would actually walk through a bridge that came by the Thoroughbred barn then, right behind Mr. Bob's house, the Main House, and then to the commissary and on to school.

There were fewer houses at Lauro's Hill. The Ranch named that spot for Lauro Cavazos. Lauro Cavazos [Sr.] was the Headquarters foreman in charge of the division, the first Mexican American to have that job. There were no more than six houses, and that's where Martín Mendietta, Miguel Muñiz, Candido Mendietta, Silvero Martinez, and Martín Martinez Jr. lived. The ones that were farthest away were Lolo [Alberto V. Treviño] and his brothers and sisters. They were maybe a couple of miles away in the pasture La Posta, near the old racetrack in town near where the Javelina Stadium [at Texas A&M–Kingsville] stands today. And they would come on horseback through the pastures and through the gates, and they would actually leave their horses behind Eugeñio Quintanilla's house. He was a horse boss at one time and he had a pen behind his house, and there's where Lolo and Pedro and Gilberto and David, Reymundo, and Ramón Treviño would all unsaddle and leave their horses and go to school.

Later my dad managed to find a Shetland pony for my younger brother, Lee, and I, and we would ride horseback back and forth to school. There was a stable at the Chon Barn near the schoolhouse where we could leave the pony there with shade and food and water. That's the barn that's shown in the Ford commercials today. My dad actually got a pony that belonged to a member of Dr. Northway's family, and a saddle. And Jim Sedwick, who was in charge of the Saddle Shop for many years, as was his father, Gene Sedwick, was nice to let my dad borrow saddles that I could use. Then he actually built me a brand-new saddle I could use with that Shetland pony. Then Dr. Northway had a pony he was able to find for Lee, and a saddle. We outgrew those Shetland ponies and went into bigger horses. So we would ride horseback back and forth to school, but my sisters walked to school.

There was no lunchroom. At that time we had all the veal in the world with the baby Jerseys at the dairy. So my mama would prepare those *taquitos* of veal, and we would take them to school for lunch.

Students in the Santa Gertrudis School on King Ranch, circa 1936. Beto Maldonado is seated, third from left. Courtesy of Beto Maldonado.

> The *taquitos* we were hiding from everybody because we were ashamed that we were eating *taquitos*. And now everybody eats *taquitos*. We had water at school—we had a fountain.
>
> ALICIA MALDONADO

There were very few times that she [Ella] wasn't able to prepare lunch for all six of us. The commissary was right across from the schoolhouse. Whenever she didn't prepare lunch for us, she would give us a dime each, that's when we would buy a can of potted meat for three cents a can and a box of saltine crackers for a nickel. That's what we would do. We drank water. I still remember the water fountain. I still have dreams of that water fountain in front of the old school.

WE LEARNED TO COOK AND SEW AND THE WHOLE SHEBANG

Later they [King Ranch] built a brick building that was used as the home economics department, where people would learn how to cook and sew and the whole shebang. That's when I actually joined the sewing class and managed to make that apron. At the home economics class we would also do carpenter work; we would borrow a tool from the carpenter shop near the maintenance department. And we would work on a garden, have our own garden with vegetables.

Then, of course, we had wood heaters. Some of us older boys would go to the sawmill and saw wood for the heaters. A guy by the name of Charin Hinojosa was the one in charge of the sawmill. It was a big ol' blade operated by electricity . . . and I now think how in the world we managed not to get hurt, I don't know. But that was about the only way that we could do it. We would actually cut wood and bring it into the building.

LATER I REGRETTED IT

When we started to school, we still had work to do. My younger brother, Lee, and I would get up at five o'clock in the morning. That's when they would finish milking those cows and would bring them up to the barn, and we would put hackamores on the baby calves and pull the baby calves away from the mamas at a very early age to milk the cows. So Lee, and I would go and help halter those calves, tie them in the barn, feed them out of a bucket, go to school, and after school we'd clean out the stables and bed them down for the next morning. We would chop wood before dark and bring it in and have it ready to start a fire in the morning for cooking.

We would do all the homework. And we would prepare our kerosene lanterns so we could have light to study with. I think we had two of those lanterns in the kitchen and two in the living room. What we did, we washed those globes with soap and water every day or two to get the lampblack off so the light would shine through. Then we'd fill them, the lanterns, with kerosene.

I continued my education here at the Ranch to the eighth grade and passed to high school and actually enrolled in high school. I was required to live in Kingsville to attend high school there, and I lived with my aunt Inez Treviño. She lived on Lee Street, close enough that I could walk to school—I'd say maybe a half a mile away. There were no problems because I was from the Ranch and the teachers were real nice. But still I missed my family and the familiar life on the Ranch. There was initiation at the school, like putting shoes in trees. I came late, so they wouldn't initiate me. It was a big change, and I was maybe a little scared that I might fail. Besides, most Kineño children, both boys and girls, quit school by the time they were thirteen or fourteen. One day I just checked my books in and headed back to the house. I didn't tell anybody—I just left. And my dad was real upset. What he should have done, he should have taken his belt off and given me a whipping and sent me back to school. He was real mad, but he let me quit. Later I regretted it. I was sorry I quit and missed school so much that I used to dream about being back there in school.

That's why that ad in the *Kingsville Record* about the GED classes was a dream come true.

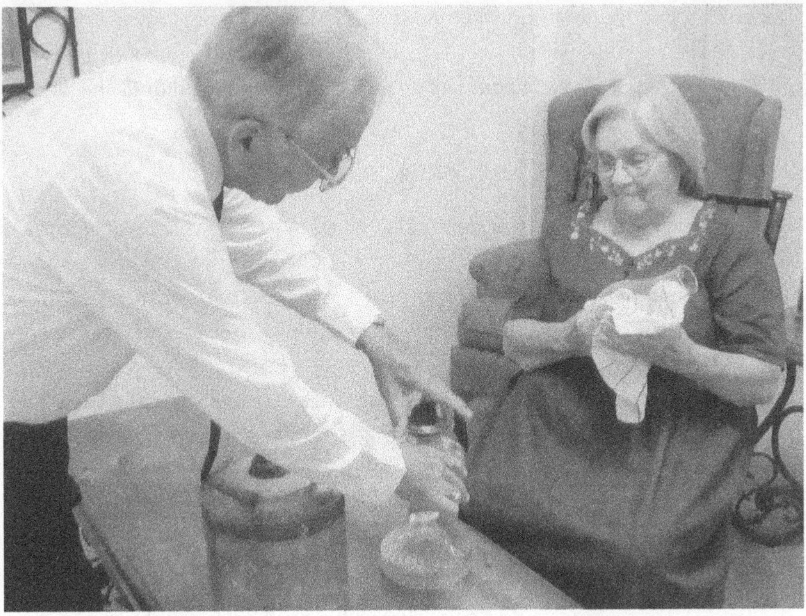

Beto and Alicia Maldonado demonstrate how they cleaned and filled lanterns with kerosene as children so they could see to do their homework. Photo by Betty Bailey Colley.

THE SCHOOL BOARD MEMBER

I actually served on the Santa Gertrudis Independent School District board of trustees from 1970 to 1979, and at one time I served as vice president, from 1974 to 1979. My brother Plácido served on the school board from 1962 to 1974. The school board met at the schoolhouse—it was a pretty good-sized building, and they had a kitchen there. I'm trying to remember correctly, but I think most of the time we met there at the school.

READING ABOUT MARILYN

At Dora's and my house there were newspapers. Juan Gaytan, one of the men who worked at the racing stable, brought me the Corpus paper [*Caller-Times*] every day, and I would read it. And I would buy magazines to read, and later my daughter Dora did as a gift *National Geographic, Life* magazine, and *Look* magazine, and I would still have to buy something to read. The kids read those things too. We didn't have TV. It took a long time for us to get TV because it cost a whole bunch at that time.

I can tell you the whole story about Marilyn Monroe. She was my girlfriend. I would go see her movies, and any magazines with Marilyn Monroe articles or pictures, I would buy. I read all about her when she was a young girl until she died.

A TRUE APPRENTICESHIP

We all worked for King Ranch except my twin sisters—they did not work for the corporation. I think they wanted to stay home and help mom. At first Alicia and Plácido worked at the veterinary department, and my younger brother, Lee, and I worked with my dad at the dairy for the longest time. Later, when Plácido went to World War II, I was moved to the veterinary department to take his place. It was located at the same place as the dairy, so I was still with my dad a lot. When Plácido came back from the service, he worked at the veterinary department, and I continued to work with my dad and the Santa Gertrudis cattle and we would halter-break them and show them around the country. Of course, I had followed my papa's footsteps since I was a little one, and he taught me a lot of things.

> You [children on the Ranch] had a school education, but the other part of it was that if your father or your uncle worked with the bulls, that's where you worked. If your father or your uncle worked with the horses, that's where you went. If your dad was in a fence crew, that's where you went. If your dad was with the windmills, that's where you went. It was a very important part of the education system because, in order to have a future [for the Ranch], you had to have people understanding and learning and coming up. Well, who was better to teach you than your family that was doing it? They were the mentors. And you learned from experience, not from being told.
>
> TIO KLEBERG

MALDONADOS CONTINUE TO VALUE EDUCATION

All of Beto's children finished high school, and some of them attended Texas A&I. Granddaughter Veronica Garcia recently earned a master's degree in agriculture from Texas A&M–Kingsville, where she was the first freshman to be selected a president's ambassador and helped host dignitaries such as President George H. W. Bush, Dr. Ruth, Governor Rick Perry, and several state representatives and senators. Veronica began showing lambs at age eight. She knew she wanted to be a teacher in second grade, and she knew she wanted to be an agriculture teacher by fifth grade. She taught agriculture courses in grades nine through twelve in Robstown, Texas. Veronica's older sister, Sonia, also attended Texas A&M–Kingsville.

Granddaughter Monica Lee Quintanilla graduated cum laude with a bachelor's degree in theater, TV, and film from the University of Texas–Pan American and is employed at Entravision Communications. Her brother Mario received an associate's degree in computer science from South Texas Community College and works as a network engineer.

7

THE MASTER TOUR GUIDE

I cannot tell you how wonderful it was to visit the King Ranch. . . .
But what I believe made the tour so fabulous for us . . .
was our tour guide, Beto Maldonado.

Letter from Kim Monroe of Chesapeake,
Virginia, November 28, 2006

Inviting people to visit King Ranch is a natural outgrowth of the legacy of hospitality established by Captain and Mrs. King, who welcomed all who came their way with food and beverage and lively conversation. Although strangers were still occasionally welcomed to the Ranch in the 1930s and 1940s, the visits became a bit more formalized in 1950 when greater numbers of people began driving through the front gates at a time when the Ranch was eager to show its Santa Gertrudis breed, which would be offered for sale that year at the first King Ranch auction. The Loop Road, built in the 1940s, was opened, and people began to drive their private cars for "do it yourself" tours; they had no printed information or signage to explain the locations they were seeing. In the 1980s the Ranch offered a cassette tape for purchase and loaned visitors a tape player, if their cars did not have one, so that visitors could at least learn about the buildings and a bit of Ranch history. Later a brochure with numbers designating sites was added.

In the late 1980s, security and safety became challenges. The great shift away from an agrarian society by this time left many people with little or no knowledge of any phase of the agriculture industry. Errors in judgment on the

Ranch were almost guaranteed because of this prevailing lack of exposure. One day, one of the managers was driving down the Loop Road and saw a vacant car pulled over, and he thought he had better investigate. He got out of his car and began checking the pasture, and sure enough, there was the driver of the car. The lady was driving herself on a tour, and she had just pulled over and crawled over the fence into the pasture with the Longhorn bulls so she could photograph them close-up. She had no idea she was in any danger. Then, when two cars were observed drag racing on the Loop Road, management and the family knew that it was decision time; either they had to close the Ranch to the public, or they needed to figure out a better way of handling visitors. They made the decision to welcome the public to King Ranch and establish a Visitor Center where guests could view a video based on the King Ranch story and take a bus tour with a seasoned, knowledgeable guide. The self-guided tours came to an end.

After careful research, shuttle buses like ones used at airports were selected as the most comfortable and easily accessible for riders. Beto went to Houston to check out those buses, and the Ranch bought three of them that held twenty passengers each. Today the Visitor Center uses two buses, one with a capacity of twenty-four and one with a capacity of twenty. Two vans and two Suburbans have been added for smaller groups and private tours.

As with any new venture, the Ranch did not quite know what to expect, even whether enough people would be interested in the new arrangement to make the tours feasible. The closing of the Loop Road was controversial, as it was seemingly alien to King Ranch philosophy since its first days. With this in mind, the first bus tours were designed to emphasize traditional, but modified, Ranch hospitality along with the history and actual workings of the Ranch. Visitors stopped at the Rancho Plomo Pens, where one of the cowboys, Adolpho Chapa, served steaming mugs of coffee and camp bread made to his recipe, while Lolo Treviño explained the use of the branding irons and other ranching tools, then mounted a King Ranch Quarter Horse to demonstrate cutting a calf from a small herd. Next they visited the reopened weavers' house, where Robert Caldera, who had agreed to come back to weave saddle blankets, demonstrated his craft. Following the tour, the Ranch offered lunch for the charter bus tours in an authentic camp house. Janell Kleberg told about organizing the tour:

> We talked to Scott Conard at Young's Pizza, and we said, "Would you cater lunches for us at the camp house?" And so he cooked for us. Scott Conard, just a great guy, put on a cowboy hat and he was jolly—he turned out to be the best entertainer we had of the whole group.
>
> Leonard [Stiles] gathered up the branding wagon. We had a chuck wagon in the barn in storage, and we got Lolo's saddle and chaps and

> spurs—we were just grabbing everything and putting it over there [at the Rancho Plomo Pens]. We put Leonard and Lolo and Beto together, and we said, "We'll bring them in—you handle them." And so Lolo explained about the branding irons, and Leonard and Beto did the tours.

Any doubts about the success of the tours vanished when 15,000 people climbed aboard the passenger buses the first year, and that number soon climbed to as many as 50,000 a year. Since 9/11 the numbers have been closer to 35,000 to 40,000 annual guests who take the original historical/agricultural tour or more comprehensive half- or full-day private tours for special interests such as cattle/horse operations, farming, or feedlot/feed mill operations. Visitors may also choose one of the guided nature tours, several of which are designed especially for birdwatchers.

KINGSVILLE LOSES DOWNTOWN

The numbers of tourists started to grow. A huge economic shift occurred when sunseekers from the North began coming to the Rio Grande Valley instead of Florida for the winter. Tour operators out of the Valley began selling commercial tours, which included a stop at King Ranch. Ranch management was surprised when tourists began streaming off those buses. The Loop Road became jammed with buses and Airstream trailers. One thing was clear: it was time for King Ranch to begin its own tours.

At the same time that tourism was flourishing on the Ranch, the city of Kingsville was dying. Wal-Mart built a store a mile or two out of town, and malls opened in Corpus Christi. Shoppers' habits changed. Soon retail stores were closing in downtown Kingsville until only a few remained—Harrel's Kingsville Pharmacy, Wilson's True Value Hardware, and a few others.

Thousands of visitors now coming to the Ranch were a built-in market, a huge opportunity for Kingsville to recapture its downtown. The tourists were spending no money in town; they visited the Ranch, got back on their buses, and continued their tours. If their Ranch tour could be followed by having lunch in town and visits to interesting specialty shops in a historic setting, they would be more likely to come and perhaps return and stay overnight. The resulting tourism dollars could fund marketing and thus further renovation of downtown. Everybody would win.

Janell Kleberg was aware of this opportunity and set about working to revitalize the downtown area. She spent a year researching tourism with the Texas Tourist Development Agency and the Texas Historical Commission. Historical markers for downtown buildings were applied for, and the first was granted and

Dr. J. K. Northway (*left*), Librado Maldonado, and Tom Armstrong welcome Kathryn and Bing Crosby to King Ranch. Courtesy of King Ranch.

B. K. Johnson (*left*), Mrs. Johnson, former governor John Connally, Nellie Connally, Bobby Shelton, Tio Kleberg, and Librado Maldonado with a King Ranch Santa Gertrudis bull. Courtesy of King Ranch.

installed at the John B. Ragland Mercantile Company Building, 201 E. Kleberg Avenue, now listed in the National Register of Historic Places.

Next a group of women in town formed an artisan's co-op. They set up in a vacant building in town to sell arts and crafts and baked goods, and soon craftsmen from all over the area joined them. A huge leg up occurred when Kingsville was chosen for a Texas Main Street designation during the state sesquicentennial celebration and was in the program from 1982 to 1985. A renovation of historical buildings was soon begun. The City of Kingsville commissioned a tourism agency funded with the hotel tax, about $40,000 that year. That funding would climb to $130,000 over a five-year period, but this was no accident.

The Main Street program advised that to restore a historic street to viability, a successful business was needed at each end as anchors. An H-E-B grocery store was already located in town, and H-E-B chairman and CEO Charles Butt was contemplating a new one, the site uncertain. Other businesses were moving out to the loop. Butt began sending Charles Blackburn, head of real estate development for the chain, to every Main Street hearing before the city commission and the public. Blackburn observed the work that had been done to get both a historic district designation and historical designations for buildings, including the Ragland Building, which, when restored to its original condition, could be one anchor.

A fortunate decision for Kingsville was that Charles Butt opted to keep his store in town. He bought the quarter block next to the old store, including several retail buildings housing insurance offices and the like, tore them down, and built the flagship of his new concept for the H-E-B chain. It was the first of the H-E-B "Super Stores." It became the other very important anchor for the Main Street project. King Ranch moved the Saddle Shop from the old lumber company to 201 East Kleberg Avenue, and its profits increased tenfold almost immediately. The revitalization of Kingsville was under way, hand in hand with the growth of tourism on the Ranch.

THE DUMBWAITER

One of the more humorous stories the Klebergs recounted about the meteoritic rise in sales at the King Ranch Saddle Shop, from $1,000 to $10,000 a day, was the story of the dumbwaiter. The demands for sales at the Saddle Shop were overwhelming because the Ranch started scheduling more tours than even Beto and Leonard Stiles could handle. So the Ranch hired Amanda Alvarez, along with other college students who had grown up on the Ranch, to help out over at the Visitor Center. But the Saddle Shop was even more overwhelmed

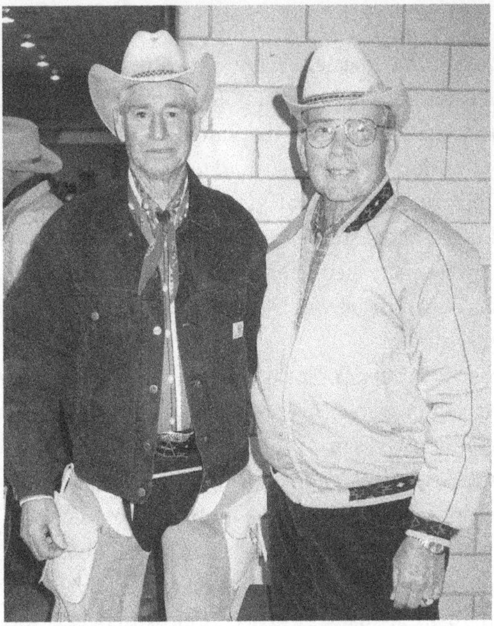

Albert V. "Lolo" Treviño (*left*) and Beto Maldonado helped facilitate the first King Ranch bus tours initiated in 1990. Beto led the tours, and Lolo demonstrated vaquero skills to visitors at the Plomo Pens. Photo by Catalina Maldonado Yaklin.

with customers, and Jamene Toelkes and anyone who was free came to help. There was one cash register in the beginning, and people lined up out the door to check out. Sometimes Janell and Tio would be there until midnight, changing the windows or ringing up sales, especially on Christmas Eve, when people who had forgotten came to get a gift or gift card. Customers would come from out of town and call, and no matter what time it was, Tio and Janell would go down and take care of the customers.

One Christmas Eve the couple were down at the Saddle Shop, taking care of last-minute pickups. Much of their inventory was in the basement or on the third floor, and a dumbwaiter made servicing the retail shop on the second floor much easier. This night Tio unknowingly locked the door to the basement while Janell was down there, and he left the building. When Janell, dog tired, put her hand on that doorknob to come to the second floor, it was totally unresponsive—not a good thing to happen on Christmas Eve just before midnight when you still have to do Christmas for kids at home. Thoroughly exasperated, Janell didn't hesitate to climb into the dumbwaiter and pull herself up by the pulleys to the second floor, where she had access to the exit. But it was not a happy time. Janell said, "I was so mad! It's like, Tio, you locked the door to the basement and I'm down there getting . . ." And by that time Tio, Janell, Beto, and the authors were laughing so hard, she couldn't finish the story.

SPECIAL EVENTS WERE A MUST

The Main Street program indicated that special events were a must to attract tourists and bring in cash for sustaining the renovation program. Among several special events added to the tourism plan was the Ranch Hand Breakfast, started in 1991 as a way to attract visitors to Kingsville and to pay for Christmas lights downtown, including lights for every animal, vehicle, and person in the night parade, even hundreds of high school students. The lighting of downtown Kingsville and the night parade were patterned after the Wonderland of Lights in Marshall, Texas, with generous assistance from leaders of that program, and this festive special event continues today.

At the Ranch Hand Breakfast, members of local civic groups, businesses, and neighbors such as Naval Air Station personnel cook and serve the breakfast of eggs, refried beans, biscuits and gravy, sausage, tortillas, coffee, and juice. The breakfast is held on the Saturday before Thanksgiving at the Ranch arena, where team roping, horseshoeing, rawhide braiding, and cow camp cooking demonstrations are part of the activities. Lined up way ahead of time, guests are greeted by Kineños stoking a campfire keeping a coffeepot steaming hot, while others on horseback guide them to ample parking space. Approximately 5,000 attended the breakfast in 2007. All profits from the breakfast are earmarked for City of Kingsville projects.

But the first Ranch Hand Breakfast did not go so smoothly. Janell Kleberg described a humorous and hectic scene:

> We were trying to break eggs one at a time at this first one here in the parking lot, and we had *a* coffeepot—we tried to do it the old way. I mean, you couldn't make it fast enough. George Meyer was in the restaurant business, ran GEM's Restaurants, and he said, "They have eggs already cracked in cartons that you can just pour in the skillet. You can buy these biscuits already done and kinda brown 'em—you know, commercial style." So George saved us, because we were expecting maybe 50, and we had 150. He went to his restaurant and got probably two gallons of eggs, and we poured them in there and saved ourselves. George said, "If you're gonna do this, there's an easier way. I can order. Just tell me how many people you want to feed with the biscuits and the sausage and all that. I can do that."

Like Beto says, "That's where you get to visit with your friends and make more friends." In addition, guests may choose to spend the rest of the day on one of the Ranch tours, have lunch in town at one of the restaurants, and shop in a number of attractive retail businesses.

Tales
of
the
Wild
Horse
Desert
B 15
Tales of the Wild Horse Desert
A musical play featuring South Texas ranching history
Texas A&M University-Kingsville Jones Auditorium
8 p.m. November 18
B 15
Sponsored by King Ranch, Inc.
Texas A&M University-Kingsville and Kingsville Volunteers
Proceeds donated to Kingsville Community Projects

For the City of Kingsville's eightieth birthday celebration, Janell Kleberg enlisted the help of the Texas A&M University Theater Department in producing a musical history of the city. The 10,000 tickets sold each year for two years helped restore the old opera house. Courtesy of Beto Maldonado.

The city continued its quest for visitors by creating special events of sufficient interest to merit publicity in newspapers in Kingsville and Corpus Christi. The City of Kingsville's eightieth birthday was a perfect opportunity for Janell Kleberg to research the history of the founding of Kingsville and write the story, enlist the expertise of Dave Deacon of the Texas A&M Theater Department to create a script, and the Music Department to write the music for *Tales of the Wild Horse Desert*. The history-based musical with a cast of 250 Kineños and townspeople, from age eighty to a baby born during the run, played to standing-room-only crowds at the Texas A&I Jones Auditorium during two weekends for two years. Proceeds from the 10,000 tickets sold each year saved the university's faltering theater department and went a long way toward restoring the old opera house. Special guests attending the musical were Ranch retirees, including Beto. "We had the two front rows reserved at every performance, and we spaced it out and gave two tickets to every single retired person from the Ranch," said Janell. "And every one of them came." Beto has the signatures of all the retirees who attended and laments that at least two-thirds of them are gone now.

Since the King Ranch Visitor Center opened in 1990, management has sought the best possible tour guides to be the face of the Ranch and to exhibit the same hospitality for which King Ranch has been known for more than 150 years. Beto Maldonado remains a master guide for tours and for other public occasions as needed.

> Beto was already on board because we knew, from the sales and from his father's genetics, that he knew how to manage people and livestock. So we knew we had Beto we could count on to develop these [tours] so that they fit within historical parameters of the way that people were used to being hosted at King Ranch.
>
> JANELL KLEBERG

THE VISITOR CENTER

Cathy Henry, a twenty-nine-year employee of King Ranch, is in charge of the Visitor Center, including guided tours. Her history major comes in handy as she trains the guides to include the historical significance of the Ranch while pointing out significant sites and relaying factual information. A number of the guides are Kineños who grew up on the Ranch, retired employees, or retired teachers from the Santa Gertrudis Independent School District, and they know a great deal about the Ranch. Instead of following a set script, guides are encouraged to add their own personal stories and experiences along with the remarkable history of King Ranch, so no two tours are exactly alike.

A U.S. map and a world map are posted on a bulletin board in the Visitor Center, and when visitors come in, they can stick a pin on their home location, an interesting, economical way to do quick research without bothering guests with questions or forms to fill out. Men, women, and children of all ages come for the tours. The youngest of record was two weeks old, and the oldest had reached one hundred years and was very proud of it. Offered a lift to board the bus, he declined, "If you don't rush me, I can get on just fine," and that he did.

Visitors learn that the Ranch was named a National Historic Landmark in 1961. This designation is not one that is sought with pages of documentation and recommendations but is awarded, unsolicited, by the U.S. Department of the Interior to locations that have great significance in American history. King Ranch no doubt received this prestigious award because of its reputation as "the cradle of the ranching industry" in the United States.

When asked about working with Beto, Cathy Henry had this to say:

> Well, he's a gentleman, knowledgeable, articulate, unassuming but confident. We all go through life, but some of us don't think about it as we're going through it. Beto does, and he has a terrific memory. He thinks seriously and he remembers accurately—what a great combination.
>
> People like Beto's tours. We get calls for him many, many times from people who have taken a tour or have a friend, and they want Beto as their guide. They say, "Is he available? Can we get him?" We always try to fill those requests.

Beto Maldonado (behind the counter) welcomes Jorja Kimball, chamber of commerce manager, and Ruben "Spike" Garcia to the King Ranch Visitor Center in preparation for its opening in January 1990. Clipping courtesy of Beto Maldonado.

Cathy Henry, director of the King Ranch Visitor Center, examines the identification buttons Beto Maldonado used for entrance into cattle shows across the United States and in several foreign countries. Photo by Betty Bailey Colley.

Mary Lewis Kleberg, the widow of Richard M. Kleberg Jr. and the mother of Tio Richard III, Scott, and Sally Kleberg, said this about Beto's work with the Ranch tours: "Talking about tourism, he [Beto] knows the most. He is one of a kind. He has the gift of gab."

Beto retired from working the A-Herds the same year the Visitor Center opened, and he was immediately chosen to lead tours in the Ranch's new venture. He continues to make a name for himself as the jovial, knowledgeable ambassador for King Ranch. He conducts mostly private tours these days, often by specific request, and his passengers have come from across the United States and from nineteen foreign countries, among them Germany, Canada, Italy, North Africa, and Mexico.

I GOT TO MEET A LOT OF PEOPLE

This is what happened. In 1990 I retired. At that time they wanted me to work part-time with the Ranch in public relations, occasionally with a special auction sale, and what have you. But I wound up with the Visitor Center, and I've been there the last eighteen years. Tommy Cornelius and I were the only ones who gave tours in the beginning, and Leonard Stiles helped us after he retired. I remember when we started those tours, we would run them about an hour and a half. We were sacked with so many tours that by the time we got back, they would ask me if I could go on another one, and I would say, "Well, let me go get a drink of water and I'll do the next one."

I got to meet a lot of people from all over the world. The oldest one I had was a hundred years old. He came all dressed up in a khaki outfit with a cowboy hat, and he stood straight up. He came with his daughter.

What I do now is half-day tours and take two or three people in a vehicle; the private tours started soon after we opened in '90. I actually took Mr. Beretta on a tour last year. Mr. Beretta is from Italy, and his family has manufactured those firearms for the past three hundred years. I also gave a tour to the people doing the repair work on the stained glass in the Main House—the whole crew from Conrad Schmidt Studios from New Berlin, Wisconsin. Jim Walton, [Wal-Mart founder] Sam Walton's brother, took my tour. And I had an assistant editor, Susan Hawthorne Nash, of *Southern Living* one time and she wrote me a letter, and this is part of what she said:

> It was the tour you gave us of the great Ranch that added color and richness to the story I wrote about the Ranch. . . . Beto, it is Kineños like you that have truly made King Ranch a legend. Thank you again for sharing your thoughts and experiences so freely.

When President [George H. W.] Bush came to make a speech and give out diplomas at Texas A&I [in June 1990], I was put in charge of guiding the White House Press Corps and taking them around. There were four of them. I picked them up in a Ranch Suburban at the Naval Air Station, where the president's plane—Air Force One—landed, and took them to Javelina Stadium and then back to the plane. I remember it was pretty well guarded where the plane was going to land, and anybody who was going to do anything there had to go through a little gate for security. As a matter of fact, I went through that gate two or three times. Dr. Lauro F. Cavazos Jr., who was secretary of education and the first Mexican American to serve in a president's cabinet, was with President Bush that day. His father was Lauro Cavazos Sr., who at one time was foreman of the Santa Gertrudis Division.

During the Ranch's 150th anniversary celebration in 2003, four people were picked to work in that field [public relations], and I was one of them. I was assigned to three or four people who were from a company that was hired to make videotapes for members of the family only. I was the guide and took them around where they needed to go. I introduced them to people that I know and

Beto Maldonado proudly displays the ring presented to him in 1990 by King Ranch for fifty years of service. Photo by Catalina Maldonado Yaklin.

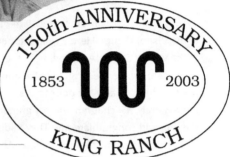

150th ANNIVERSARY
1853 2003
KING RANCH

King Ranch employees and retirees continue to be an integral part of Ranch life and are included during celebrations such as the 150th anniversary of the Ranch. Courtesy of Beto Maldonado.

C. Bryan Stuckey, D.V.M.

September 28, 2004

Albert Maldonado
P.O. box 5038
Kingsville, TX 78363

Dear Beto,

Julie and I cannot find the words to express how we feel about the wonderful time we spent with you Friday, September 3, on the Ranch tour. Our daughter could not have chosen a nicer anniversary gift. You helped make the Tour Day one of the most memorable days of our lives. Seeing my longtime friend and colleague, Dr. John Tolkes, and "Badger" were just icing on the cake.

The deep feelings you have for the Ranch are expressed in every word you speak. I wish we could have a week to spend touring the Ranch with you as our guide. We hope the Ranch and the visitors you take on tour realize what an irreplaceable treasure you truly are. Please continue sharing your memories and character with the rest of the world. We remembered your mentioning how much you liked Rudy' Bar-B-Q, so as a token of our deepest appreciation for the great day you gave us, accept the gift certificates to Rudy's and enjoy the time with your family when in San Antonio. If you like and have the time, call ahead and we will meet you there, as it is only 10 minutes from our home in Boerne.

We have two requests that came to mind while touring with you. The first and most important is we would like to have an autographed copy of your book when it is published. If you will let us know when it is ready, we will come to the Ranch to visit and pay for the book. **For history's sake, please finish the book.** The second request is that when you get the video of the "twin" D-8 Caterpillars demonstrating the brush control, we would like to have a copy for our family. As you said, these were the first and only ones to have ever been used in this manner. What an engineering feat and important part of our Texas history.

Thank you again for a most memorable day.

Sincerely,

Bryan & Julie

Bryan and Julie Stuckey

Letter courtesy of C. Bryan Stuckey, DVM.

members of the [Ranch] family, and they would ask them questions. We spent some time at the Main House, taking pictures and me telling them all about the house. I took them over to the auction sale grounds. We would walk to one of the foremen, introduce them, and they [the video crew] would talk to them and ask them questions, and they kept on going to other people, and my family too. We stood at the auction sale, and they taped a lot of the animals that were going through the auction ring.

FIFTY YEARS' SERVICE

In 1990, I was actually presented with my ring for fifty years' service to the Ranch at the Visitor Center. Here's what happened. One day I was called to a meeting at the Visitor Center. As usual, I got there early and noticed that no other people were there for the meeting. I kept waiting and nobody came, and I didn't know what to think. Finally the door to the video room opened, and there was my entire family, my children and my grandchildren; they had come to see me get the ring and congratulate me. They had parked their cars behind the building so I would not know they were there. Anyway, Jody Gabbert was in charge of the Visitor Center then and she presented the ring to me, and we had cakes, cookies, and punch, and I am still real proud of that ring. It is a gold ring with seven diamonds and the Running W. For forty-five years' service, the Ranch gave me an oval tie pin with three diamonds and the Running W on it.

INSIDE THE MAIN HOUSE

One of the first times I went to the Main House was to help Leroy Curry do something in the house for a special occasion or whatever. Later we got together for a Christmas party, and all of the people that worked at the Tourism Department had dinner there. They gave us a tour of the house. We also got a tour, and they took us all around when they were restoring the building, so we could talk about it on the tours.

Hundreds of visitors to King Ranch have heard Beto's upbeat, good-natured storytelling as he points out major points of interest that mirror his life on King Ranch. He hosts more than a hundred guests a year. Over the years, many of these guests have said to Beto, "You have to write a book." To have his and his father's story on King Ranch written became Beto's second dream. *The Master Showmen of King Ranch* is the realization of that dream.

EPILOGUE

THE MALDONADO FAMILY TODAY

Beto and Dora Maldonado still live on King Ranch in the same house that was built for them in 1949, and Beto's sister Alicia lives next door in the house originally built for Librado and Ella Maldonado. One of Beto's twin sisters, Amelia, lives in Kingsville. His brothers, Plácido and Librado Jr. (Lee), and his sister Aurora are deceased.

The Maldonado family remains very close, with almost daily contact with each other. The oldest daughter, Dora Maldonado Garcia, and her husband, Joe T. (Chepe), live in Kingsville next door to the younger son, Samuel (Sammy), and his wife, Jo Anne. Samantha Garcia Castillo (Dora and Chepe's daughter) and her family live nearby. The older son, Alberto Jr. (Tico), retired after thirty years as a manager with AT&T, lives in San Antonio. Norma Maldonado Quintanilla, the middle daughter, works in banking, and she and her husband, Onisimo, who is a teacher, live in McAllen, Texas, as do their two children, Monica Lee and Mario and his family. The youngest daughter, Catalina "Cata" Maldonado Yaklin, has been employed by King Ranch since 1974, even before she graduated from high school. She and her husband, Pete, live in Riviera, Texas, with their two children, Tracy Renee and Daniel.

When he is not leading private tours at the Ranch or catching up on news with his friends in town, Beto does the shopping and helps Dora make tamales, still her favorite pastime, other than their frequent visits with family members, including five grandchildren and three great grandchildren. Or he might occasionally check his coins he has been collecting for at least fifty years, since back before President John F. Kennedy's time. Most of Beto and Dora's evenings are spent watching television until around 10:30. Now that some of their favorite programs such as *Bonanza, Ed Sullivan, Name That Tune, To Tell the Truth,* and *The Lawrence Welk Show* are no longer broadcast, their favorite program is one from Peru that is broadcast in twenty-five countries.

Beto and his family have witnessed sweeping changes on King Ranch. A management corporation now operates the Ranch as a more diversified business; when Tio Kleberg resigned his position as vice president and took a seat on the board in 1998, it was the first time since Captain King established the Ranch in 1853 that a family member was not involved in the daily management of the Ranch. By 1991 the foreign and non-Texas properties had been liquidated except for the 20,000-acre Florida farming operation, and the number of employees on the Ranch reduced from around 1,200 fifty years ago to about 300 today, of which only 45 are cowboys (Gwynne 124). Third and fourth generations of vaqueros working thousands of cattle from horseback in a boiling cloud of dirt have been replaced by helicopters that coax cattle to pens in a half day instead of a week, with the help of just a few cowboys on horseback. Branding irons are electric now. Though the quality remains the same, there are fewer cattle and horses on the Ranch now; the number of cattle is down from 95,000 in 1925 to 33,000 in 2007. The camp houses are closed, standing like mute monuments to men who worked from before sunup to sundown from the saddle, often for weeks at a time. Now such men come home at night, thanks to modern ways of handling cattle, pickup trucks, and miles and miles of paved roads. Chuck wagons, those portable prairie diners from which the tantalizing smells of camp bread and fresh beef sizzling over an open fire signaled mealtime for the vaqueros, are now retired. One is in the King Ranch Museum in the Henrietta Memorial Center in Kingsville, and perhaps one or two are in a barn, where they are dusted off for display on special occasions.

One thing that has not changed is the pride of Beto Maldonado in his lifelong association with King Ranch, still one of the most famous and successful ranches in the world.

KING RANCH TODAY

King Ranch continues its leadership of exemplary ranch management into the twenty-first century. Santa Gertrudis cattle, the Ranch's premier contribution to cattle breeding, now thrive in harsh ranching climates all over the world and remain the most prevalent breed of cattle in Australia. The composite breed King Ranch Santa Cruz, developed over a ten-year period, is testament to the Ranch's sensitivity and response to changing market preferences. As of 2006, approximately three hundred Quarter Horses remained part of the cutting-horse breeding and development program.[1]

While maintaining its legendary ranching enterprise, the Ranch continues to diversify. Farming enterprises in Texas and Florida include cotton, milo, sod, sugarcane, vegetables (sweet corn, green beans, and specialty lettuce), and citrus fruit; King Ranch is the largest orange juice producer in the United States, with 40,000 tree-planted acres in Florida (King Ranch website).

In the fall of 2006 the Ranch announced the acquisition of Young Pecan Shelling Company, one of the largest pecan-shelling facilities in the United States. With processing housed in Las Cruces, New Mexico, and distribution facilities in Florence, South Carolina, the company sells processed pecans to major food processing companies, wholesalers, club stores, and grocery retailers. In August 2007, Jack Hunt, president and CEO of King Ranch, Inc., announced the acquisition of Turf Grass America, making the company the largest grower of turf grass in Texas and one of the largest in the country; Turf Grass America has a farm in Bastrop, with distribution centers in Bulverde and Austin, as well as other locations in Texas and across the South (*San Antonio Express-News*).

As a result of the Ranch's historical allegiance to stewardship of the ecosystem, it is a mecca for hunters, with arguably the largest population of wild bobwhite quail and white-tailed deer on a single ranch in the country, as well as an abundance of deer, wild turkey, quail, javelina, wild hog, and nilgai antelope. King Ranch is considered the birthplace of Texas game conservation because of its deliberate game management initiatives, begun in 1910 when deer and wild turkey had been almost eliminated in South Texas due to unregulated hunting. While a majority of wildlife acreage is leased for private recreational hunting, guided hunting tours are also available to the general public.

In the interest of continuing a state-of-the art ranching industry, King Ranch has moved into the field of education. The Caesar Kleberg Wildlife Research Institute, established in 1981 to honor the pioneer of wildlife habitat enhancement programs on the Ranch and in the state of Texas, is located at Texas A&M University–Kingsville. It attracts researchers, educators, and students from a variety of disciplines who study a myriad of wildlife topics.

In 2003, in commemoration of the 150th anniversary of King Ranch, the Ranch, its family, and friends established the King Ranch Institute for Ranch Management at Texas A&M–Kingsville. The mission of the institute is the training of experienced graduate students in a unique and multidisciplinary systems approach to ranch management, along with the ability to think their way through to success and innovation for the industry (King Ranch website).

Today the Ranch's retail businesses include the King Ranch Saddle Shop, Robstown Hardware Company (established 1913), Kingsville Publishing, and tourism.

NOTE

1. From Joe Roybal, "Not That Complicated," *BEEF*, December 1, 2006. Reprinted with permission of Penton Business Media. Copyright 2006. All rights reserved.

APPENDIX A

Individuals Interviewed

Castillo, Samantha Jo Garcia—daughter of Dora Maldonado Garcia and Joe Garcia and granddaughter of Dora and Beto Maldonado; works at the King Ranch Saddle Shop.

Due, Sonia Garcia—daughter of Dora Maldonado Garcia and Joe Garcia and granddaughter of Dora and Beto Maldonado; worked as a tour guide in the King Ranch Visitor Center while attending Texas A&I.

Garcia, Dora Maldonado—oldest daughter of Dora and Beto Maldonado; worked for King Ranch.

Garcia, Francis—facilitated the interview with Alberto Maldonado Jr.

Garcia, Veronica—daughter of Dora and Joe Garcia and granddaughter of Beto and Dora Maldonado; holds a master's degree in agriculture and is academic adviser of the Dick and Mary Lewis Kleberg College of Agriculture, Natural Resources and Human Sciences at Texas A&M University–Kingsville.

Groves, Helen Kleberg—daughter of Robert J. Kleberg Jr. and an accomplished horsewoman who remembers playing with Kineño children as a child on King Ranch.

Henry, Cathy—director of the King Ranch Visitor Center.

Kleberg, Janell Gerald—accomplished horsewoman, photographer, author, and wife of Stephen J. "Tio" Kleberg.

Kleberg, Mary Lewis Scott—widow of Richard M. Kleberg Jr. and mother of Tio, Richard III, Scott, and Sally Kleberg.

Kleberg, Sally—daughter of Mary Lewis and Richard M. Kleberg Jr. and great-great-granddaughter of Captain Richard King.

Kleberg, Stephen J. "Tio"—great-great-grandson of Captain Richard King, son of Richard M. and Mary Lewis Kleberg, member of the American Quarter Horse Hall of Fame, vice president for agribusiness for King Ranch (1988–1998), and presently a member of the board of directors, King Ranch, Inc.

Maldonado, Alberto, Jr.—older son of Dora and Beto Maldonado and grandson of Librado Maldonado.

Maldonado, Alberto "Beto," Sr. —son of Librado and Ella Maldonado who was born on King Ranch and, like his father, became a master showman of King Ranch Santa Gertrudis bulls.

Maldonado, Alicia—sister of Beto Maldonado who has lived next door to him all of his life.

Maldonado, Dora Ruiz—wife of Beto Maldonado for almost six decades.

Maldonado, Jo Anne C.—wife of Sammy Maldonado who, along with Sammy, graciously opened their home for interviews for this book.

Maldonado, Samuel "Sammy"—son of Dora and Beto Maldonado; furnished valuable information and family recipes for this book.

Marshall, R. P.—executive director of Santa Gertrudis Breeders International until he joined King Ranch as director of marketing in 1971.

Moncrief, Monte, DVM—veterinarian at King Ranch (1949–1979); worked closely with Beto and Librado Maldonado.

Parish, Norman—animal physiologist at King Ranch (1962–1986); worked closely with Beto Maldonado.

Parish, Seba—wife of Norman Parish; worked for Santa Gertrudis Breeders International as a statistical analyst.

Perez, Aurora Maldonado—sister of Beto Maldonado and twin sister of Amelia Maldonado Alvarado.

Quintanilla, Norma Maldonado—daughter of Dora and Beto Maldonado.

Silguero, José—right-hand man to Librado Maldonado; helped Beto with the auction sale bulls after Librado died.

Toelkes, Jamene—wife of Dr. John Toelkes and former employee of the King Ranch Archives.

Toelkes, John, DVM—King Ranch veterinarian.

Yaklin, Catalina Maldonado—daughter of Dora and Beto Maldonado; has worked with King Ranch since she was a junior in high school in 1974.

APPENDIX B

Individuals Referenced

Acevedo, Daniel—worked as a cook in cowboy camps on King Ranch for many years and on retirement opened his own restaurant, the Royal Café, in Kingsville, where Beto and his friends often ate before attending movies.

Alvarado, Amelia Maldonado—daughter of Librado and Ella Maldonado and twin sister of Aurora Maldonado Perez.

Alvarez, Amanda—worked at the King Ranch Visitor Center, the Henrietta Memorial Center, and the King Ranch Saddle Shop.

Amaya, Manuel—filled milk cans for the people at Headquarters and the commissary when King Ranch had a Jersey dairy; also worked as a clerk at the commissary.

Anderson, Billy—a good buddy of Beto's when the two were in New York visiting the King Ranch's racing operation.

Anderson, Oscar—may have observed Librado Maldonado's ability handling Jerseys at a livestock show and offered him a job with King Ranch.

Armstrong, John—husband of Henrietta Kleberg Larkin and former vice president and president of King Ranch.

Armstrong, Tobin—rancher and brother of John Armstrong; attended King Ranch auctions.

Bass, Perry—built an oil fortune with his uncle Sid W. Richardson and attended King Ranch Santa Gertrudis cattle auctions.

Batista, Fulgencio—called by some a dictator whose Cuban government was overthrown by Fidel Castro in 1959.

Beretta, Giuseppe—an owner of the Beretta Holding Group of Italy, a firearms business dating back to 1526; took one of Beto Maldonado's private tours.

Blackburn, Charles—head of real estate development for H-E-B grocery stores when the chain's first superstore was built in downtown Kingsville.

Bowie, Gerald—auctioneer for the first airborne cattle auction to Hawaii and the U.S. Bicentennial Santa Gertrudis sales at the Adolphus Hotel in Dallas and the Shamrock Hilton in Houston.

Bracher, Bob—writer for the *Santa Gertrudis Journal*.

Braga, George A.—joint partner with King Ranch in a ranching operation in Cuba.

Briggs, Mrs. Robert—member of the Briggs Syndicate; often attended King Ranch auctions and stayed at the Main House.

Britten, Colonel Walter—auctioneer at every King Ranch auction (1950–1985).

Burford, Bill—represented the Texas Art Gallery at the Santa Gertrudis/art auction at the Adolphus Hotel in Dallas, 1976.

Butchofsky, Robert, DVM—football teammate of Dr. Monte Moncrief at Texas A&M whom Moncrief was telephoning when the train, with Assault and the jockey, left Moncrief behind in El Paso.

Butt, Charles—of H-E-B grocery stores; built the flagship of his new concept of H-E-B superstores in downtown Kingsville.

Byington, Alfredo and Anna Belle—Beto Maldonado's uncle and aunt who were his attendants at his wedding to Dora.

Byington, Allie—sister of Sammy Byington and Beto Maldonado's aunt; was a *padrina* at Beto's first Communion.

Byington, Sammy—Ella Byington Maldonado's brother; a *padrino* at the first Communion of his nephew Beto Maldonado.

Caldera, Robert—weaver of King Ranch saddle blankets; returned to the Ranch to weave saddle blankets for Visitor Center tours.

Cantu, Ambroso "Sambo"—seventh-grade student who helped Beto Maldonado cover his book on Beto's first day of school.

Castillo, Rudy—husband of Samantha Garcia Castillo.

Castillo, Samantha Garcia—daughter of Dora and Chepe Garcia and granddaughter of Dora and Beta Maldonado.

Cavazos, Lauro F., Jr.—son of Lauro Cavazos Sr. and U.S. Secretary of Education (1988–1990).

Cavazos, Lauro F., Sr.—first Mexican American to serve as a King Ranch foreman; foreman of Santa Gertrudis Division (1926–1958).

Cavazos, Steve—helped Beto Maldonado and Tomás Rodriguez identify names of uninvited attendees at the Kineño Christmas dances.

Chamberlain, Hiram—an ordained Presbyterian missionary who brought his daughter, Henrietta, to Brownsville, Texas, in 1850 to establish the first Protestant church on the Rio Grande. Henrietta became the bride of Captain Richard King.

Chapa, Adolpho—served camp bread cooked according to his own recipe to visitors at the beginning of King Ranch tours in 1990.

Cheeseman, Bruce—author and former archivist at King Ranch.

Clegg, George—sold a colt later named Old Sorrel to King Ranch; Old Sorrel became the foundation sire for the King Ranch Quarter Horse family.

Clement, Illa—wife of James H. "Jim" Clement Sr., who was president of King Ranch (1974–1987).

Clement, James H. "Jim," Sr.—president of King Ranch (1974–1987).

Clement, Leslie—daughter of James H. Clement Jr. and Illa Clement.

Clements, William "Bill"—two-term governor of Texas (1979–1983, 1987–1991).

Clyde, Allen M., Jr.—son of Clyde M. Allen Sr.; worked with his father in the Allen Furniture Company business.

Clyde, Allen M., Sr.—owner of the Allen Furniture Company, which was also used for a funeral home.

Collins, Tilford—from San Antonio; catered some of the Friday night parties before the King Ranch auctions on Saturday.

Conard, Scott—owner of Young's Pizza who catered lunches for tourists during King Ranch Visitor Center tours in the 1990s.

Connally, John—thirty-eighth governor of the State of Texas (1963–1969) and a Santa Gertrudis breeder who often attended King Ranch auctions.

Cornelius, Tommy—conducted tours at the King Ranch Visitor Center when it opened in 1990.

Cortez, Alfredo—a groom who delivered a horse to Chicago at the same time Beto Maldonado delivered a horse to Santa Ana, California.

Cortez, Herman and Lina—hosted Beto and Librado in their home in New York when Librado and Beto returned from Morocco; Herman was a groom for King Ranch racehorses.

Crocker, Emert—foreman of the Santa Gertrudis Division for whom Tio Kleberg worked when he returned from the U.S. Army to work on King Ranch in 1971.

Cude, Susan—secretary and meticulous record keeper for the King Ranch Quarter Horse operation.

Curry, Leroy—lived and worked at the Main House and helped with the King Ranch auction Friday night parties.

Davey, Martin L., Jr.—wrote a letter of thanks to Tio Kleberg for handling of his cattle purchase following a King Ranch auction.

Deacon, Dave—member of the Texas A&M University–Kingsville theater department; helped create a script and music for *Tales of the Wild Horse Desert.*

Diaz, Nick—coordinator of the Ranch's Christmas party for the Kineños.

Dobie, J. Frank—American folklorist and writer who depicted life in Texas during the days of the open range.

Douglas, Larue—owned a ranch in Georgetown, Texas, where Beto and Macho [Santa Gertrudis bull] spent the night on the way to the Dallas/Fort Worth Airport to "buy" Macho a ticket to Hawaii.

du Pont, William—flew his private plane to King Ranch to attend auctions.

East, Robert—rancher and member of the King family who attended the first King Ranch auction in 1950.

East, Sarita—of Kenedy Ranch; attended the first King Ranch auction in 1950.

East, Tom—rancher and member of the King family who attended the first King Ranch auction in 1950.

Egan, William, Jr.—veterinarian inspecting cattle coming in and out of the United States at the Port of Houston when Librado and Beto took Santa Gertrudis bulls to Morocco.

Egan, William, Sr.—racehorse trainer at King Ranch.

Ellis, Gary, Mrs.—Beto Maldonado's first-grade teacher at the school on the Santa Gertrudis Division of King Ranch.

Embruck, Delia—one of Beto Maldonado's teachers when he started school on the Santa Gertrudis Division of King Ranch.

Espy, Kip—Sally Kleberg's husband; accompanied Sally, John Armstrong, and Julia and Andrew Jitkoff to Spain and Morocco to evaluate King property following the death of Bob Kleberg in 1974.

Estrade, Raul—foreman of King Ranch operations in Rabat, Morocco.

Fender, Freddy—the judge whose friend won the tamale contest when Dora Maldonado's tamales were in the finals of the Channel 3 TV station in Corpus Christi.

Gabbert, Jody—in charge of the Visitor Center and a surprise party when Beto Maldonado received a diamond ring commemorating fifty years of service with King Ranch.

Garcia, Cipriano—listened on the radio with Beto and Librado when Assault won the Kentucky Derby in 1946.

Garcia, Cipriano, Jesus, Juan, Lupe, and Samuel Jr.—children of Samuel Garcia Sr. who played baseball with Beto and his friends and family.

Garcia, Emiliano—made baskets for yarn, processed wool, and wove King Ranch saddle blankets; also was a barber.

Garcia, Joe T. "Chepe"—husband of Dora Maldonado Garcia, Beto and Dora Maldonado's daughter.

Garcia, José "Pastel"—jockey with Dr. Monte Moncrief and Assault when the train left Moncrief behind in El Paso while they were on the way to the Hollywood Gold Cup in California.

Garcia, Ramón—listened on the radio with Beto and Librado when Assault won the Kentucky Derby in 1946.

Gaytan, Juan—worked at the racing stable and brought the *Corpus Christi Caller-Times* to Beto Maldonado every day.

Gilliam, Leslie—licensed to take bets at the party celebrating fiftieth anniversary of Assault's winning the Kentucky Derby.

Godfrey, Arthur—TV star who showed Tennessee Walking Horses at the Chicago International Fair and purchased the Grand Champion steer.

Gonzales, Andre—by chance, met Plácido Maldonado in Italy as Plácido, a medic, was checking out soldiers to return home following World War II.

Gonzales, José Angel "Chancle"—one the jockeys for the kids' horse race when Helen "Helenita" Kleberg, B. K. Johnson, and Alice Kleberg competed for a box of Whitman's chocolates.

Gonzales, José "Chino"—one of the jockeys for the kids' horse race when Helen "Helenita" Kleberg, B. K. Johnson, and Alice Kleberg competed for a box of Whitman's chocolates.

Guerra, Melissa—author of *Dishes from the Wild Horse Desert.*

Gutierrez, Alejos—a vaquero who discouraged party crashers at King Ranch Christmas celebrations.

Hall, S. K. "Kid"—full-time farrier at the Thoroughbred race track.

Harrison, Steve—chairman of the organizing committee for "the World's First Airborne Cattle Auction" in 1985.

Hassan II—King of Morocco when Beto and Librado attended the International Fair in Casablanca.

Henderson, J. Y., DVM—veterinarian for Ringling Brothers and Barnum and Bailey Circus when King Ranch Quarter Horses were featured as an act.

Henderson, Minnie Rangel—Kingsville ISD board member when Beto Maldonado earned a GED certificate; sister of Irma Mae Rangel, a member of the Texas Legislature from 1977 to 2004.

Hinojosa, Charin—in charge of the sawmill where Beto Maldonado and his schoolmates went to cut wood for the heater at the school on the Santa Gertrudis Division of King Ranch.

Hirsch, Buddy—son of Max Hirsch and trainer of King Ranch Thoroughbreds in California.

Hirsch, Max—expert trainer of King Ranch Thoroughbreds in New York.

Holmes, Mona—a good friend of Bob Kleberg's who often attended King Ranch auctions and stayed at the Main House; had Santa Gertrudis cattle on Kona, Hawaii.

Hughes, Michael—in charge of King Ranch operations in Morocco and Spain when Beto and Librado flew with Santa Gertrudis bulls to Rabat, Morocco.

Hunt, Jack—president and CEO of King Ranch, Inc.

Jackson, Stout—owner of Teatro Carpa, where Beto attended movies as a young boy.

Jaramillo, Pedrito—one of the most famous *curanderos* in Mexico and South Texas; Librado and Ella Maldonado visited his shrine in Falfurrias for cures.

Jitkoff, Andrew and Julia—accompanied Sally Kleberg, John Armstrong, and Kip Espy to Spain and Morocco to evaluate King Ranch property following the death of Bob Kleberg in 1974.

Johnson, B. K.—nephew of Robert Justus "Bob" Kleberg Jr.; grew up in the home of Bob and Helen Kleberg.

Jones, Mark—author of "Librado Maldonado—Dean of Cattle Showmen," which appeared in the *Kingsville Record*, February 13, 1983.

Kenedy, Mifflin—Captain Richard King's lifelong friend, business partner, and founder of Kenedy Ranch.

Kennedy, C. Bernard—helped Clyde M. Allen with the mortuary business, a part of the Allen Furniture Company.

King, Henrietta Chamberlain—wife of Captain Richard King, founder of King Ranch.

King, Captain Richard—founder of King Ranch in 1853.

King, Richard, II—son of Captain Richard King and Henrietta Chamberlain King.

Kleberg, Alice King—youngest daughter of Captain Richard King and Henrietta Chamberlain King.

Kleberg, Helen Campbell—wife of Robert Justus Kleberg Jr., who ran King Ranch from 1918 to 1974.

Kleberg, Mamie—wife of Richard Kleberg Sr.

Kleberg, Richard Mifflin, Jr.—great-grandson of Captain Richard King and chairman the board of King Ranch (1969–1979).

Kleberg, Richard Mifflin, Sr.—son of Robert Justus Kleberg Sr. and Alice King Kleberg; he served in Congress (1931–1944).

Kleberg, Robert Justus, Jr., "Mr. Bob"—grandson of Captain Richard King who ran King Ranch (1918–1974).

Kleberg, Robert Justus, Sr.—son-in-law of Captain Richard King and Henrietta Chamberlain King.

Lasater, Ed—a premier breeder of Jersey cattle on Lasater Ranch near Falfurrias, where Librado Maldonado lived and worked as a vaquero as a young boy.

Lea, Tom—wrote and illustrated the two-volume history *The King Ranch*, published in 1957.

Lee, General Robert E.—helped his best friend, Captain Richard King, select the site for his home on King Ranch.

Lewis, Gideon K. "Legs"—a Texas Ranger who was Captain King's first ranching partner; at his death in 1855, owned half interest with King in the Rincon de Santa Gertrudis and the Santa Gertrudis de la Garza grants.

Maldonado, Ella Byington—wife of Librado Maldonado and mother of Beto Maldonado.

Maldonado, Librado "Lee," Jr.—Beto's younger brother; worked as a groom with King Ranch racehorses in New York until his death in 1971 at age thirty-nine.

Maldonado, Librado, Sr.—"the Master Showman" who paraded Santa Gertrudis cattle at every King Ranch auction from 1950 to 1979.

Maldonado, Lillie—wife of Plácido Maldonado.

Maldonado, Plácido—Librado's father and Beto's grandfather.

Maldonado, Plácido—oldest of Librado and Ella Maldonado's children, born September 21, 1921.

Marchman, Joe—a prominent Santa Gertrudis breeder.

Marroquin, Johnny—Dora Maldonado's uncle; introduced Dora to Beto Maldonado.

Marroquin, Lillie—Dora Maldonado's aunt; gave Dora's and Beto's wedding reception.

Marroquin, Manuela—Dora Maldonado's grandmother whom Dora was visiting in Kingsville when she met Beto Maldonado.

Marshall, Geneva—wife of R. P. Marshall

Marshall, R. P.—executive director of Santa Gertrudis Breeders International, who left that position to work for King Ranch in 1971.

Martin, John—a rancher from Alice, Texas, who attended the first King Ranch auction in 1950.

Martinez, Martín, Jr.—a vaquero who lived at Lauro's Hill on King Ranch.

Martinez, Silvero—lived at Lauro's Hill on King Ranch when Beto Maldonado was growing up.

Maud, Colonel Harry—owner of a cattle operation in Cuba.

Mayorga, George—a vaquero who took King Ranch Thoroughbreds by train to Kentucky with Dr. J. K. Northway and Beto Maldonado.

McFarland, Helen—one of the speakers at the Kentucky Derby Day Gala celebrating the fiftieth anniversary of Assault's winning the Kentucky Derby.

Mehrtens, Noreen—wife of jockey Warren Mehrtens.

Mehrtens, Warren—jockey who rode Assault to win the Kentucky Derby, the Preakness, and Belmont Stakes in 1946.

Mendietta, Candido—lived at Lauro's Hill on King Ranch when Beto Maldonado was growing up.

Mendietta, Cipriano—a vaquero who helped Beto with vaccinating horses at the Headquarters Division.

Mendietta, Martín, Jr.—a vaquero who worked with horses and cattle and was a *caporal* on the Santa Gertrudis Division for twenty years.

Mendietta, Martín, Sr.—lived at Lauro's Hill on King Ranch when Beto Maldonado was growing up.

Mendietta, Roberto—filled milk cans for the people at Rancho Plomo when King Ranch had a Jersey dairy; worked as a vaquero.

Mendietta, Serafin "Pepiño"—drove a bobtail truck and often gave Beto and his friends rides back to the Ranch following movies.

Meyer, George—owner of GEM's Restaurants who "saved" the first Ranch Hand breakfast.

Mohammad V, King of Morocco—visited Bob Kleberg Jr. at King Ranch.

Monroe, Kim—of Chesapeake, Virginia; wrote a letter complimenting Beto on his tour.

Montalvo, Elva—contributed recipe for flour tortillas in the *King Ranch Cookbook.*

Morales, Dionicio—husband of Alicia Maldonado's daughter, Mally.

Morales, Mally—daughter of Alicia Maldonado and granddaughter of Beto and Dora Maldonado.

Moreno, Ramón—son-in-law of Valentín Quintanilla.

Morris, Robert, Dr.—of the Ozark Valley Farm in Mountain Home, Arkansas; attended the first airborne cattle auction on the way to Hawaii.

Muñiz, Miguel—filled milk cans for the people at Lauro's Hill when King Ranch had a Jersey dairy; also a vaquero and a horse trainer.

Nanny, Oliver—principal of the school on the Santa Gertrudis Division of King Ranch when Beto Maldonado entered first grade.

Nash, Susan Hawthorne—an assistant editor of *Southern Living* who took Beto's tour of King Ranch.

North, John Ringling—of Ringling Brothers and Barnum and Bailey Circus; a friend of the Klebergs and Dr. J. K. Northway who called them for a recommendation when hiring veterinarian Dr. J. Y. Henderson.

Northway, J. K., DVM—longtime veterinarian at King Ranch (1916–1973).

Ochoa, Avelino, Gilberto, José, Juanita, Pablo Jr., Olidio, Pedro, and Preseliano—children of Pablo Ochoa Sr.; could make up a family baseball team when Beto Maldonado was a boy playing baseball at the end of the day.

Ochoa, Miguel—helped Librado show Jersey cattle; listened to the radio with Beto and Librado Maldonado when Assault won the Kentucky Derby in 1946.

Ochoa, Pablo, Jr.—listened to the radio with Beto and Librado Maldonado when Assault won the Kentucky Derby in 1946.

Ochoa, Pablo, Sr.—listened to the radio with Beto and Librado Maldonado when Assault won the Kentucky Derby in 1946.

Parker, Marjorie Hodgson—author of *Assault: The Crippled Champion.*

Perez, Joe Henry—Beto Maldonado's nephew from Alabama; met Beto and Librado in New York when they returned from Morocco.

Perry, Rick—forty-seventh governor of the State of Texas (elected in 2000); toured Texas A&M University–Kingsville with Veronica Garcia as his guide.

Quintanilla, Eugeñio, Sr.—allowed the Treviño brothers to leave their horses in the pen behind his house while they attended the school on the Santa Gertrudis Division of King Ranch.

Quintanilla, Mario—Norma Maldonado Quintanilla's son and Beto and Dora Maldonado's grandson.

Quintanilla, Monica Lee—Norma Maldonado Quintanilla's daughter and Beto and Dora Maldonado's granddaughter.

Quintanilla, Onesimo—husband of Norma Maldonado Quintanilla; teaches school in McAllen.

Quintanilla, Valentín, Sr.—rode horseback two miles from his home in Rancho Plomo to the dairy to get milk from Santa Gertrudis cows for Robert J. Kleberg Jr., who preferred it to milk from Jersey cows.

Rangel, Irma Mae—state representative from Kingsville (1977–2004).

Rhoad, Albert O.—internationally recognized geneticist and scientist who came to work for King Ranch in 1951; taught classes in English, Spanish, and Portuguese in North, South, and Central America and authored numerous scientific articles and two nonfiction books.

Richardson, Sid (1891–1959)—Texas oilman, cattleman, and philanthropist who attended King Ranch auctions to shop for Quarter Horses and Santa Gertrudis cattle for his ranch.

Rockefeller, Winthrop—third-generation heir to the Rockefeller oil fortune and governor of Arkansas (1967–1971); attended King Ranch auction sales to purchase Santa Gertrudis bulls for his Winrock Farms in Arkansas.

Rodriguez, Ramón—fed and brushed Assault every day after Assault retired to the Ranch in 1950.

Rodriguez, Refugio—a Kineño who was a trusted assistant to Librado Maldonado and traveled with Beto to help with the bulls at livestock shows.

Rodriguez, Ruben—helped Beto Maldonado take the bull Macho to the Dallas/Fort Worth Airport to "buy" Macho a ticket to Hawaii for the first airborne Santa Gertrudis auction.

Rodriguez, Tomás—helped Beto Maldonado and Steve Cavazos identify uninvited attendees at the Kineño Christmas dances.

Rogers, Roy—popular western movie star who visited Bob Kleberg at King Ranch several times with his movie star wife, Dale Evans.

Ruiz, Renaldo—father of Dora Maldonado.

Salazar, Edwardo—helped his brother José run Salazar Store after the death of their father, Vicente Salazar.

Salazar, José—managed Salazar Store after his father, Vicente Salazar, died.

Salazar, Nicolas—helped his brother José run Salazar Store after the death of their father, Vicente Salazar.

Salazar, Vicente—owner of Salazar Store in Falfurrias and later in Kingsville, where the Maldonados shopped.

Saldano, José—in charge of the fence crews that put up the tent for King Ranch auctions prior to construction of the permanent arena.

Salinas, Lorenzo—in charge of milk deliveries on the Ranch and to employees living in town when King Ranch had a Jersey dairy.

Secundios, Pete—a young man whom Beto Maldonado met at the Chicago International Fair in 1957; came to visit Beto at King Ranch in 1994 and 2007.

Secundios, Sue—wife of Pete Secundios; showed the grand champion steer, purchased on her honeymoon in San Antonio, at the Chicago International Fair.

Sedwick, Gene—modified commercial halters to prevent painful rubbing on the noses of cattle.

Sedwick, Jim—like his father, Gene Sedwick, he modified commercial halters to prevent painful rubbing on the noses of cattle.

Shelton, Bobby—nephew of Robert Justus "Bob" Kleberg Jr.; grew up in the home of Bob and Helen Kleberg.

Silguero, Samuel—contributed recipe for roasted armadillo in the *King Ranch Cookbook.*

Silva, Bobby—a Kineño who went with Beto Maldonado to show cattle in Coleman, Alabama, and helped him take the bull Macho to the Dallas/Fort Worth Airport.

Silva, Rogerio—vaquero who helped Beto Maldonado vaccinate horses on the Laureles Division.

Smith, R. E.—an early Santa Gertrudis owner who told his foreman to buy Monsanto, a King Ranch prize bull, no matter what the cost.

Stiles, Joe—became manager of the King Ranch horse operation in 1971.

Stiles, Leonard—foreman of the Santa Gertrudis Division of King Ranch; after his retirement, worked in the Visitor Center conducting tours.

Stivers, Joe—from San Antonio; catered some of the Friday night parties before the King Ranch auctions on Saturday.

Strange, Don—of Don Strange of Texas Inc., San Antonio; catered some of the Friday night parties before the King Ranch auctions.

Stuckey, C. Bryan, DVM—of Boerne, Texas; wrote a thank-you letter to Beto Maldonado following a King Ranch tour in September 2006.

Sublett, Collier, MD—a physician in Kingsville who expressed dismay that Kineños often treated themselves when they had health problems.

Tash, Lowell H.—manager of Compañia Ganadera Becerra in Cuba, a Santa Gertrudis cattle venture of which King Ranch was 50 percent owner.

Treviño, Alberto V. "Lolo"—a vaquero from a family on the Wild Horse Desert since before Captain King came; broke Assault, the 1946 Kentucky Derby winner.

Treviño—David, Gilberto, Pedro, Ramón, and Reymundo—brothers of "Lolo" Treviño who rode with him to school.

Treviño, Inez—Beto Maldonado's aunt with whom he lived in Kingsville while attending ninth grade at Henrietta King High School.

Walton, Jim—brother of Wal-Mart founder Sam Walton; took Beto Maldonado's private tour.

Welch, Buster—a West Texas rancher and expert horse trainer who came to help develop the King Ranch Quarter Horse commercial breeding program in 1974.

Welch, Sheila—expert horsewoman and wife of Buster Welch.

Williams, Barula—Ella Byington Maldonado's aunt who served as midwife during the birth of Ella's children.

Wortham, Gus—called an insurance tycoon and cattle baron, he attended the King Ranch Santa Gertrudis auction sales and held the Houston area's first registered Santa Gertrudis sale.

Yaklin, Daniel—son of Norma and Pete Yaklin.

Yaklin, Pete—husband of Catalina Maldonado Yaklin, Beto and Dora Maldonado's daughter.

Yaklin, Renee—daughter of Norma and Pete Yaklin.

Zapata, Juan—carpenter who made a loom and a spinning wheel from a Model T Ford steering wheel for Emiliano Garcia to use for weaving King Ranch saddle blankets.

APPENDIX C

Maldonado Family Tree

Librado Maldonado Sr. [b. April 3, 1898 d. February 10, 1983]
[m. May 20, 1920]
Ella Byington [b. June, 1898 d. March 30, 1986]

- Plácido L. Maldonado [b. September 21, 1921 d. March 18, 1993]
- Alicia Maldonado [b. June 9, 1923]
- Mally Maldonado [b. December 14, 1948]
  [m. December 30, 1964]
  Dionicio Morales
- Amelia Maldonado Alvarado [b. December 16, 1925]
- Aurora Maldonado Perez [b. December 16, 1925 d. July 31, 2008]
- Alberto "Beto" Maldonado Sr. [b. January 16, 1930]
- Librado "Lee" Maldonado Jr. [b. May 16, 1932 d. July 19, 1971]

Alberto "Beto" Maldonado Sr. [b. January 16, 1930]
[m. February 6, 1949]
Dora Ruiz [b. April 16, 1930]

- Dora Maldonado [b. November 6, 1949]
  [m. September 11, 1970]
  Joe T. "Chepe" Garcia [b. September 19,1946]

Sonia Garcia [b. February 16, 1974]
[m. August 9, 2008]
Matt Due [b. December 3, 1971]

Dylyn Due [b. August 6, 2007]

Veronica Maldonado Garcia [b. August 8, 1980]

Samantha Garcia [b. August 22, 1984]
[m. September 10, 2005]
Rudy Castillo [b. October 21, 1980]

Jose Andres Castillo [b. April 18, 2005]
Makayla Castillo [b. September 14, 2007]

Alberto Maldonado Jr. [b. April 13, 1952]

Norma Maldonado [b. December 8, 1954]
[m. April 5, 1975]
Onesimo Quintanilla [b. March 25, 1950]

Mario Quintanilla [b. September 24, 1978]
[m. October 2, 2005]
Neri De La O Rodriguez [b. January 5, 1977]

Lorraine Rodriguez [b. March 28, 1993]
Noe Rodriguez III [b. January 10, 1997]
Molly Rodriguez [b. March 15, 2000]

Monica L. Quintanilla [b. September 30, 1982]

Samuel R. Maldonado [b. August 5, 1955]
[m. February 17, 1990]
Jo Anne Cantú [b. November 7, 1967]

Catalina Maldonado [September 14, 1956]
[m. February 8, 2003]
Pete Yaklin [b. June 24, 1957]

Tracy Yaklin [b. April 12, 1990]
Daniel Yaklin [b. September 2, 1992]

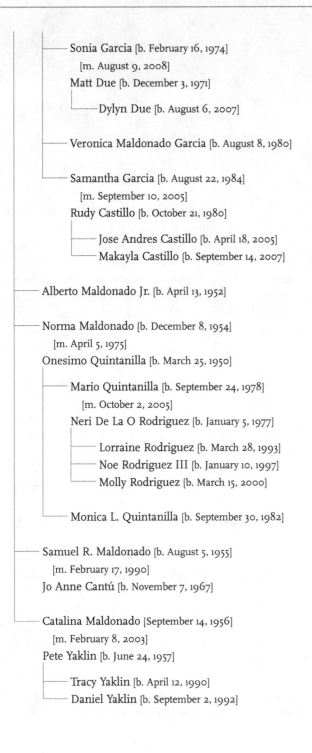

APPENDIX D

Maldonado Family Recipes: Good Food Is a Four-Generation Tradition

One of Beto's favorite memories as a child is of his mother, Ella, cooking in the kitchen. He shared how his day began as a small boy at home.

As the light broke over the horizon of the Wild Horse Desert to announce a new day, Beto smelled the wonderful odors coming from their kitchen. Ella had been up hours before the children, getting the woodstove going, preparing coffee for their dad, Librado, before he left to check on his Jersey "babies" in the barn, and beginning to prepare for the busy day ahead. When the children had completed their chores, Ella would have their breakfast of fresh flour tortillas, eggs, and potatoes ready. They also had plenty of fresh milk to drink from the dairy near the house. Ella fried crisp strips of veal to be placed in tortillas to make the taquitos the children would take to school for their lunch. Then the children were off to school.

In the middle of the day, Librado and Ella always took a break for a *merienda* about three o'clock in the afternoon. Librado worked close to the house at the dairy so he could come home. Ella would prepare coffee that had been boiled with the grounds and sugar together. She always found time to make sweets like her molasses cookies, three- or four-layer yellow cake with pineapple preserves or coconut, or—Librado's favorite—chocolate. Sometimes she made empanadas with pumpkin or pineapple filling and, of course, always a homemade crust.

Beto remembered that his mother always wore an apron and was a wonderful cook. His favorite was her lemon pie, and he said she made the best in the world. Regretfully we do not have that recipe but below you will find some of the family recipes. Ella's kitchen was filled with love, good cooking, and memories that she passed on to her children and grandchildren. The tradition of excellent cooking has continued in the family, and today two of Ella's grandchildren, Dora Garcia and Sammy Maldonado, often cater for large parties. Most of the recipes below have been shared by the family, but when we did not have one that the family especially mentioned, we have included a recipe that was similar or that came from another Wild Horse Desert cook.

BUÑUELOS

Makes 4 dozen

5 to 6 cups flour
½ teaspoon salt
½ teaspoon baking powder
3 tablespoons sugar
1 egg
½ hand of lard
1 cup water

Mix ingredients well, roll out on floured board or counter, and cut. Fry in hot grease till crispy. Sprinkle with sugar and cinnamon if desired.

ELLA MALDONADO

HOT CHOCOLATE FOR 30

Hot chocolate was the traditional drink served on special occasions like wedding receptions, after baptisms and first Communions, and at holidays like Christmas.

16 cups milk
2 cans Pet evaporated milk (3 cups)
48 teaspoons cocoa
60 teaspoons sugar

Mix cocoa and sugar together. Gradually add milk, stirring till blended, and heat.

ELLA MALDONADO

PAN DE POLVO

Makes about 500 cookies

This wonderful cinnamon-and-sugar cookie was served at most important occasions, especially at Christmas.

1 cup boiling water
4 sticks cinnamon
6 pounds flour (Gold Medal)
2 teaspoons baking powder
¼ teaspoon salt

3 pounds Mrs. Tucker or Crisco shortening, melted
½ cup sugar
¼ cup ground cinnamon

Boil cinnamon sticks with the water for 10 to 15 minutes; make it strong, remove cinnamon sticks, and keep it warm.

Put flour, baking powder, and salt in a large bowl, and mix well. Add melted shortening, and mix well.

Add the cinnamon water, and blend well. Make eight balls of dough, and blend well on board. Place wax paper on the board, place one ball of dough on top of it, and place another piece of wax paper on the top of the ball. Roll the dough until it is not too thick and not too thin, about ⅛ to ¼ inch; repeat for each ball of dough. Cut with mold of your choice. Bake in oven at 400 degrees. When the cookies look brownish, remove from oven and liberally sprinkle with sugar and cinnamon, using a large flat pan to coat the pieces.

ELLA MALDONADO

VARIATION: The following smaller recipe makes about 12 dozen.

Tea
2 cups water
2 sticks cinnamon

Dough
5 cups all-purpose flour
2¾ cup vegetable shortening
1¼ cups sugar
1½ teaspoons baking powder
1 tablespoon ground cinnamon

Sugar Topping
1 cup sugar
1 tablespoon ground cinnamon

To make the tea, boil cinnamon sticks and water in a small pan for 5 minutes. Remove the sticks, and let tea water cool.

To make the dough, combine the flour, shortening, sugar, baking powder, and ground cinnamon in a large bowl. Knead until smooth. Add ¾ cup of the cinnamon tea, and continue to knead until tender. When the dough is well combined, let it rest under a clean towel for 15 minutes. Preheat the oven to 350 degrees.

For the topping, combine the sugar and cinnamon in a shallow dish. Roll out the cookie dough on a floured surface to a ¼-inch thickness, and cut into 2-inch cookies.

Place on an ungreased cookie sheet, and bake for 12 to 15 minutes until golden in color. Roll the cookies in the sugar topping while hot, and let cool on a rack.

MELISSA GUERRA, *Dishes from the Wild Horse Desert*, 229

CHILI GUISADO

Makes 6 servings

6 ounces sliced bacon
½ medium-sized onion, chopped
1 ten-ounce can Ro-Tel tomatoes, normal or extra hot
1 eight-ounce can tomato sauce
2 tablespoons flour, cooked

Cut sliced bacon in small pieces, about 2 inches by 2 inches, and fry in a skillet or pan till well done. Remove bacon from pan. Reserve a portion of the bacon grease, and drain bacon on a paper towel. Add chopped onions, and cook for a minute or two in the bacon grease. Add tomatoes and tomato sauce, and cook for 5–10 minutes.

In another small skillet, cook the 2 tablespoons flour in about ½ teaspoon of the bacon grease until it is medium brown. Use cooked flour to thicken the sauce, if needed, after all the rest is done.

BETO MALDONADO

DORA'S FAMOUS TAMALES

Makes 15 dozen

10 pounds boneless beef brisket
5 pounds pork meat
1 head garlic
1 small package (1 ounce) *comino* (cumin) seeds
3 three-ounce bottles of Gephardt chili powder
6 tablespoons flour
10 pounds masa or powdered *masa seca*
32 ounces pork lard
2 tablespoons salt (more or less to taste)
5 packages corn shucks (husks)

Cut beef and pork in small pieces, about 2 inches by 2 inches, and cook for about an hour in water to cover; then remove meat from water and let cool (reserve the water). Grind the meat and garlic in batches in food processor for about 20 seconds or until ground. Use just enough of the reserved water from the cooked meat to mix *comino* seeds and chili powder to make a paste. Cook flour with oil in a skillet to a brown point; then add all spices and chili powder to the cooked flour. Bring reserved meat water to a boiling point; then add the already-cooked ground meat and spices, and cook to a point not too soft or dry. Soak corn shucks in hot water about 30 minutes, and let the shucks half-dry. Mix masa well with lard and salt; then roll into small balls the size of a golf ball, add one ball to a shuck, and spread in center of shuck, leaving room at both ends to fold the shuck under. Spread 1 to ½ tablespoons of the meat mixture on the masa, and roll up. Fold ends of shucks under.

Place a steamer in the bottom of a big tamale pan with a lid. Add tamales to the pot, seam side down. Add 2½ quarts water, and cook for one hour.

DORA MALDONADO

CARNE GUISADA

Makes 3 servings

1-ounce box whole black pepper
1-ounce box ground cumin
2 tablespoons chopped garlic
1 pound stew meat
2 tablespoons vegetable oil
¼ cup diced onion, or to taste
¼ cup diced bell pepper, or to taste
8 ounces tomato sauce
Salt to taste
2 tablespoons flour

Grind the black pepper, ground cumin, and chopped garlic together in a blender until smooth. Set aside.

Put stew meat into an iron skillet with the vegetable oil, and brown. Once browned, add diced onion and bell pepper, and cook for a few minutes. Add enough water to cover. Add no more than 1 teaspoon of the spices; save the remaining spices for later use. Add the tomato sauce and salt to taste. Simmer until meat is tender, an hour or two. Just when ready, add flour to just enough hot tap water to make a thin paste, and add a little at a time to the skillet to thicken, as desired.

SAMMY MALDONADO

VARIATION: Alicia Maldonado flours her meat before browning to make gravy. She adds garlic, *comino* seeds, black pepper, salt, onion, and water to make the gravy. She covers hers with a lid and cooks until tender, for 1 to 2 hours.

READY SPICES

These are preground spices and vary from cook to cook but are a must in every kitchen in the Wild Horse Desert.

1-ounce box whole black pepper
1-ounce box ground cumin
2 tablespoons garlic, chopped
2 cups water

Place ingredients in a blender and blend until spices are pureed. Use immediately, or mix with 2 cups water and pour into ice cube trays and freeze. They are now ready to add to recipes as needed.

SAMMY MALDONADO

SPANISH RICE

Makes 8 servings

1 cup rice
3 tablespoons vegetable oil
¼ cup onion, chopped
¼ cup bell pepper, chopped
½ cube Ready Spices (See Ready Spices recipe above.)
8 ounces tomato sauce
2 cups water

Brown rice in a cast iron skillet with oil, stirring often. Add onion and bell pepper, and cook a few minutes. Add enough water to cover rice about 1 inch, and then add ½ Ready Spices cube and tomato sauce, and boil uncovered until tender, about 20 minutes. Pull the skillet from heat, cover, and let it set a few minutes before serving.

SAMMY MALDONADO

VARIATIONS: Alicia Maldonado gets her rice very brown and adds *comino* and garlic along with the water. Her mother, Ella Maldonado, added onion and canned tomatoes to the recipe.

FRIJOLES A LA CHARRA

Makes 12 servings of ½ cup each

1 pound dried pinto beans
¼ cup onions, chopped (more if desired)
1 fresh tomato, chopped
2 slices bacon, chopped
½ cup fresh cilantro, chopped
Salt to taste

Soak beans overnight in water to cover. Rinse thoroughly after soaking. Place beans in a slow cooker, and add water to about 2 inches over beans. Add chopped bacon. Once beans start to boil, add chopped onions. After beans soften and are done, add the chopped tomato, cilantro, and salt to taste, and enjoy a delicious cup of frijoles *a la charra*. Cooking time is about 6 to 8 hours in a slow cooker at low setting or about 3 hours on high setting.

SAMMY MALDONADO

PAN DE CAMPO (CAMP BREAD)

Makes 6 rounds about 12 inches in diameter

This recipe was given to the Maldonado family by King Ranch cowboy cook Adolpho Chapa, who made this and served it to tourists on the early King Ranch Visitor Center tours on the Santa Gertrudis Division.

5 pounds flour
4 tablespoons baking powder
2 tablespoons salt
1 tablespoon sugar
1 cup powdered milk
2½ cups shortening
9–12 cups warm water, depending on consistency

Mix all the dry ingredients. Cut shortening into flour mixture with two knives or pastry blender. Gradually add water, and mix thoroughly. Form into flat circles (disks) about 12 inches in diameter, and bake in greased black cast iron skillet or camp bread pot (black cast iron pot with three legs, flat bottom, and flat indented top for holding coals out on the range; available at some hardware stores) at 550 degrees for about 10–12 minutes.

ADOLPHO CHAPA

CORNBREAD

1 cup Pioneer cornmeal
1 cup flour
2 teaspoons baking powder
½ teaspoon salt
1 egg
1 tablespoon oil
⅔ cup milk

Mix all ingredients well, and pour batter into a greased black cast iron skillet. Bake until golden brown in hot oven (about 425 degrees).

ELLA MALDONADO

BRER RABBIT SYRUP CANDY

Ella Maldonado made candy out of Brer Rabbit syrup. She added other ingredients, like a little butter and vanilla, boiled the mixture until it was thick, and then let it cool. Before it was hard, she would work it with her hands, as is done today with saltwater taffy machines, until it was a pretty blond color. Beto would often help her make it.

VARIATION: Molasses Taffy
Makes 1½ pounds

2–3 tablespoons butter, softened
2 cups dark molasses
1 cup granulated sugar
½ cup dark brown sugar
¾ cup water
4 tablespoons butter, cut into ½-inch bits
2 teaspoons distilled white vinegar
¼ teaspoon baking soda
¼ teaspoon salt
2 or 3 drops of oil of peppermint, or vanilla to taste

Spread a shallow baking pan with softened butter. Combine molasses, granulated sugar, brown sugar, and water in a heavy pan over high heat, stirring constantly until the molasses and sugar dissolve. Reduce heat to moderate, and boil uncovered until the temperature reaches 200 degrees on a candy thermometer. Then, stirring deeply and constantly with a wooden spoon, continue to boil until it reaches 250 degrees, or until a few drops form a firm ball in ice water. Remove the pan from the heat, and beat in the butter bits, vinegar, soda, salt, and the flavoring. Pour the candy into the buttered pan, and let it cool about 10 minutes.

While the mixture is still warm, coat hands with softened butter, pinch off about one fourth of the candy, and pull it into a ropelike strand about 1 inch thick. Fold it into thirds and stretch it out again; repeat until it is a pale brown color and begins to stiffen. Stretch it into a rope, and cut it into 1-inch lengths; repeat for the rest of the taffy. Serve at once, or wrap the pieces of taffy in wax paper and twist the ends and store in a covered container.

Time-Life, American Cooking: New England, 141–142

FRIED RABBIT

Makes 8 pieces

Dora Maldonado Garcia said that her grandfather Librado Maldonado fixed meat like fried turtle, jackrabbit, and armadillo with chili powder. These were common foods for the men and women who occupied the Wild Horse Desert.

1 five-pound rabbit, cleaned, dressed, and cut into pieces
2 cups corn oil
2 cups milk
2 eggs
1½ cups all-purpose flour
Salt and pepper to taste

Heat the oil to 350 degrees in a 12-inch skillet. Whisk the milk and eggs in a bowl.

Mix the flour, salt, and pepper in a shallow dish. In batches, dip the pieces of rabbit into the milk mixture, and dredge in flour mixture. Fry the pieces of rabbit in the skillet slowly about 10 minutes until golden brown. Flip the pieces over, and fry about another 10 minutes. Remove the pieces, drain on a paper towel, and serve immediately.

MELISSA GUERRA, *Dishes from the Wild Horse Desert*, 216

ROASTED ARMADILLO

Makes 5 servings

1 armadillo, cleaned
1 teaspoon cumin
1 teaspoon chili powder

1 teaspoon salt, or to taste
¼ teaspoon black pepper
4 cloves garlic
2 tablespoons all-purpose flour

Soak the cleaned armadillo overnight in slightly salted water. Remove from the water, rinse well, and pat dry. Place in baking dish, which has been sprayed with a nonstick vegetable spray. Combine the spices, and rub the meat with them inside and out. Make a slit in each leg where it joins the body, and insert a clove of garlic in each slit. Place the armadillo, stomach side down, in the dish and sprinkle with flour. Pour water into the dish to about ¼ inch deep. Cover with a lid or aluminum foil, and bake 350 degrees for 1½ hours or until golden brown. If it does not brown while cooking, remove the lid and bake uncovered for 15 minutes or until browned.

If you are a novice at field dressing an armadillo, extreme caution must be exercised to avoid puncturing the gall bladder, as it spoils the meat.

SAMUEL C. SILGUERO, ERCILIA SILGUERO'S FATHER, SANTA GERTRUDIS RANCH, *King Ranch Cookbook*, 91.

EMPANADAS

Makes 30

Ella Maldonado made empanadas like this, but she filled hers with pineapple and pumpkin. You may also use a sweet potato filling or strawberry, peach, mango, or guava jam.

Dough
4 cups all-purpose flour
¼ cup sugar
1 teaspoon salt
1 ¾ cups vegetable shortening
1 egg
½ cup water
1 tablespoon vinegar

Mix the flour, sugar, and salt. Knead in the shortening briefly with your hands, about 30 seconds. Add the egg, water, and vinegar, mixing well to form a soft dough. Form the dough into a ball, wrap in plastic, and chill 1 hour.

Preheat the oven to 350 degrees. Divide the dough into 30 portions by first dividing it into equal halves, then each half into 3 pieces, then each piece into 5 equal portions.

Using a tortilla press or a rolling pin, flatten the dough into circles about 3 inches in diameter. Fill each circle with 1 tablespoon of filling; do not overfill. Fold the dough over the filling to form a half circle, and pinch the edges together with a fork to make a crimped pattern. Place on an ungreased cookie sheet, and bake for 20–35 minutes until browned.

MELISSA GUERRA, *Dishes from the Wild Horse Desert*, 216

FLOUR TORTILLAS

These tortillas were made throughout the Ranch and the Wild Horse Desert. They were often served at all three meals, and the women of the households could make them light and tender so they melted in your mouth.

4 cups flour
1 teaspoon baking powder
2 teaspoons salt
½ cup shortening
1½ cups hot water

Mix dry ingredients together. Add shortening and mix thoroughly, using fingertips. Add water, and stir until soft dough is formed. Dough should be pliable but not sticky. Knead for about 10 minutes. Divide dough into small walnut-size balls. Roll out to about 1⁄16-inch thickness on floured board. Cook on hot griddle or hot cast iron skillet, turning three or four times.

ELVA MONTALVO, LAURELES RANCH, *King Ranch Cookbook*, 2

APPENDIX E

Family Album

Ella and Librado with their children. *Back row*: Beto, Amelia, Aurora, Alicia, and Plácido.

Ella Maldonado holding her granddaughter Sonia Garcia, with Librado Maldonado.

Thirty-plus years after the above photo, John David, Daniel, Michael, and Eloy Morales with their great-grandfather Librado Maldonado. They are the sons of Mally M. Morales and grandsons of Alicia Maldonado.

above: Norma and Cata on Norma's wedding day, April 5, 1975.

left: Beto and his sister, Alicia Maldonado, have lived in the same house or next door to each other since Beto was born in 1930.

Back row: Cata, Sammy, Dora, Albert Jr., and Norma. *Front row*: Beto and Dora.

Beto and Dora Maldonado with their family. *Back row, left to right*: Catalina M. Yaklin, Sammy Maldonado, Dora M. Garcia, Albert Maldonado Jr., and Norma M. Quintanilla.

Catalina M. Yaklin and Norma M. Quintanilla with Barbie dolls they received at a King Ranch Christmas party when they were children.

Dora M. Garcia with grandson José Andrés "Andy" Castillo, great-grandson of Beto and Dora Maldonado.

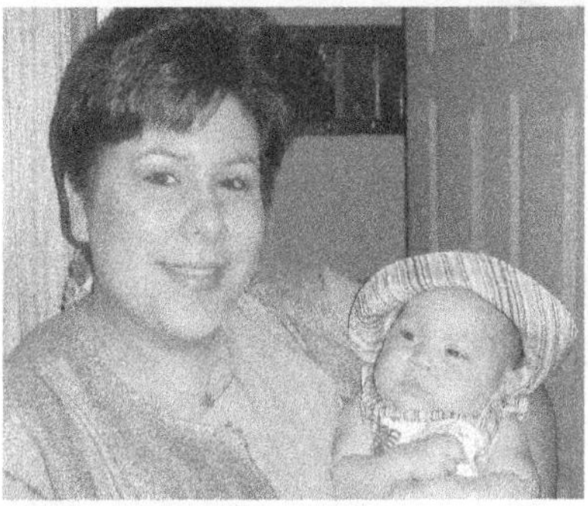

Sonia Garcia Due, granddaughter of Beto and Dora Maldonado, with Dylyn Matthew Due, seven weeks old.

Albert Maldonado Jr.

Rudy Castillo holding Andy Castillo and Samantha Jo Garcia Castillo holding MaKayla Jo Castillo. Samantha is Beto and Dora's granddaughter and Andy and MaKayla Jo their great-grandchildren.

Catalina M. Yaklin's family. *Left to right*: Tracy Yaklin, Pete Yaklin, Catalina Yaklin, and Daniel Yaklin.

Sammy and Jo Anne Maldonado.

Norma M. Quintanilla's family. *Back row, left to right*: Norma M. Quintanilla, Mario Quintanilla, Onesimo Quintanilla, and Monica Quintanilla. *Front row, left to right*: Lorraine Rodriguez, Noe Rodriguez, Molly Rodriguez, and Neri Rodriguez Quintanilla.

The Maldonado family. *Back row*: Mario Quintanilla, Monica Quintanilla, and Onesimo Quintanilla; Pete Yaklin, Tracy Yaklin, and Daniel Yaklin. *Middle row*: Neri Quintanilla, Lorraine Quintanilla, and Noe Quintanilla; Dora M. Garcia, Norma M. Quintanilla, Alicia Maldonado, Catalina M. Yaklin, Albert Maldonado Jr., Jo Anne Maldonado and Sammy Maldonado. *Front row*: Molly Rodriguez, Dora Maldonado, and Beto Maldonado holding Andy Castillo. *Not pictured*: Veronica Garcia, Samantha G. Castillo, Matt and Sonia Garcia Due, and Dylyn Due.

GLOSSARY

ALFARESA. Illness.

AMULET. A charm.

BANDELÓN. A Mexican guitar with a big fat back.

BAILE. Ball, or dance.

BUÑUELOS. Tortillas fried in deep fat, then tossed with a cinnamon-sugar mixture.

CAPORAL. Cow boss.

CARNE GUISADA. Mexican meat stew.

CASA GRANDE. Great house.

CASCARONES. Emptied eggshells filled with bits of festive paper.

COMINO. Cumin, a spice used in Mexican cooking.

CORRIDA. Cow camp; basic work unit of a ranch in which ten to thirty men work together.

CURANDEROS. Folk healers.

DESPACIO. Slow.

DÍA DE LOS MUERTOS. All Saints' Day.

EMPANADAS. Individual pastries filled with fruit or vegetables, then baked in the oven.

ENTRADA. The group of people who came from Cruillas, Mexico, with Captain King to help establish his ranch.

FARRIER. A person who cares for their hooves and puts shoes on horses.

GRAHITOS. Sour grass on King Ranch that children liked to chew.

GUAYABERAS. Cuban shirts common to Mexico and South Texas.

GUITAREROS. Guitar players.

GUITARRONES. Large Mexican guitars.

HACKAMORE. Bridle.

HEADSTALL. The part of a bridle or halter that fits over a horse's head.

HUISACHE. Bright yellow, sweet-smelling wildflowers found on King Ranch.

KINEÑOS. King's men.

LAGUNA MADRE. Mother lagoon. Two long bays along the western coast of Texas and Mexico separated by an outlet of the Rio Grande.

LA MADAMA. A name of respect given to Henrietta King by the Kineños.

LA PATRONA. Boss, mistress, or patron saint.

LATIFUNDOS. Immense ranching estates found in Northern Mexico when Captain Richard King founded his rancho in 1853.

LOTERÍA. Mexican bingo.

MADRINA. Godmother or sponsor of a girl, selected for the girl's first Communion.

MANTILLA. Lacy headdress worn by women.

MANZANILLA. Chamomile tea.

MASA. Finely ground corn meal used to make tamales.

MERIENDA. Afternoon snack.

METATE. Flat stone used for grinding corn.

MOLCAJETE. Traditional Mexican version of a mortar.

MOÑO. A bun formed with hair at the back of the head.

MORRAS. Sweet, purple, wild berries that children ate for treats on the Ranch.

PADRINO. Godfather or sponsor of a young boy, selected for the boy's first Communion.

PALO MARCADO. Name of working pens once located on the Laureles Division.

PAN DE CAMPO. Camp bread.

PAN DE POLVO. Pastry cut into cookies, baked, and covered with a sugar and cinnamon mixture.

PAN DULCE. Sweet bread.

QUITA Y PONE. A game made in Mexico that the Maldonado family played.

SEGUNDO. Assistant or second in command.

SUSTO. Fright.

SUBIBAJA. Seesaw.

TAMALES. Common Mexican fare made of masa with a spicy meat filling, rolled in corn husks and steamed or baked.

TAQUITOS. Small corn tortillas filled with potatoes and spicy meat, sometimes with chili.

TARLATAN. Scottish cloth.

TROCAR. A copper ring, originally designed to relieve bloating in cattle. On King Ranch it was placed in a bull's nose through a hole in the septum and used to attach a short rope to aid in controlling the bull.

VAQUEROS. Mexican cowboys.

VEVE LECHE. Hopscotch.

WELITA. Grandmother.

YAGA. A sore.

YERBA BUENA. Mint.

BIBLIOGRAPHY

BOOKS

Britten, Walter S., with J. DeArman. *"Sold!"* Bryan, Tex.: Newman Printing, 1988.

Cavazos, Bobby. *The Cowboy from the Wild Horse Desert.* Houston: Larksdale.

Cavazos, Lauro F. *A Kineño Remembers.* College Station: Texas A&M University Press, 2006.

Cheeseman, Bruce S. *My Dear Henrietta.* Austin, Tex.: W. Thomas Taylor, 1993.

Collins, Jim. *Good to Great.* New York: Harper Business, 2001.

Corpus Christi Caller-Times. "King Ranch, 100 Years of Ranching." 1953.

Cypher, John. *Bob Kleberg and the King Ranch.* Austin: University of Texas Press.

Dobie, J. Frank. *Cow People.* Boston: Little, Brown, 1964.

Forgason, Caroline Alexander, and Paul Genho. *Wildlife on the King Ranch.* Corpus Christi, Tex.: Grunwald Printing Co., 2003.

Graham, Joe S., ed. "The Role of the Curandero in the Folk Medicine System of West Texas." *American Folk Medicine.* Berkeley: University of California Press, 1976.

Groves, Helen Kleberg. *Bob and Helen Kleberg of King Ranch.* Albany, Tex.: Bright Sky Press, 2004.

Guerra, Melissa. *Dishes from the Wild Horse Desert: Norteño Cooking of South Texas.* Hoboken, N.J.: John Wiley and Son, 2006.

Henderson, J. Y., DVM. *Circus Doctor.* Boston: Little, Brown, 1951.

Hunter, Cecelia Aros, and Leslie Gene Hunter. *Historic Kingsville: Guide to the Original Townsites.* Kingsville, Tex.: Kingsville Historical Development Board, 1994.

Jackson, H. Joaquin, and David Marion Wilkinson. *One Ranger.* Austin: University of Texas Press, 2005.

King Ranch Cookbook. Kingsville, Tex.: King Ranch, Inc., 1992.

Kleberg, Janell. *Waiting for Daylight.* Ketcham, Idaho: Stoelklein Publishing and Photography, 2003.

Kleberg, Sally S. *Kineño Christmas.* Self-published, 2003. Available at King Ranch Saddle Shop.

Lea, Tom. *The King Ranch.* 2 vols. Boston: Little, Brown, 1953.

Monday, Jane Clements, and Betty Bailey Colley. *Voices of the Wild Horse Desert: The Vaquero Families of the King and Kenedy Ranches.* Austin: University of Texas Press, 1997.

Monday, Jane Clements, and Frances Brannen Vick. *Petra's Legacy: The South Texas Ranching Empire of Petra Vela and Mifflin Kenedy.* College Station: Texas A&M University, 2007.

Nettles, Gala. *King Ranch and Little Peppy: The Legacy and the Legend.* Groesbeck, Tex.: LMH Publishing Co., 1996.

Nixon, Jay. *Running W: Stewards of a Vision; A History of King Ranch.* Hong Kong: Everbest, 1986.

Parker, Marjorie Hodgson. *Assault: The Crippled Champion.* Albany, Tex.: Bright Sky Press. 2005.

Torres, Eliseo. "Cheo." *Healing with Herbs and Rituals.* Albuquerque: University of New Mexico Press, 2006.

PERIODICALS

Aschoff, Susan. "Cattle Auction Held On Plane." *Dallas Morning News,* January 10, 1985.

Associated Press. "Auction Draws $3.4 Million in Ballroom." *Houston Chronicle,* 1976.

Associated Press. "Santa Gertrudis Auction Strictly Black-Tie." *Dallas Morning News,* 1976.

Bracher, Bob. "First Showman of the Santa Gertrudis Breed." *Santa Gertrudis Journal* (September 1972): 12, 64–65.

Bray, Ralph G. "Great American Ranch." *Texas Farming and Citriculture* (September 1940): 18–26, 56, 59.

Broyles, William, Jr. "The King Ranch." *Texas Monthly,* October 1980, 271.

Buranen, Margaret. "Assault the Clubfooted Comet." *Texas Co-Op Power,* September 2006, 25.

Currie, Barton W. "A Farm as Big as Delaware." *Country Gentleman* (Philadelphia), August 28, 1915, 1, 4, 24.

El Mesteño. *Recipes.* Edited and published by Homer Salinas Vera, Premont, Tex., 2003. www.el-mesteno.com.

Gonzales, John W. "King of the Coastal Plains." *Houston Chronicle Magazine,* October 5, 2003, 6–10.

Gwynne, S. C. "The Next Frontier." *Texas Monthly,* August 2007.

"Inside King Ranch." *Cowboys and Indians,* November 1998, 106–107.

Jones, Mark. "Librado Maldonado—Dean of Cattle Showmen." *Kingsville Record,* February 13, 1983, 1, 12.

King Ranch, Inc. King Ranch 29th Annual Auction Letter from the President. In *The Heads of the Class of 1980.*

Libby, Leanne. "Modern Methods Displacing Older Ways at Landmark, Which Turns 150." *Corpus Christi Caller-Times,* September 28, 2003, 1.

Manning, Victoria. "Age-Old Cures Still Thriving in Modern World." *San Antonio Express-News,* August 6, 2007.

Rhoad, A. O. "The Santa Gertrudis Breed." *Journal of Heredity* 40, no. 5 (May 1949).

Roybal, Joe. "Not That Complicated." *BEEF,* December 1, 2006.

San Antonio Express-News. "King Ranch Makes Texas Turf-grass Deal." August 23, 2007, E2.

Santa Gertrudis Breeders' Association (Australia). *Santa Gertrudis Review* (Brisbane), July 1983.

Thomas, Les. "The Ranch That Would Be King." *Southern Living,* March 1992.

Time-Life Books. *American Cooking: New England.* Foods of the World. New York, 1970.

Torres, Eliseo. *Curanderos and Shamans in the Southwest.* University of New Mexico, November 4, 1996.

Uhler, David. "Don Strange and His Family Carve Out a Catering Dynasty." *San Antonio Express-News*, June 7, 2007.

Vera, Homero Salinas. *El Mesteño* 3, no. 1 (Winter–Spring 2003).

BULLETINS FROM KING RANCH

"How the Silver Lady Sale Came About."

King Ranch Auction Catalogue, 1985.

"The Silver Ladies and Their Sterling Pedigreed Bulls."

"Some Sterling Pedigreed Quarter Horses."

UNPUBLISHED SOURCES

Kleberg, Robert J., Jr. "The Santa Gertrudis Breed of Beef Cattle." King Ranch, Tex.

Kleberg, Robert J., Jr. "A Review of the Development of the Breed." King Ranch, Tex.

Marshall, Geneva. "Geneva Remembers." Self-published.

WEBSITES

BEEF magazine. www.beefmagazine.com.

King Ranch. www.king-ranch.com.

Kingsville Chamber of Commerce. www.kingsville.org.

TSHA Online: The Handbook of Texas Online. www.tshaonline.org/handbook/online/.

Torres, Eliseo. "Don Pedrito Jaramillo." *The Folk Healer: The Mexican-American Tradition of Curanderismo.* Nieves Press. www.unm.edu/~cheo/DonPedrito.htm.

U.S. Census Bureau. http://factfinder.census.gov.

INDEX

CPSIA information can be obtained
at www.ICGtesting.com
Printed in the USA
JSHW051733180920
7923JS00002B/6

9 780292 719439